TONY KREIT

CHILDHOOD'S END

I dedicate this series of Books to my Three Children

DARRAN   GAVIN   and MEERA

In the hope that someday they will be able to find answers to some of the questions that they might wish to ask when I am no-longer around to answer them.

I would like to make one further dedication to my old school-friend Robin Wilks whose efforts to contact me some 50 or so years after we both left school enabled me to return a book that I had borrowed from him all those many years earlier.

I now have two dedications to persons who began the process of opening the world up for me. In no particular order then-

Peter Vansittart it was who taught me how to love my own language but with no particular emphasis on its Grammar. Many thanks.

Ruth Richards it was who taught me both French and the need for Grammar in any language. Merci Beaucoup Ruth.

Prologue Page 3

<u>Prologue: Childhood's End</u>

This collection of short stories is about a boy and his friends. It is a collection of memoirs, adventures and collected anecdotes that a reader may find interesting, perhaps even sometimes amusing as well as entertaining. It is a collection of true accounts of a selection from events in a life and of people who one has met or worked with during a long, interesting, and sometimes chaotic life. As a reader you will meet real people and true events but from which names have been changed here and there for the sake of confidentiality. These true stories tell about the life of me, my family, and friends and of a period in England, London in particular that is little known to most of you, and which is rich in modern historical interest both in humour and tragedy as well as people behaving both well and badly, sometimes downright unkindly.

I wish to make one further statement at this point. All the experiences, incidents episodes and explorations in these pages are true BAR ONE. I have diverged deliberately into one short episode of pure fiction because the subject intrigued me. I have done my very best to weave it into the fabric of my young life. I have included a clue in the last words of this work so that the inquisitive can search it out. If and when you think you've worked it out you can contact me on my email. (tonyinthewritingbox@btinternet.com). I will reply to any or all contacts.

I was born in the March before WW2. I have said it before, and I really mean it; a child needs to grow up quickly during wartime'. I was going to and from school alone or with other childhood friends, at the age of five years, from day two of my school career. That was a four-times a day journey because I did not want to stay for school lunches and my Mum could not spare the time to take me to and fro. My school journeys were sometimes completed to the sound of an Air Raid Siren. Mum's instructions under those circumstances were to run either home or back to school whichever was the closer. That was in 1944 when conventional air raids by the Luftwaffe were a thing of the recent past but by when there were daily attacks on London by rocket and doodlebug. One learned to tell the difference between the sounds of the two at a very young age. Even so I am absolutely certain that I was in less danger then from the Nazi War machine than a lone child would be today at the mercy of modern traffic.

I have to say that I lived a Huckleberry Finn type of life much of the time when I was young. Children and young people had a much wider permitted personal, spatial, and temporal horizon when I was a young child and teenager than they began to be permitted as the generations came and went. One hopes that this will become clear from these reminiscences. Spatial horizons along with a feeling for, or knowledge of, the natural world around them, have, unfortunately, narrowed for children along with the quickly passing years.

Tony Kreit   10-04-2022

Chapter One

A Family in Wartime

Boy Meets Mum

He stared back at his mother's glare; he knew he would be in trouble over this. "You been in that bloody brook again boy?" "No Mum." Was all he could think to say, and then he followed her glare down to his feet. The tell-tale puddles of water seeping from his shoes onto the shiny lino of the kitchen gave the lie to his answer; tiny lakes on the shiny, oh so shiny heavily polished lino of the kitchen. He tried offering that cheeky grin, the one he knew might steal her heart yet again but no! Punishment seemed imminent, damned water! Sussed and 'hoist once more and by your own Petard'!

Glimpses

Short trousers, cold knees, wintergreen ointment, cold houses, furniture circled around the fire, fireplaces, in every room, ice on windows even the inside, much loved on 'Houses under the Hammer' sash windows always sticking, fireplaces creating thick killer smog. Coal shot in the house into the coal cupboard under the stairs then, when this was used as an air-raid shelter, through the house and into the back yard. Rationing of anything you really wanted. 'Women's work was never done', the unimaginable tedium of the week's schedule, the outside loo with its wooden slatted door and gaps top and bottom. Smoking and the promotion of smoking Fuel shortages, power-cuts gas powered lighting in school, hot water bottles, both hard and soft. These were all very well remembered features of the times.

On the other hand, there were still trees in streets, freedom to play, streets without cars, freedom to explore, a scarcity of the immediacy of bad news invading from a hundred sources into the home. There was always home cooking, a variety of good bread choices and no sliced bread except what you had sliced for yourself with a bread saw. Front door keys hanging on a string behind the letter box. There were also; tradesmen's rounds, generosity of spirit and my two bikes; Hercules Jeep and my beloved Claude Butler. The man who sold baked potatoes on Edmonton Green after Saturday morning kids' pictures and the good old River Lea and Edmonton Green! Yes, dear old Edmonton Green much changed nowadays.

Mum Meets Dad

They tell us that the times were hard, and they were, what with the bombing, the separations, and the interminable rationing; but then we lived them and got on with them and didn't realise that life was as hard as it was; so we enjoyed ourselves anyway.

I was born on the 8th of March 1939 in a flat in Angel close 'Upper' Edmonton in North London. It was quite near the Regal cinema. I was of course born at home just as the large majority of babies were in those days, particularly working-class babies; this was after all almost ten years before the inception of the NHS. My parents moved soon after my birth to a rented house in Stanley Road just off Church Street in 'Lower' Edmonton. Shortly after that they moved yet again to -where I grew up and where my Nan, one Uncle and two Aunts lived at No.222. I remember that during the War, which had begun just before that final move, a congregation of Aunts collected from time to time at my Nan's house. She rented the whole house but sub-let the top half later to her daughter, my Aunt Rose, and her husband Ted. I always felt comfortable in my Nan's house. When I was a child it seemed to me to be always busy with family hustle and bustle. Nan always had a piano which my Uncle Les. Nan's youngest son could play quite well by ear. Uncle Les was also quite a good artist; it was a tragic shame that young working-class people like him did not have the avenues in which to explore and develop their talents in those days as they do nowadays. There was also a dog, Bob, who was some kind of very agreeable canine mixture. Bob and I got on very well. He had a dog 'cave' in the large space that had been allocated to him at the bottom of the Welsh Dresser. That particular piece of furniture appeared to be standard in those terraced houses. We also had one at 180 but our house was the other way round to Nan's; that is the ground floor rooms of our house ran off to the left of the long passageway whereas in Nan's house they ran off to the right of the passage; the upstairs rooms followed this 'opposite' orientation; in other respects the two houses were identical.

I am convinced that I begin to have glimpses of direct memory of my surroundings of the house, the family, and the War at about the age of three and a half years. This is in addition to the multitude of tales that I absorbed as and when they were related within the family as I grew. I have to agree though that the mixture of the two is a complicated bundle. I can certainly remember the night that my maternal Grandad died. Mum and I were sleeping at No. 222 for family comfort due to the possibility of air Raids. Mum and I were in the back room upstairs. Nan and Grandad were in the middle room and Aunt Rose and Aunt Joan, her younger sister were in the larger front bedroom. This room had a beautiful Bay window that let in 'bags' of light. Rose's husband Ted was away from home more than most during the War. He was with the British Expeditionary Force; yes, the one that had to be evacuated from the beaches of Dunkerque early in the War. He was thankfully one of those rescued from that debacle of British planning. Uncle Ted returned to England very briefly, he was re-trained and sent off to the Far East to fight in what was then Burma. Every soldier had a tough war, but Ted had one of the toughest.

There were two air raid shelters at No. 222 my Nan's house. In the garden there was an Andersen Shelter which was basically a hole dug in the ground with a roof of curved corrugated iron; all further protected by as many sandbags as possible. This would be little protection from a direct hit of course but pretty good against nearby explosions. It could also be made quite comfortable. The second shelter was in Nan's kitchen and was a construction known as a Morrison Shelter. This was a rectangular construction with four angle iron uprights held together by a roof of steel plates and in-all about two-foot six high. There were fixtures on all of the uprights where screens of wire mesh could be fixed to prevent debris from invading the space. They were not pretty objects but were apparently easy to construct and saved many a life during the war. They were cosy and offered a feeling of safety. They could also be used as a table, an ugly cumbersome table but useful nonetheless in that regard.

I woke up one terrible night to the sound of Grandad groaning and crying out in pain. He was dying and I was four years old, and my Grandad was in pain as he was dying, and they prevented me from going in to see him. I hung around but did not understand what truly was happening. That is all of what I remember of the passing of my Grandad; He was in pain, and they didn't want to let me see him. I did not really know exactly what dying was although I had heard, even seen, some of it during that damned War. All I know now, as a Dad and Grandad, is that if the last thing I might see on this earth would be just one of my children or grandchildren I would take that any day and sod the pain! Let it mind its own bloody business! The sight of a loved one would always be a comforting pass into whatever comes next!

 My Dad was a Taylor, not unusual for a young Jewish man in the 1930s but he yearned for much more for me and, later, for my sister who was born eight years after me; just another way that the War separated families! Dad was born in Cable Street in the East End of London. When he was about nineteen, he met a young woman, non-Jewish and tried to introduce her to his family, an orthodox Jewish family. There was no way that they could or would ever have come to terms with a son having a non-Jewish girl friend or 'God forbid' a shiksa as a wife. Now Shiksa (pronounced shick-suh) is a Yiddish word that refers, often very unpleasantly, to a non-Jewish woman who is either romantically interested in a Jewish man or who is a Jewish man's object of affection. It was commonly said in Jewish circles that the shiksa represents an exotic "other" to the Jewish man, someone who is theoretically forbidden and, thus, incredibly desirable. It is in fact also commonly used as an unpleasant expression for any non-Jewish young woman who the speaker does not like for any reason. It is a generally quite unpleasant word. I do not like the word and have never used it myself other than as here, in description of its usage and meaning.

Shiksa is certainly a word that Dad's family, in fact my family of course, would have used against any young non-Jewish woman in whom Dad was showing an interest. At that point in his life Dad was not able or willing to stand up to the pressures to which some members of his family notably his mother and some of his sisters would have subjected him. In desperation he left both the girl and his family and went off to wander around France for six months or so. That part of my Dad's story was told to me by my maternal Aunt Joan after Dad had passed away. I do know that he had acquired some French in his younger days and that must have been the period of his life when he did so. I was later able to confirm some aspects of the story with my paternal Uncle Ruben, but he knew nothing about Dads activities during his period in France. Such is life, full of mysteries. We always forget to ask the questions when the loved one is alive. Added to this we frequently do not know what questions to ask until after the passing.

Dad returned to England, to his family home in the East End and, rejecting religion totally, he joined a branch of the YCL, a Young Communist Fraternity, in Stamford Hill North London. It was there that he met my mother, also not Jewish just like his first amour. Determined not to allow his plans to be disrupted yet again he married my Mum at a local registry office. He then went home and announced his 'fait accompli'. Oy a Gevalt! [See that; three languages in one sentence.] 'Gevalt' is a Yiddish word that means violence in English. And violence there was. Dad's Mum and two of his sisters ganged up when they heard the news and began to throw all his belongings out into the street until Dad's older brother, my Uncle Harry intervened and forced them to stop; saying that he was not going to allow his brother's possessions to be treated in that way. Dad left home immediately, as he had planned. He hardly ever spoke to his mother or of her again until I intervened years later when I was twenty-three and in the RAF. I have related that story in chapter 18 of my first book (A Road Ran Through It). I used the fact of being in the RAF as a device to visit my Bubba, my Jewish Grandmother, without incurring the pressures that my parents would have put on me if they had known of my intentions beforehand. Such are the deviances that family life can sometimes force upon us when we do not have the stomach for the inevitable storm that will erupt when we confront directly as we should!

Mum and Dad were therefore married under difficult circumstances as far as most members of his family were concerned. As far as that went, and with the female contingent mostly; Dad was dead to his family. They urged my Uncle Isaac to say the Kaddish prayer in Synagogue; just as if Dad were dead. This is widely held to be the prayer of mourning for Jews It was not always thus however: - Kaddish originated not in the synagogue but in the house of study (Beit Midrash). After a scholar had delivered a learned discourse, students and teachers would rise to praise Gd's holy name. During the mourning period for a rabbi or teacher, students would gather to study in his honour, and his son was given the honour of leading that prayer. Over time, reciting Kaddish replaced studying as the tribute given to a scholar. Eventually the custom extended to all mourners– not only the survivors of rabbis and leaders. By the sixth century, Kaddish was part of synagogue prayers, and during the 13th century, when the Crusades threatened universally the Jewish communities of Europe, it became inextricably linked to loss and mourning. For over two decades my Dad, being one of ten siblings; five sisters and five brothers, had no contact with the majority of his family; just two of his brothers my Uncle Harry and my Uncle Ruben were the only two who refused to join the family ostracism of their brother. Uncles Harry and Ruben remained friends to Dad and then to me for the rest of their lives after Dad passed away.

Over the years I became very close to both of those Uncles. In fact, I travelled up to Manchester with my Uncle Ruben when my Uncle Harry was ill and in hospital there. During the journey I noticed that my uncle was becoming more and more emotional. He could hardly speak to me for the tears that were clearly welling below the surface. At first, I assumed that he was concerned over the possibility that his brother might be close to death. I made to re-assure him that we had no reason to fear the worst. He held his hand up very quickly to stop me in my tracks.

"No Tony, it's not that; I am worried about Harry of course but it's not that." He then went on to tell me much more about the early months of his marriage and the tragedy that befell him and my Aunt Doris; all totally without the support of his family. I am still sometimes surprised at the confidences that he related to me. The vast majority have remained confidences since Ruben [Alev Ha Sholem] has passed away and will remain so...

It seems that although My Aunt Doris was from a perfectly respectable Orthodox Jewish family Ruben's family, our family of course, would not take to her, they even, for some unconscionable reason insisted on referring to her as a Shiksa. At the time they were all living in Manchester. In the passage of time and in the natural way of things my aunt became pregnant with their first child, a boy, who was born badly disabled with what used to be called commonly as 'Water on the Brain'.

In the past, the condition of hydrocephalus was often referred to as "water on the brain" by the general public and outside of the medical profession... However, the brain is not surrounded by water but by a fluid called cerebrospinal fluid (CSF). CSF has three important functions: firstly, it protects the brain from damage; it has the function of removing waste products from the brain; it also provides the brain with the nutrients it needs to function properly

My dear old Uncle Ruben finally managed to steady his emotions to explain that, of course, they were young, he and Doris and that this baby was their first born and that they dearly needed the support of a family. Ruben's family was living quite close to him and Doris, but they received no support from them. In fact, what they mostly received from Ruben's family was total and ignorant rejection of their son. Then there came the cruncher for my uncle on our train journey to Manchester. It turned out that Harry had been hospitalised in the very same hospital in which their baby had died. By the time he got to that point we were both in tears. I stretched across the table between us to take his hand. At that my uncle nodded towards me and grasped my hand quite hard, almost fiercely. For obvious reasons Uncle Ruben foreswore his religion entirely. He did not wish nor have any intention of having normal family relations with his own birth family other than my Dad and my Uncle Harry and, as time passed, with me I'm pleased to say.

The reception for my Mum and Dad's marriage was all very different as far as my Mum's family was concerned, to that which both Dad and my Uncle Ruben experienced from their family. The young couple had little or no rejections, only congratulations from Mum's family. I do not remember any one of them ever having a bad word for my Dad. In fact, my Aunt Joan is [keyn aynhoreh], still with us as I write. She has also been a great friend to me all my life and often sings the praises of my Dad.

CHAPTER TWO

My First Days at School

"All things bright and beautiful.

All creatures, great and small.

All things wise and wonderful.

The Lord God made them all".

It was November 1944. Edmonton. North London. The day was dark, a typical, gloomy, England in November. In the overcast late afternoon of that autumn of 1944 the flickering gas lamps gave but a poor yellow light in the high classroom. It was a very high room, far too high for economy of heating in the single-story Victorian building of the old school. The white-washed or, rather, yellow washed walls were at least fifteen feet high with two tiers of windows set into them. These windows could be opened, with great difficulty, by using a long pole which had a horizontal 'S' hook fixed at the end of it. This hook had a downward curve for opening and an upward curve for closing. The contraption required both effort and practice to be able to use it with any semblance of ease and grace. The appropriate part of the hook had to be juggled into a ring fixed to the upper part of the wooden window frames which pivoted along their horizontal axes.

Opening or closing these windows was almost always a vexatious undertaking particularly when attempted by a short person to one of the upper windows, up to which the pole would then only just reach. It was tippy toed brinkmanship in wet, sticky, weather when the wooden frames had swelled and made the operation next to impossible. The poor teacher was often left, swinging, in vain and undignified rage at the end of the useless pole. It has to be said that the operation of those windows provided much innocent entertainment to pupils in the empty days before classroom television. Windows, once open could be fixed at the required angle by tying a dangling cord to a hook on the wall. The reverse operation, to close the window, had to be done equally expertly with a sharp upward shove or it would not shut quite completely. Otherwise, the real expert could tug the lower cord to bring the window neatly into place. Any mistake in either of these operations left the wind to whistle through the resulting gaps. This made disconcerting noises and created cold draughts to discomfort already chilly necks. Those were the days in which chilblains were the epidemic of winter for boys who always wore short trousers due to a national shortage of cloth and were expected to endure the rigours of an English winter with global fortitude. Chilblains attacked any vulnerable extremity such as ears or knees or toes and were very painful, the, then famous 'Wintergreen' ointment being the only remedy readily and odorously available.

There were two other openings to the outside elements, the skylights, which were set on either side of the high apex of the ceiling and were almost flush with it. The skylights were opened and closed by means of a long 'Heath Robinson' rod and ratchet arrangement which started at the frame of the 'light' proceeded down the wall and was operated from below by a square key and handle which turned one of the rods through a universal joint. The upward movement of this was transmitted to the window through the series of joints and rods. It should have worked in theory, but the fact was that the windows could never be shut quite tightly enough. A combination of age, wear and sheer distance between the operator and the device on the frame meant that the small six-inch key could not generate enough leverage to bring the frame back fully into position. It was not surprising, therefore, that whenever it rained water would seep under the 'light', down the rod and ratchet combination to the socket on the wall, down the wall and then make a puddle on the floor, like a distant and invisible ghostly cat. A patch of green mould at that point bore silent testimony to the years of repeated soakings to which the parquet tiles had been subjected. As the apex of the roof ran almost the whole length of the room there was a row of desks on either side of the central aisle which had to be moved every time it rained hard otherwise the permanent occupants of those desks might well have been rendered mouldy too. Strangely, it never occurred to anyone to re-arrange the desks on a once-and-for-all basis.

The gas lamps, which were the only source of lighting in those far off days, hung from the ceiling down to a height of about seven feet. Rings on chains on either side of the lights were the means by which they were turned on and off, pull one side for on and the other for off, provided the pilot light had not gone out and also that the mantle was in good order or that the police or air raid warden had not been round to issue orders not to use gas appliances or that Hitler had not been about his erstwhile daily business of dropping bombs or sending rockets or doodlebugs. When this had happened during the recent years everyone had had to file out to the air raid shelter in the playground, where the lesson usually continued in stoic British manner, often in near darkness but with that rugged determination not to be outdone by the 'filthy Hun'.

I had real cause to remember one particular afternoon in that classroom, in the autumn of 1944 for the rest of my life; for it was in that room on that certain afternoon that I was made to stand by my desk. I remember that I was nervous and looked about myself, in vain, for some comfort from just one of my classmates. I looked up at the lamps; it was so dark outside that I could not see into the black void above them. As I stood there I prayed for inspiration. The long chains hung down and I prayed longingly for inspiration into the deep shadows beyond them. I had no time to search the shadows with my panicky, racing eyes. What could she mean, that teacher? She already knew my name.

"What is your name boy? This was followed by another long, desperate silence until I, convinced that the world had suddenly gone mad, felt that I had to break the silence, I replied.

"Tony Miss err, Miss Brown." I felt it prudent to be as polite as possible. I knew that I would remember that woman's face for as long as I lived, like a scar.

"Tony what? Stupid boy! Not your Christian name, we all know that." She seemed to smirk around the class to the, by now, sniggering audience. I felt myself licking my lips, my mouth had gone very dry, and I was only five and this was my own first year in school in fact. She was a new teacher to the school, having arrived only two weeks before, just after the beginning of term. She was a new teacher but was at least a thousand years old which lent to her a much more imposing aspect to my very tender years. She had picked on me ever since she had arrived, but this was the worst. I remember that I did not even understand what she was driving at.

"Please Miss you've got it in the register." Her grip tightened on the blackboard duster, and I hastily decided that this was not what she wanted or expected.

"Kreit Miss, Tony Kreit." I smiled at her then, sheepishly, naively, more out of hope than belief that I was now off the hook that the ordeal was over. I looked around the class, searching, again in vain, for the oasis of a friendly face amid the suddenly hostile sea staring back at me. Giggles and smirks there were, at my discomfort but no succour to be seen at my distress. She paused and, in that pause, lay such hidden menace. Her shoulders twitched and she continued the attack, for that was what the impromptu inquisition had become.

"Kreit, Kreit." She rolled my name in her mouth like an unpleasant sweet, in a tone I had never heard before, like a bad word. She was speaking to me in a way no adult had ever spoken to me before, hard and spiteful.

"That's a strange name, Kreit, for an English classroom, um, Kreit" My name was repeated by that woman, and I did not understand why, why strange? Why was my name so strange?

"Where on earth did you get a name like that boy?" My knees trembled and nearly gave way under me. My body shook with fright. Why did she keep going on about my name? I could no longer answer her; I had become numb, numb, and dumb.

"Well? I'm waiting."

The exchange had gone far beyond my understanding. I remember that I was answering by instinct alone, and not very well at that. I prayed for the lesson to end or for a bomb to drop. Neither blessed event occurred. The inquisition continued.

"It's a strange name, boy, for an English classroom" She repeated herself. "It's a German name, isn't it?" I suddenly felt the colour drain from my face, I could not answer her, I could not say anything, and I am certain that I would not have been able to move at that moment. I had no idea where Germany was, but I knew well enough that all Germans were evil, everyone said so. How do you get to be a German, or have a German name? Did I have a German name? The evil witch had just said so. My previously secure world had just been shattered, it lay smashed about me, reflected in the blank stares of my classmates and the look of hate from this teacher, this wizened harridan. A tear began to edge towards the corner of my eye. I fought to control the tear by blinking hard, but it welled out of control, and I was forced to cuff it aside and hope the no-one had noticed it.

"Dunno miss, I don't think so?"

"Yes, it is." She almost screamed at me. "It's a German name." Red faced, she paused for breath.

"We've been at war with the Germans." She spoke as if to the whole class for continued support, but the atmosphere had got too far out of control even for their taste. They had lost interest, using the opportunity of her pre-occupation to make faces among themselves. They all knew there had been a war on. None of them could remember anything but the war. Peace might be with them soon, everyone hoped so, but it was just a word to them, war had been their only reality. They had all fought Germans too, in the playground with makeshift Tommy guns and sparking fingers pointing at the sky, at any plane, friend or foe, for they knew no difference.

I have returned mentally to look back and frequently, on that afternoon, in later life and my blood has always run cold. That woman had been beside herself with rage and hatred, directed at me, a boy of not six years of age.

I stared at her; I had reached that age with almost no experience of anger from my own adults. My Dad, on the very few occasions I had seen him, was a calm quiet man who obtained respect and obedience without recourse to anger. With Dad away in the army my Mum, and gran; plus a whole basketful of Aunts had woven a quiet, protective, female cocoon around me which shielded me from a world tearing itself apart in a multitude of terrible conflicts.

I stared at the teacher; she had a sudden splash of angry spittle on her chin. I knew nothing about names. How did you get to be a German? I kept asking myself the same question but could not even guess at the answer. What was a German name? How could you know if you'd got one?

I sat down without permission and before I realised what I'd done. I gasped at my own folly, looked up quickly, half expecting her to explode into another tirade. I was so surprised and relieved when nothing happened that I risked giving my desk-mate a playful nudge. In those days we were still using double desks. I got the cold shoulder though from him; a scaly boy with red skin, red hair and a dribbling nose, John, his name was John. I had started out by sharing the desk with my first ever girlfriend, the lovely Rose but Miss Brown had stopped all that when she arrived. She did not approve of boys and girls sharing. She had done her damage yet again, for my desk mate was now giving me the full silent treatment.

I didn't like John much but could have used some support at that moment. It was as if a silent shiver went around the room. I had only ever had one or two class friends anyway. My real friends were the ones I had been brought up with in my own road, the road where many of us had been born and where most of us were to grow up. There were none of those friends in that classroom, no friendly faces, not even the lovely Rose. My eyes searched the room hopefully as I fingered the metal catch on my desk. My tormentor had evidently burned herself out, finally. She glanced around the room as if daring criticism but, in reality, I no longer cared what she was doing. I was engaged in an intense study of my desktop, for a quiet, stubborn, teardrop had nestled in the corner of my right eye. I was yet again in the throes of a mighty effort to rid myself of it without moving a muscle lest I should attract attention to myself. This silent battle seemed to take ages. Deep breaths and sniffs and gentle movements of the eyelids all combined in a mammoth battle to disperse the tear without resort to cuffing it.

"Slates and chalks children!"

The strain was suddenly and unexpectedly lifted. Amid the general clatter and bustle of desk lids opening and closing to the teacher's command I managed to knuckle the tear and rid my nose of the shameful and imminent danger of the miniature waterfall.

I could not concentrate on the word task set by the teacher, however. My ABCs were lost for the moment behind the bitter taste of tears and the newly acquired worry over my name. I stared and stared at the big map on the wall. It was the Empire map; brightly it shone as it stood boldly and uncompromisingly red, over huge areas of the world. I searched in vain for Germany. I had been shown where it was, but I had forgotten, and my reading ability was not up to the struggle at that distance. I turned my attention to Miss Brown. I glared at her, praying very hard to shrivel her with that glare. The Gods were not hearing me; however, I dug my fingernails into the chalk, the hard stick of chalk in my still sweating hands.

I felt true hatred for this woman but what was worse, I feared her. For the first time in my life I was afraid of an adult, so afraid that my stomach was sick at the thought of what she had said. How could it be that I had a German name? I had never been afraid before, not like this, not even when the stick of bombs had fallen, only a few houses away, and the blast had shattered all the windows and had blown the back door off. Grandad had been in the shelter with me and had pretended to put a drop of whisky into my night-time drink of hot milk. I had not been afraid when my Dad had gone off into the army. Everyone's Dad had done the same, and besides, your own Dad couldn't get hurt! I had not even been afraid on that bad, hazily remembered morning, when I woke up to hear the noises of my Grandad dying. My Grandad and friend of those cosy nights in the garden bomb-shelter was dying and the world just carried on as if nothing was happening that morning, in our little 'Andersen'. He must have been in very bad pain. They tried to make me leave, to go downstairs. I understood their quiet lies, I knew in my innocent heart, and I refused to leave. They did not force me to go. Grandad died in great pain without ever kissing me again. I was not afraid though, because I knew that Grandad would go to heaven. My Nan said so. I did not know where heaven was, but it could not be a bad place. My Nan spoke about it so softly.

I had recently reached four and could not, myself, remember much about Grandad now. They would tell me, but I could not remember, even trying hard, that, after a long day at work my Grandad would often sit me on his lap and share his dinner with me, his little boy. It was just the two of us in that cramped shelter. As a boy, however, I could remember the smell of the shelter though, the Grandad smell of it. The oil and sweat from the heat of the iron works, the smell of his pipe and the pint he would sometimes have on his way home. They had filled our little hole in the ground and that became a permanent memory of him. I missed him desperately.

I dug my penknife into the chalk and gently began to carve at it as I contemplated the floor and the terrible and so sudden, prospect of being somehow different. A rug had been pulled from under my feet and no power on earth would ever be able to put it back the way it had been.

"Please Miss". From behind me a voice I knew well brought me back to reality for a moment. I looked around. David Brownlow's hand was up in the air, his fingers twitching in the timeless manner of a boy who has left it just a bit too late before asking to be excused. Girls do not seem to be subject to this condition to the same level of immediacy that overcomes boys. They are either too sensible to leave it to the last moment or they are able to 'bottle' it better than boys if they do. Miss Brown was in no mood to bring relief to anyone that afternoon.

"No boy, wait 'till the end of the lesson. You can wait that long surely"? She began to make her way down the aisle between the desks, checking the work done by each boy or girl in turn. There was a nod here or a scowl and a cuff there. She came alongside my desk and her rage flared anew as she saw my blank slate.

"What have you been doing all this time"? She snapped the question at me.

"Where's your chalk? What on earth have you been doing with your chalk boy?" The pitch of her voice rose with each question. She stared down at me and the tell-tale scattering of chalk dust at my feet and on my clothing.

"What have you done to that chalk?" She repeated the question, this time pointing at my hands, chalky with unconscious carving. I looked down at last and opened my left hand. I closed it quickly. My heart jumped to my gullet and froze there. There in my left hand was the result of my five minutes of industry. I opened my hand again as if to check the evidence of my own eyes. Lying there, carved in perfect white miniature was a fine, hand worked, erect and circumcised penis. I was never sure how she recognised it so quickly for what it was, but it was certain that she did. She leaned over me, rigid with awful menace. She picked it up, finger and thumb, like a dead mouse or the real thing, from my unresisting hand.

"You dirty, filthy, little boy!" It was all she said and all she had time to say for, as she turned with her trophy, a second catastrophe was about to fall. It was enough, anyway, to distract her attention from me and the chalky dick.

It began unnoticed, as a mild rustle. Almost a whisper at the back of the mind as the brain fought to identify it before the ears had heard it. Then it became the sound of a hose directed at the side of a bucket as if to hide the noise. It was a trickle, then it was a flow which rapidly became a torrent as the dam burst and the waters poured forth in uncontrolled and uncontrollable bliss. It was the teacher's turn to freeze as the dreadful truth was made to dawn in the form of a bawdy and unidentified shriek from the back of the class.

"Brownlow's pissing on the floor!"

The whole back row disintegrated in exaggerated reaction as the boy-made river ran back to meet them. Evacuation was rapid and complete. Miss Brown fled.

The breakup of the lesson brought temporary relief. The inquisition and its knock-on effects were, however, destined to remain to haunt me through the years.

Two important things happened the next day; the first being that my Mum and my maternal Nan came to the school to interview Miss Brown. It would have been great indeed to have been a fly on that particular wall that day!

The second, and more important, was that they took me into the front room and began to talk to me. They began to relate the story of my family which opened some remarkable windows for me. I certainly did not understand it all at that time. Much of the meaning and implications needed to fall into place gradually over the years. The young 'me' though was both mystified and grateful for the explanations. When I began to understand them, moreover, it seemed that my father, when he had to go into the army, had left instructions that those left behind should try to hide the fact that he was just one element of a large Jewish family. That was his unrealistic attempt at an insurance policy for us in case the Nazis managed to cross the channel. What he had not taken into account though was that, in north London at that time, I was convinced that it was a bloody sight easier to be a Jew than for people to think you might be a German! That childish conviction established in me a series of future choices that became firmly established over the next few years.

I repeat though that it remains one of the great mysteries and sadnesses of my life that I was not a fly on the wall that day to hear…

Chapter Three

Dad Goes Away and Comes Home.

Mum and Dad were married in 1938. I was born in 1939 and War was declared just six months later. It disrupted the lives of virtually the whole population of Europe as well as Africa and Asia for six years in one way or another as well as the USA from December 7, 1941, after the Japanese attack on Pearl Harbour. On 11 December 1941, just four days after the Japanese attack on Pearl Harbour and the United States declaration of war against the Japanese Empire, Nazi Germany declared war against the United States, in response to what was claimed to be a series of provocations by the United States government when the U.S. was still officially neutral during World War II. The decision to declare war was made by Adolf Hitler, apparently off-hand, almost without consultation. It has been referred to as Hitler's "most puzzling" decision of World War II. He may even have been taken by surprise at the Japanese attack on Pearl Harbour. He had after all declared war on the USSR on June 22nd earlier that year. It was, even for him, a big year for errors of strategy.

Dad was called up before the end of 1941 for training in the R.A.S.C. I was only a few months old when he had to go away. We saw him for a few days here and there over the next several years, but his presence made little impression on me. Mum became pregnant on two of the occasions of Dad's visits home. She suffered miscarriages during each of those pregnancies. Dad requested compassionate home leave on each of those bereavements. His C.O. refused permission on both requests. He actually used the accusation that Dad had either manufactured the idea of miscarriages or had even more seriously that Dad had himself organised and paid for illegal abortions. I still have the letter written by my Dad to my Mum, in now very fading pencil, in which he tries to explain to my sick and desperate mother the reason that he had been refused permission for home leave for the second time. I was far too young to understand the reasons for Mum's distress at the time. I can only hope and believe that she would have received substantial support from her nearby family.

I was even too young to really understand what "Dad" meant. We did not get together as father and son until he was de-mobbed late in 1945. It was not a relationship made in heaven for many months, years even. I had lived in the company of my Mum, my Nan and a collection of Aunts for the whole of my life up to the age of six. I had only seen Dad during a couple of brief leave periods that he was granted. I was, therefore used to him coming home for short periods when he brought with him such goodies as he could acquire by hook or by crook, often the latter, we had some fun and he went away again...

It became clear on this occasion though, after days and then weeks had passed, that he was not going away anywhere or anytime soon. It was also clear that he was determined to be a new force in town! I resented this big change in my life, together with the constant arguing, night after night, that had begun between Mum and Dad. This conflict persisted to the extent that I began to wet my bed. I spent many months, even years being dragged by Mum or Dad, sometimes both, to Great Ormond Street Hospital to no avail. The bed-wetting was the bane of my young life. It continued until my early teens on and off until I met my first girlfriend! I have since qualified as a psychologist, but I can only hazard 'reasons' for my eventual cure! I am quite clear in my mind however as to the reasons for the onset of the condition. I discuss these in greater depth in a while.

There were some aspects of Dad's return home that appealed very much to my childish sense of greed, however. He brought with him some true riches that he had collected during his travels through France Belgium and Germany. There was a huge Grundig radio that he had 'found' in a German railway station , there were also two trains sets, one electric, the other a beautiful clockwork model of the Flying Scotsman Engine, complete with its Tender. It was a beautiful example of its type and seemed very strange, coming from Germany at that time, after six years of war. Additionally, there was a meccano-type set with parts made of wood and much larger than the metal ones with which we later became familiar. That is when we could afford them in the years after the war. In this majestic collection of goodies there was also a cine projector with films. All of these films were in black and white, but we were used to that at the cinema in those days. A few of the films were German Wehrmacht training films but others were comedy greats such as, Laurel & Hardy, The Marx Brothers, and W. C. Fields who all reached their creative peaks in the 1930s, as did Mae West. 'Our Gang' also known as 'The Little Rascals', there may even have been one of the Three Stooges, I just cannot remember everything in that collection of riches. I can definitely remember one final item though. It was a wooden box-tray containing a double layer of bunches of black grapes. I did not know how or where Dad gained those. I did not care either because fruit of that type had become an unobtainable delicacy for the whole of my life up to that point. I am happy to say now that Dad distributed some of those black delicacies to friends and family. I now also realise that so many grapes, which had already been in the tray for some days, might well have 'gone off' by the time that we had managed to scoff the lot. None of us had seen grapes before. Once tasted I was enthusiastically quite prepared to risk damage to my digestive system in an effort to eat as many of the tasty little devils as humanly possible. I never did get the chance; I am now pleased to say.

As I have said my Dad was in the Royal Army Service Core. As a part of training, he learned to both drive a lorry and ride a motor bike. In these capacities he was involved in the D Day landings known officially as Operation Overlord, also known as the codename for the Battle of Normandy, the Allied operation that launched the successful invasion of German-occupied Western Europe during World War II. The operation was launched on 6 June 1944 with the Normandy landings. A 1,200-plane airborne assault preceded an amphibious assault involving more than 5,000 vessels. Nearly 160,000 troops crossed the English Channel on 6th June and my Dad was a part of all that.

Dad was billeted for a short period with a French family in Langrune Sur Mer. I maintained a friendship with one member of that family on and off for many years from the age of twelve until she passed away three years ago at the age of 93. She was therefore a young woman living in a Northern Coastal town of France throughout a heavily manned military Nazi occupation. She must have witnessed many scenes and activities of real interest, even value and some danger. In all the years that I knew her, of the times we met of the many occasions that we corresponded or met I never once asked about her war experience [What a Clot!] Just once and I still have her letters; she wrote to me and mentioned Dad's first meeting with her family. She explained that Dad arrived at their door to introduce himself. Her Mum met him at the front door at which point he stammered an apology to the fact that by standing orders he was armed with a Sten gun. It seems that her mother burst into tears and threw her arms around his neck. Dad's apology after years of Nazi occupation switched on her Mum's emotional taps. That was all I ever learned about my Dad's war and not from him. He, like many men would never speak of it even when asked direct questions.

Mum once told me that Dad was with the British troops who opened up Belsen Concentration Camp. If that were true it would have been a traumatic experience for a Jewish man albeit a man who had foresworn religion. I have actually found some photos of my Dad with his motor bike and in his RASC uniform .I got to thinking about why a man in Northern France during that period of intense warfare would have been required to use a motor bike. The only reason that I have been able to come up with is that he must have been a despatch rider. If that were so, and it does seem likely, it could have been quite dangerous at a time when military boundaries were quite changeable, quite fluid in fact. I guess that many of us leave it too late to discover as much as we would have liked to do before the death of a parent.

 I did not wonder as a six-year-old boy just how my Dad managed to bring home all his 'ill gotten' but very welcome gains. I have to tell you in the same breath that the same six-year-old boy did not care a single jot. His Dad was though a man with but the one back and two arms allocated to any of us. It was not until many years later that I fell upon a likely answer to the conundrum during a period when it was, too late to ask the questions. Thinking about my parents though it occurred to me that there was a real puzzle in the question of how in blazes did he do it? I was recently reading an article about British troops being shipped home after hostilities had ceased. Apparently, they were told that the customs officials in British ports had been ordered to challenge and seize any items from soldiers that looked as if they might have been looted or in any other manner could be viewed as contraband.

The rumour circulated that charges were going to be brought….whereupon items of, shall we say of extra-curricular status were being disposed of over the side of the ship. Clearly Dad did not resort to this action; his return home made that very clear. Then the penny dropped; he must have used his lorry! Dad was a lorry driver in the RASC. He was in charge of his lorry until he had to have it signed off sometime between his 'Return to Good Old Blighty' and his discharge from the Army. I don't know just how he managed it but it stands to reason that his lorry must have been involved in some fashion. I know for sure that that was just what I would have done. In Retrospect I, once again, take my hat off to him, My Dad, the smuggler! His immediate return home with all those goodies made one little boy very happy.

By the time that we get to the Normandy landings in June 1944 the Allies had, some four years previously lost the Battle of France on the Western Front, the Battle of Dunkirk was a victory achieved from almost total near defeat. It involved the defence and evacuation to Britain of much of the retreating British and other Allied forces in Europe from 26 May to 4 June 1940. About 350,000 British and Allied forces were saved and brought back to this country by ships of the Royal Navy, the Merchant Navy and a virtual flotilla of small boats that were recruited into service or which simply joined voluntarily in the massive effort to evacuate the various military forces from the wide, open beaches of Dunkirk.

....

Chapter Four

Dad Comes Home

WITH THESE FOLLOWING WORDS Neville Chamberlain, THE UK Prime Minister at the time, announced the declaration of war against Germany on the BBC Home Service, Sunday 3 September 1939, 11:15

"I am speaking to you from the cabinet room at 10 Downing Street. This morning the British ambassador in Berlin handed the German government a final note stating that unless we heard from them by 11 o'clock that they were prepared at once to withdraw their troops from Poland, a state of war would exist between us. I have to tell you now that no such undertaking has been received, and that consequently this country is at war with Germany."

And so, we were at War.

My Dad fortunately had managed to avoid being involved in the near catastrophe of The Battle of Dunkirk which was fought in and around Dunkirk, France, during the Second World War, between the Allies and Nazi Germany. Dad was still undergoing his military training at the time that the expeditionary forces of the Allies were being surprised and overwhelmed by the better trained better organised and better equipped force of the Wehrmacht. My Uncle Ted was one of those fortunate soldiers evacuated from the beaches of Dunkirk. He also had the real bad luck to be sent to the Far East where he became entangled in the Burma campaign. Uncle Ted had a real hard war.

When Father Comes Home Part 2

I was always very fond of my Uncle Ted. There was always the cheery "hello boy" greeting when I met him and that was quite often because he and my Aunt Rose [Mum's immediately younger sister] lived in a few rooms in my Nan's house after the war. Mum had one further younger sister who is my Aunt Joan; she is still alive and now in a nursing home in Enfield. She has been a constant friend to me all my life.

I worked for my Uncle Ted for a couple of years in my teens when he was working as a bakers' delivery man, for the co-op, around Stamford Hill. My favourite lunch by far when with him on those Saturdays was beans on toast. He always bought me a lunch in the same 'greasy spoon' and I also received five bob in wages. I look back with some affection to those days with my Uncle. They were stress free. Ted, and he did ask me to call him by his first name, as did some other of my Uncles when I reached my older teens. Nonetheless I still think of him as 'Uncle' Ted. My thoughts on that are that I might know many 'Teds' in my life but I'll only ever have one Uncle Ted. The same principle goes for all of my Aunts and Uncles.

It was when I was working in Stamford Hill that I first heard the term "Shabbos Goy" used as it was used, in reference to me when I was kind enough to help an orthodox Jewish woman by lighting a fire for her on a Saturday morning. She had asked my Uncle if he could help but he naturally didn't want to risk getting dirty. I looked at him as if to say, 'what about me?' He grinned and pushed me gently forward. Saying to the astonished woman "he's good at lighting fires." This was actually true as I tended most of the fire-lighting duties at home.

As I entered the house I noticed a small boy, about 5 or 6 years old. He moved nervously towards his mother asking, in Yiddish "What's he doing Mummy?" "It's okay darling – he's just the Shabbos goy". I bristled fiercely at this because Shabbos goy is not a complimentary term. It is also doubly insulting in my view when a person has been very decent enough to enter your home in the middle of other work in order to help you out.

My Yiddish has never been perfect. At that age I knew just enough to understand what the woman had said to her son as well as to appreciate the dismissive nature of it. Over the years I have acquired a better understanding of the language. At that age though I knew just enough to cobble together some sort of response in English though as I finished lighting the fire and was on my way out of the house. "By the way Mrs I'm no Shabbos goy!"

I took great personal delight at the look of disbelief on her face as I left the house to re-join my Uncle at the trusted three-wheeler.

Mum and Dad sadly did not have an altogether peaceful, or happy marriage, in fact they had a marriage that should in reality have ended in divorce. They argued constantly and I am convinced that my sister would bear witness with me that our parents had a terrible marriage. It was more like a battleground than a marriage. From my point of view, I loved them both very much moreover they were both nice people when taken separately. They were just not good friends and friendship has to be the basis for any permanent union. As a child and young teenager, I hated going to bed because I knew that soon after I left my parents alone, they would begin their nightly routine of hateful and very loud argument. I dreaded night times because my sole lullaby was the noise of their fiercely angry exchanges. As I have thought about this many times over and over again through the years, I am convinced that there are two possible reasons as to why these two good people would be so far out of touch and permanently so very angry with each other.

The first of these was the absolute attitude of my father that "no wife of his would go out to work." He just would not discuss the matter other than forbidding it. For him the topic was closed. For him it was an absolute question of roles. This would be seen nowadays as the perfect example of patriarchy at work but my Dad had loved my Mum and saw it as his role to provide for his family. Britain at that time was at the very beginning of what we now see as the very justified women's 'movement for equality' and the only too gradual move towards equal rights for women. My Dad had not moved at all in that direction. My Mum desperately wanted to go out to work as a means of relieving herself from some of the tedium of domesticity that was her entire life. She was however battering at a door that just was not going to open, not ever!

It was therefore a fact that Mum's life was one of domestic drudgery just as her Mum's had been. The difference between the two was that My Nan, Mum's Mum, would have been on my Dad's side in any open family forum on the subject. It never got that far though because it was a subject that Dad would never allow into discussion. Thus, my Mum's life was what it was; it was a life defined in the ritual of domestic chores. She was unfortunately tied to the backward conventions of the time; so too was my Dad in his own sadly stubborn way. Those times were also stubbornly tied to difficult to-open divorce proceedings. I do not wish this document to become a historical study but the short summary that follows gives a very brief insight to how and when the laws on divorce became more freely available to ordinary folk.

Both World Wars caused a spike in divorces, but it was not until the Divorce Reform Act 1969 that they reached towards the level we are familiar with today. This legislation marked an important shift not merely because it added further grounds for divorce, on the basis of two years' separation with the other party's consent, or five years' without, but because it removed the concept of 'matrimonial offences' and hence the idea of divorce as a remedy for the innocent against the guilty. By 1969 my parents had been married for over thirty years and the old prejudices against divorce still persisted in many minds even after the review of the law. Mum and Dad continued to exist in their state of unhappy disharmony.

Mum's routine was almost identical to that of the majority of women at that time. Mondays were washing days. One only had to travel by train to any destination in the country on a Monday for this to become obvious and confirmed; you would have seen washing lines bedecked with the family wash. This would have carried over to the next day in large families. After the washing women were faced with other mundane chores such as ironing the collection of different items that had to be ironed. The couple of days that followed, between washing and ironing were days occupied with other housework; for Mum this included whitening the stone boiler in the corner of the scullery, as well as doing the front doorstep; black-leading the kitchen range and red-leading the two-foot approach to the front doorstep. To these were included in the to my mind, huge range of other demeaning aspects of the whole domestic scene as far as women were concerned. At least a half of my memories of my Mum were of her on her knees polishing or whitening or red leading or black leading some or other part of the family domesticity.

It is also the case that most women also saw it as a duty to keep clean and tidy that part of the public pavement in front of their own house. This often extended to that of an elderly neighbour or one with a disability. It also extended to the snow and slush of winter as well as the dust of summer. There was much less worry and concern in those days as to the implications if for example a person were to slip on some ice left over in the wake of inadequate snow clearance. Neighbours seemed to be of a mind that the risk was worth the candle in exchange for a kindly act.

Friday of course was main Shopping Day. The world knows that well that Britain was the nation of orderly queues of course and there were, as-yet no supermarkets to ease the system as far as the choosing of items was concerned. There were general shops that catered for almost everything and specialist shops for the rest, fishmongers, butchers bakers and even, probably, candlestick makers. There were also many small specialist hardware stores where a long-term employee would cheerfully climb three sets of stairs to bring you your request of four candles or was it fork-handles? At all of these individual shops there were queues. At the head of most of those queues was a woman (it was mostly women who did these chores) who was telling the shopkeeper her choices, often one by one whilst she also gossiped to him at the very moment that he achieved each of her choices thus slowing him down interminably. It can be seen then that shopping for a whole household could easily take the best part of a day. On top of all this was the preparation of food for breakfast lunch and dinner, the meal of supper was usually informally acquired. It is though, no wonder to me that women, many of whom had been supporting the country by working in industry during the war, began to rebel against the domestic abys that was how many of them saw the then current status-quo. Mum was up against an even harder granite wall than most in her frequent attempts to argue for more freedom.

I am trying to understand what it was like in the 1950s for families who had mentally ill members to take care of. My family was in my view among that number because in that possible category was my mother; in that she suffered two Nervous Breakdowns that each required a period spent in a care home. These homes were under that name of Mary McCarthy homes or something very similar. What is important here though is that I can speak from my own experience as a young child; that Mum needed to go away for two lengthy periods of rest. Whether recuperation occurred is another matter; perhaps it had too steep a hill to climb?

Mum suffered these two episodes and was probably never free of issues regarding her mental well-being. Nervous breakdown is a term that was and is sometimes used to describe symptoms of intense mental and emotional distress. These feelings make it difficult or even impossible to carry on normal functioning and complete daily tasks.

As a child my only concern was that Mum would return to us as soon as possible. As an adult now I am able to look back on our family life at that time and allocate large portions of responsibility to the relations between our parents and the fundamental lack of opportunity for women in the day and for my own mother in particular.

In this observation I am certainly not pointing blame at my father; he was a kind and generous man. I once had an argument with a female instructor on this general subject when I was undertaking a course as a social worker; she was all up for 'blaming' men in general for the totality of this intense social inequality that society imposed on women.

My memories of the mores of the time were that they were couched within terms such as "a women's place…" and "a man's responsibility." Society was not yet ready to hold these generalisations to the fire. Even after two world wars during which women had upheld the reins and strains of the industry of the nation there were still women who were content to go back to their former roles. Many were not of course and having said all that the "Times they were a-Changing!" Mum could not benefit from those infant changes because Dad did not recognise that it was all happening. He saw his own role very clearly and it was as sole provider for his family, and it was damned onerous. He worked long hours and did private work in his 'spare' time'. In many ways he was just as much a prisoner of his own lack of foresight as was Mum, Bloody Sad Times!

I first worked at Lloyd's Bank for seven years after I was demobbed from my two years National Service in the RAF .At the end of those seven years I went to work with Dad in the East End; that was in 1969. Dad died from a heart attack in 1973 and I was left with a business in which I had to learn a lot about making clothes in a very short time. My Uncle Ruben helped me a lot both emotionally and practically. Additionally, though my Mum stepped into the breach by coming into work with me after Dad passed away. I was very glad to have her there with me. Mum came into work in the Mornings and left just after lunch .She took charge of the office legal/admin side of the business. I was really amazed at how very firmly but politely it was that she dealt with aspects of that work. Mum always seemed to be sad to leave the factory, but she did become tired by lunch time. It was also an indirect journey to and from Whitechapel for her home in Enfield.

Mum had never been a well woman, so I was both surprised and anxious for her. Despite my reservations however she was determined to keep coming to the factory. I also liked having her there and that period developed into the best period of my life with my Mum since the end of the War. One day I got the feeling that she was more weary than usual. When it was her time to leave I helped her into her raincoat. It was a very nice coat I thought. It had been fashioned in deep red proofed cotton and it suited her very well. I had been in the 'rag trade' for some years by then and the feel for such things had become a part of what I was. Being with Mum had also become just as much a part of my life as being with Dad had been before he passed away. I followed her that day because the emotion of seeing her so tired was in my mind. It was such a tragedy that she and Dad had not been able to work together when both were younger and fitter and able to enjoy being together. I have often been bugged through my life by a series of if-onlys…

I followed Mum down the stone staircase as usual to the courtyard and through the archway into the street; Fieldgate Street. We had said our "by-byes" upstairs as usual but instead of returning to the cutting room I waited in the street for a few moments and then began to follow her. I intended only to follow her to the corner of New Road where she passed the tiny entry of the schull [Synagogue] where I had become used to attend on Saturday mornings. Instead of watching her as she turned right into Whitechapel Road, I continued to follow her as she passed the London Hospital. The stalls were still out and plying their trade as I followed Mum along Whitechapel Waste and so on to the Whitechapel Tube station. She was stooped and very sad of appearance as she entered the station. I still have a clinging memory of that dear, still not old woman as she disappeared into the very busy deep dark mouth of that underground station and felt the weight of her effort to struggle to and fro between Enfield and Whitechapel It did not help me after Mum died when my Aunt Joan informed me that, "of course she only did it so that she could have time with you." She meant this to be kindly, but it did nothing to ease the strong feeling of guilt that has sat on my shoulder ever since Mum died.

<u>Dad and the 'birthday parrot</u>

Dad had bought a parrot in Petticoat Lane as a birthday present for Mum when I was about nine.

Petticoat Lane is London's world-famous Sunday market and nowadays sells mainly clothes for men, women and children, from street-cred club-wear to excess orders of designer goods and last year's must-haves. There was also a large amount of 'Cabbage' sold which is a local term for garments made by an 'out-worker' for a manufacturer out of cloth that he has 'saved' from the docket of cloth supplied by the manufacturer. The manufacturer regards this as stealing. The out-worker regards it as fair game as long as the manufacturer gets the number of garments he is expecting. 'Cabbage' is also one of the mysteries of the East-End that interests the Tax Authorities. They also take the view that it is stealing; not revenue from the manufacturer but the tax rather, that should have been charged on the sale of the garments. The out-worker sometimes forgets to declare this source of income.

One of the street's specialities is leather wear at the Aldgate East end and there's bric-a-brac, household goods, in fact everything you could possibly think of plus some other bits and bobs too. The market is held in and around Middlesex Street on Sundays from 9am to 3pm, with a smaller market open on Wentworth Street from Monday to Friday.

It is a little-known fact that Petticoat Lane itself doesn't exist nowadays; we have the Victorians' prudishness to thank for that. Wishing to avoid any reference to ladies' undergarments they changed the name to Middlesex Street in the mid-1800s. With more than 1,000 stalls lining the streets on a Sunday bargain hunters come in their droves, it's a great scene worth the trip even if you're not shopping. There are other areas of interest nearby, but Petticoat Lane remains London's biggest street jumble sale, but for bargain hunting with a bit of haggling thrown in, it's the original and the best.

Regulations prior to the Factories & Workshops Act of 1901 were lax, with virtually no control of working conditions for adults. The few convictions of Jewish workshop owners were for working on the Jewish Sabbath. Wages were unregulated until the Trade Boards Act of 1909.

In Britain it was forbidden to trade from a shop on Sunday, the Christian Sabbath. An exception was made for shops owned by Jews, whose Sabbath was and is on Saturday, Friday night to Saturday night in fact. Sunday markets therefore evolved at Petticoat Lane, and the surroundings of Brick Lane. It has been written that; "On Sunday Middlesex Street and its adjoining roads and street became a curious tangle of humanity… the most abiding impression it leaves on your mind as you struggle out of its seething, shouting gesticulating population is of infinite picturesqueness, and the life-stream tumbling like a swirling torrent along its course". English shopkeepers complained, however, that some Jewish owners took away their business, respecting neither Sabbath, and trading every day for long hours. As if…?

Getting back to Dad; however, he arrived home this day with a parrot that he had bought for Mum from Petticoat Lane, it was not a large parrot as these things go but it made an immediate big impression on Mum. She declared War!

"What the bloody hell am I going to do with that? I can't wear it and I can't cook it!"

Mum had right on her side, but Dad looked so miserable that I had to take pity on both him and the parrot.

"Can we call him Bill?" I asked my Mum; trying to break the ice a bit, I guess.

"You can call him bloody St Francis of Assisi for all I care. What does he do?"

I couldn't answer that. What do parrots do anyway except make other parrots?

"Bloody hell!" I muttered too loud.

Mum heard it and gave my ear a clout. "Oh Mum! He just bit me!"

I tried to explain that the little devil had just bit me as I tried to move him from the carrying box to the large cage that dad had struggled home with. She just scowled at me. Bad that! I'd done nothing wrong. I'd somehow got on the wrong side of both Mum and the damned parrot I couldn't blame the parrot though. He probably related me to the dosser who'd put him in the cardboard box an hour or so ago...

Well then Bill the Senegal Green parrot had come home to live with us. I came to like Bill very much, but I also resolved, almost immediately that I would never keep a bird in a cage myself. They are beautiful creatures and are intended to fly and live in a wild natural environment. Bill had been captured in Africa and shipped to England in bulk, in cages containing far too many other birds. His left side flight feathers had been ripped out so that he could not fly. He wanted to fly because he tried to do it when I gave him some freedom by opening his cage door and taking him onto my shoulder. This was a process that demanded some resolve on my part because there was a constant defence of my ear lobes that had to be put into effect. He was not even put off when I resorted to swearing softly at him. No! Ear lobes were in as far as Bill was concerned.

Other than that, we got on O.K. Bill and I, and he really liked the freedom of walking on the outside of his cage. It was pitiful however when he tried to fly. He knew that he should be able to do it but was so clumsy and his trips from the top of his cage always took a downward flight path.

We had a cat! He too took a one-time interest in one of Bill's early failed flights. Bill landed as usual heavily on the floor. This made him grumpy because he could not understand why he wasn't somewhere up near the ceiling. There was a scuffle, one startled screech from Bill then a series of cat screams and howls as Bill took a firm hold on Tom's long furry tail and just would not let go. It took me a while to prise the two apart and it was a match in which Bill took the prize. He finished up way- way ahead on points. Parrots have a grip with their beaks that allows them to move the lower jaw backwards and forwards under the upper, longer curved beak; this provides them with what amounts to a portable nut cracking tool. Tom's tail spent a number of long, long seconds on the 'nut-end' of that tool.

You will see from the contents of the last paragraph that our family was not BIG on fancy names for our pets.

At Mum's suggestion I put the rather large cage that Dad had struggled home with on the far corner of the wide lower work surface of the Welsh Dresser. Bill fought a bit as I put him through the door and placed him on one of the perches. He then set about breaking his bell as if it were the source of all his ills.

Our brave little parrot then set about the process of choosing long term enemies one of course was to be Tom whose tail was attacked every time it came within range of Bill's beak as he sloped around the back of Bill's cage. My Nan came first, however, on Bill's list of enemies. She came into in into the kitchen that same day. She had popped in to see Mum and to wish her a happy birthday. She sat down in her usual chair between the kitchen table and the end of the Welsh dresser right near Bill's newly established home. It was a bad move! She had been seated for very few moments when suddenly – 'whoosh' – she was doused with water from Bill's newly reconstructed bell. The bell was in the shape of a very small upside-down saucer with a clanger hanging from apex centre on a tiny chain of small metal links. Bill's idea of re-construction had been to very quickly decide that he had no use for the clacker, so he had ripped it from its roots at the apex. The bell he had decided would make a very useful dish from which to douse my poor old Nan with water dipped from his in-cage water trough. For some reason Bill had made the instant decision that he did not like Nan, she wasn't his Nan after all. Every time she came to the house, she sat automatically in the chair she had always used and every time the refrain "you old bugger!" was to be heard in the home as Nan received her usual greeting from Senegal! Her explosive vocabulary varied from "Sod"! To rotten old bleeder"! But her vocabulary rarely descended to expletives much lower than those.

It was a good job that Bill never learned to mimic the human voice though. His vocabulary would have been very rich in basic 'Street English'!

Bill and I had a long but intermittent relationship. All the time that I was at home he would be allowed out of his cage. He still tried the occasional flight with the usual sad consequences. Still, you had to give him points for trying! He even forgot to chew my ears for a while. Then I had to leave home to do my National Service and did not return to the parental home. He remained incarcerated in his cage until about 15 years later when my parents died one after the other about fifteen months apart.

There was nowhere else for the poor old devil to go. He came home to live with Joyce and me and our teenage kids. I then resumed his forays out of the cage, but he had become quite spiteful and seemed to want to take it out on my damned ears all over again. We both persevered but he improved only partially. Perhaps he blamed my ears for his years of incarceration? My lasting memory of my birdy friend is that whatever car I drove during those last years I would hear him begin to screech as I pulled up in front of the house as I returned home. I still hear the old sod screech even now sometimes as I return home in a car. That may well be a phantom memory, but I don't care. It's true enough for me. The end came finally one night when Joyce and I were sitting watching the telly. There was a dull thud and Billy was dead, in true Parrot fashion he had fallen off his perch!

My only epitaph and promise for my sometimes-spiteful old friend is "Bill I promise you that I have never and I will never keep another bird in a cage"!

<u>A further Reason to be at War?</u>

Finally, and reluctantly, I have been concerned that there may however have been a further, darker possibility for the bitter estrangement between my parents that grew quite quickly between them after Dad returned home. It forced its way into my thinking as I grew into my late teens and became more aware of the ways of the world. I was also still young enough to remember the period at the end of the War when personal life was at turmoil for the whole world. I have moreover continued to anguish over the nights of disturb, and the fierce, angry words that were exchanged continually between my parents. The unwelcome circumstance that has grown in my mind is founded on the possibility that Mum's marital loyalty may have wandered off course a bit in the period between the end of hostilities in Europe and Dad's return home. I write this only after some very careful and painful consideration. I have of course to consider that I was only six years old at the time and not at all 'au fait' with the ways of adults with reference to love and sex.

The issue, the possible issue, arose when a group of builders and decorators arrived in the street. They were charged to repair War Damage of which there was plenty all over Britain but not much at all in our house. In my young and naïve way, I began to feel uncomfortable at the amount of attention one of the men was paying to Mum. Then there was the almighty row that took place in the house of a neighbour just across the road and to the left of us. Mrs 'A' was the formidable woman who actually owned her own house had 'called a meeting' at which my Mum was the primary object on the agenda it seemed.

I stood in the street outside that house listening helplessly at the sound of my Mum being harangued inside. The front door was closed but I could hear Mrs. 'A' speaking very loudly and my poor Mum trying to reply but not getting any space to do so. This went on for an age, too long, far too long for me, a little boy, hearing my poor old Mum trying to get a word in edgeways and very emotionally to boot. There were moreover several other women, all neighbours putting their two penny worths into the mix. Mum finally came out of the house. She had clearly been in tears and would not allow me near her for several minutes after we had returned to our house.

I realise that these observations only add up to vague circumstantial evidence but Mrs A was not a close friend so it was a big surprise that she would be involved like that or, in fact in any way at all, with my Mum . It just had to be something serious...As I say, I loved my Mum and Dad. It did take me a while to get used to Dad being a permanent fixture, but we got on pretty well after a while. They did, after all, allow me a huge amount of personal freedom from quite a young age. I say I loved them which is true. The fact is however that I loved each one of them separately but did not even like them as a couple sometimes. As a young child their arguing, often for hours on end just after I went to bed really upset me. I felt that my world was being torn apart and I couldn't fix it.

 I am moreover totally convinced that my parents' discord was the root cause of my beginning to wet the bed after Dad came home. I did not wet the bed, neither before he returned permanently to the house nor during the two holidays of a week each that I spent with my Nan at Ramsgate after he came home. These holidays took place in the summers of 1946 and 1947. I remember clearly that I shared a bed with Nan, so I definitely did not wet the bed during those weeks. The apparent discord between Mum and Dad lasted for the whole of Dad's life. I can remember him saying to me on several occasions and very sadly when we sat together towards the evening in the cutting room. "You know Tone I don't want to go home." I knew that he didn't, but I still couldn't fix it! I never, ever knew how to fix it. Moreover, the trouble was I did want to go home! I had a wife and young family who I missed very much because of the hours I was working. Dad was quite happy to stay at the factory and there was a kind of emotional but unspoken blackmail that kept me there longer than was necessary. I did after all leave my house at six a.m. most mornings to get to the factory in time to start up the pressing machines

……………………………………………………..

<u>Chapter Five</u>

<u>Two B&B Holidays in Ramsgate</u> with my Nan.

I have no idea how it all came to be arranged but one tea-time in the early summer of 1946 my Mum suddenly asked me. "How would you like to go on holiday to the seaside with your Nan?" My only questions were "When Mum, when can we go?" and as an afterthought; "Where?" "Now don't get in a rush. It would be in three weeks' time to a seaside place called Ramsgate." I must have looked puzzled at this. She continued…"You don't know the place, but I can show you where it is on the Atlas, if I can find it. You'd be going on the train, and it would be just you and Nan. Is that O.K.?"

Would it be O.K.? I nearly wet myself in my excitement, the seaside, a train ride, a whole week and sure it would be O.K. just with Nan…why not? I didn't sleep much that night. I had many school friends who had never even seen the sea let alone go on holiday there, and for a whole week. What plans! What dreams! The three weeks simply dragged until the time I was walking proudly down Winchester Road with Nan, a small case with some night clothes and a change of outers together with a hanky containing five shillings in pennies. {I'm not going to explain this strange sum of money, you'll have to look it up, do you good!} Just to say that most of it had been gained lawfully as part my early wastepaper collecting empire.

Two trains later and we arrived at Ramsgate station. And yes, the air did smell different! London air was not the best in those days; it became much improved in the years following The Clean Air Act. [1956]But never up to the standard that one could breathe in Ramsgate.

A short walk and we were at the door of the B&B, The landlady a certain Mrs Roe. I only say it that way because just a few days ago I was talking to my cousin Paul, and he mentioned having holidays in Ramsgate with his Mum and Dad after the War. I have also, just a few days ago spoken to two further cousins, Christine and Janice, the two daughters of my uncle Bert, my Mum's oldest brother, and they both chuckled at the name, Mrs. Roe. Yup! They went there too! Mrs Roe apparently did well out of our family in those early post-war years.

"Not at Mrs Roe's?" I exclaimed. "Absolutely, Mum and Dad took me there a few times." was the answer; then. "How would you feel about visiting Ramsgate with me if I get down your way sometime?" And so that agreement between Paul and me has been made…

The first thing that became apparent from the start during those holidays was than Nan had no intention of being on my back all the time. She did come down to the front with me occasionally but was not keen on long forays away from her comfortable armchair and a chinwag with Mrs Roe. We did spend some time together in the amusement arcade on the promenade by the beach. That was where I invested my hard-earned pennies really wisely on ice cream and fruit machines. My five bob did not last long I seem to remember but the initial rapid disappearance of it did make me ponder a more cautious approach for the future.

At the beginning of our first holiday Nan was a bit more cautious about letting me go alone to the beach area but Mrs Roe had a son or maybe a grandson called John. I just cannot remember exactly but he was a few years older than me and was given the unwelcome responsibility of showing me around and looking after me. That responsibility was imposed on him and not much welcomed by John; he did though keep with me for quite a while and did make sure that I would be able to find my way back to the B&B. As I remember it, he lasted the whole of one morning before he sloped off to meet his own friends.

There was no invite for me to join him and quite frankly it was a new and welcome experience for me to be left alone to dig and delve into the many rock pools that existed on one of the beaches. Whether you are a beginner or an old hand you must surely be astounded by the wonder and sense of pure discovery that you can experience from the world of Rock Pools. They are the pure magic that disappears with the surging tide only to re-appear with the tide's ebb. By some miracle then the newly uncovered pool is a quite different world from the one recently covered and uncovered. I did not know half of the creatures that could be found there. Mrs Roe found me a simple, comic-style and brightly coloured magazine that opened up the beautiful and intriguing world of Rock pools. Several times I was late for a meal and on other times I had to be called from the beach before getting cut off by the rising tide.

"For a boy of seven and eight years of age who had never played by the sea before what could have beaten the unchaperoned exploration of those cool depths of a rock pool? Excitement rises as the oncoming tide is bringing with it the waves that are just now gently lapping close by, but which will soon engulf his investigations in yet another rising tide. The sun is shining down, and a fresh sea breeze does temporarily cool the sometime fiery summer air?"

It is often one of the earliest and most memorable introductions to the natural world for children and can arouse a lifelong passion for wildlife. The sights, sounds and scents of the seashore stir the senses and lift the soul. These multisided and multi sized pools of sea water are fleeting windows into the underwater world which appear each and every time the tide retreats. The sea in its many moods, leaving behind pockets of seawater trapped in the dips and hollows of the seashore. These transient mini seas offer a vital refuge for animals temporarily isolated from the sea. They offer oases of cool and shade for a variety of marine animals and plants in a desert of open, unsheltered rock and sand…

I did a lot of sea's-edge paddling too which brought me almost to the point of swimming during our second holiday there. Nan gave me a lot of freedom and, as I say, some of her time as well. I remember that we took one short train ride together on a funny old narrow-gauge train through a tunnel in the cliffs to Dumpton Park. It was not a long journey but the smoky old train smell in the tunnel has become an evocative memory of those two holidays with my Nan. Much loved and fondly remembered.

My two separate weeks away with Nan were peaceful. I owed her a lot for she was always a sanctuary for me. She never however took sides between me and my parents. I tried as best I could to repay her some of her kindness to me as a boy by keeping in touch after I moved down to Kent after Joy and I got married. My Aunt Joan was her main support and contact as time passed. I visited her quite often though especially when she moved into an Alms House in Church Street. Apart from Joan however her own children very seldom took the time to visit her. I know this because the lack of visits was a constant cry from her heart in discussions with me during my own visits to her. Nan was an ardent knitter. Nearly blind in old age she continued to knit. Her colour mixtures though were frequently SPECTACULAR!

Chapter Six

About a Boy 1945-1949

"Oyfn pripetshock brent a fayerl,

  un in shtub is heys.

Un der Rebe lernt kleyne kinderlach

  Dem alef-beys".

In the fireplace glows a fire,

  and the room is warm.

The Rabbi teaches little children

  Their A.B.Cs.

This is not a collection of stories just about myself; it is about me and some of my friends and so I changed my initial plan which was to relate only about my story because as I did so I realised that some of my friends had important places here. I do in fact meet two strangers unexpectedly here: Firstly, the harridan schoolmarm and secondly, myself in new light. I had suddenly become a stranger to myself in many ways. What was a Jew? How could I be Jewish? Why didn't I know about it? And so it had begun; the story of discovery about the stranger within me...

I remained confused for several years. The repetition of rebukes and setbacks, from both sides of the argument, regarding my Jewish heritage worked solely to confirm a decision that had its embryo in the first days at school immediately following that day of confrontation over my name. The confusion came from the secrecy of the previous five years as well as the social rebukes and confrontations I experienced and from totally unexpected quarters. I frequently asked my Dad to tell me more about his family, my unknown family but he remained stubbornly silent and perhaps naturally too bitter to get into any discussion with me on what became a more and more important matter for me. I have always had a stubborn streak, even as a child and Dad's refusal to engage me on the subject may well have been an important factor in my determination to continue along that very path of discovery and decision.

Dad entered the War as a confirmed communist but came out of it as a through and through Stalinist. This commitment of my Dad to the President of the USSR strongly inhibited me in any discussion with him about desire to investigate my Jewishness. He regarded any such discussion as an entry into a discussion of a religion which was totally against both his principles as a communist as well as his emotions as a badly treated member of a Jewish family.

 As I grew older, and my reading became wider I realised that the Stalin [Uncle Joe] so revered by My Dad and his friends was and had been one of the most-evil men on the planet for much of his life. His murderous regime was equal to that of Adolf Hitler and more, in that he was responsible for the deaths of in the region of around twenty million fellow Russians including many Jews on the same grounds as Adolf himself; that they were Jews. 'Uncle Joe' was equally a racist as Hitler. These were issues that Dad would never truly discuss. He was a confirmed Stalinist Communist and just could not see beyond that.

I heard, as a child, the stories spoken quietly over the singing crackle and bustle of the open fires in the evenings as the news rattled in from the Beeb of the Nuremberg trials and of the concerns of the US that too much time spent on these would give the Russians time to consolidate their position in Europe. I was too young at that time to fully understand the words. I took my measure of the situation from the alternate worried and angry expressions of my parents and their friends. I filled in the blanks more and more fully as I grew older and read more widely.

Someone once said that "if a person can remember their own childhood, they have the basis for a good story". To make an ending is to open up a beginning. That is why I have entitled this collection of stories as I have." Life was fun during our childhoods despite the many shortages. We had never had it, so we didn't miss it! As children and young people, we lived the vast majority of life outdoors and we truly did live it joyfully. I knew at the age of 4 years that the way to look was optimistically towards the future. My Uncle Bert, a member of the ARP had just given me a really cool imitation Tommy gun that he had made himself. He promoted me at once to "Chief of the Defence of the Realm." The ARP [air raid protection] was an organisation in the United Kingdom set up some time before WW2 and was dedicated to efforts aimed at the protection of civilians from the danger of air raids. Uncle Bert was in the ARP, he had a uniform and he had made me that wooden Tommy gun. It became my pride and joy in my daily battles with the Luftwaffe. The gun made a magnificent noise, just like the real thing as far as I was concerned. My gun had a handle that turned a large wooden cog against a fixed strip of wood. This combination made a very convincing rat-a-tat-tat noise as the handle was turned and in my little world I was convinced that my battle was with the Luftwaffe but I was four so the year must have been 1943. Most of the planes in the sky at that time would have been British or American. At the age of four I had never done an airplane recognition course and so many of my rat-a-tat-tat 'victims' may well have been Allied planes. Sorry Chaps! Anyone can make a mistake. Hey ho!

A smack in the face or/Oder A brik in di tokhes

The one is not an exact translation of the other, but it does in its own way portray the gathering exasperations that I felt as a series of put-downs begat outrage for me. It began on the first Easter at school when the preparations for Easter celebrations began. For most of my friends the power of Easter resided in whether they might get an Easter-Egg or not; chocolate in any form was scarce after all. As I say we lived in Edmonton and throughout the War the kind and thoughtful people of Edmonton in Canada sent food parcels to the children of Edmonton London. These parcels were distributed through the schools. Just after the War a shipment arrived of chocolate powder. The schools decanted this wonderful gift into appropriately sized brown paper bags and entrusted us children to convey the bags home to our mothers to be used, probably, in hot drinks. Any adult with any experience of children, especially with regard to children who have been starved from most sweet goodies for their whole lives up to that point should know what the result of that action would be; what actually did arrive home in many cases was a chocolate-stained child!

 As regards Easter however the school authorities took that all very seriously. Taking it seriously moreover apparently meant that a level of blame for the death of Christ lay firmly at the foot of the whole Jewish Nation. I was only six years old when this calumny was first levelled at Jews the identity of which population I was beginning to take on board for myself. It is difficult to explain why this decision began to grow within me at that time. I was living in a family where the murder of a member or members of the family at the hands of the Germans/Nazis was only too frequently on the suppertime menu. In my childish way I began to form the idea that me taking on board the identity of an anonymous Jewish boy I would in my tiny way replace one of the murdered hosts and thereby stick two fingers up to Adolf.

The claim that the whole Jewish nation had been and still was responsible for the death of Christ was the historical excuse for the murder of hapless millions century by century throughout history. My own paternal grandparents had flown from Poland in 1906 in order to escape a surge of Pogroms against Jews in the Easter of that year. When there came an element in a Reuters' report in 1964 that Pope Benedict, in a new book, had personally exonerated Jews of allegations that they were responsible for the death of Jesus Christ, repudiating the concept of collective guilt that had haunted Christian-Jewish relations for centuries. Jewish groups applauded the move. The Anti-Defamation League called it "an important and historic moment" and hoped that it would help a complicated theology "translate down to the pews" to improve grass roots inter-religious dialogue.

I was a young man at the time with a young family beginning. My first thoughts were "Up Yours Benedict! you need first to gain pardon for the Christian church for your part in the persecution of Jews throughout history!"

The Roman Catholic Church officially repudiated the idea of collective guilt in 1965. From my own travels and experience I am not myself convinced that the Pope's revised philosophy has as yet, in his words, fully "trickled down to the pews." We wait, more in hope than expectation. It certainly has far from disappeared in countries like Poland and many others in Europe for example.

At the age of nine or ten I went with other boys of my group to join the boy scouts. My chosen group was called something like the 12th Enfield. I got as far as buying some uniform. I was beginning to enjoy myself at the evening sessions joking and planning camping trips with other boys. I even took a couple of 'badges'; 'knots and 'semaphore' I seem to remember. It was all so long ago.

The sense of contentment all came crashing in on me one evening when AhKayler the scout leader approached me whilst I was demonstrating some knots to a new boy. She had her 'stern' face on. I looked up as she approached. "How long have you been with us Tony?" She asked me the question, but I knew that she knew full well how long I had been with the group; it was she who had greeted me and my three friends when we first arrived at the hall and stated to her that we would like to join her group. It was convenient for us, that hall, only about fifteen minutes-walk from Winchester Road. "About two months miss." I replied but somewhat puzzled. "I have not seen you at Sunday Church parade; not ever and I go every week." Oh, that was all she wanted, that was easily explained; or so I thought.

"That's because I don't go to church Miss, I'm Jewish." Well, you'd have thought I'd put a firework up her bum!

"It's a rule that you go to Sunday church parade in the scouts, and"---she took a very deep breath before she delivered the Coup de Grâce.

"This group is for Christian boys only; and they have to go to Sunday Church Parade."

She glared at my three friends who were clearly gob-smacked at this news. We were all agreed afterwards that no mention of the enforced Church Parade was made at the joining session. She had one more arrow from her sling for me, however.

"I'm sure there are appropriate groups for people like you, just not in a Christian group."

And there it was, the first time I had experienced the "People like You" dismissal.

I then went on to have a go at joining the Sea Scouts, a group over in the region of Bounces Road, this time in Edmonton proper. I don't know why but very naively I had thought that the location might make a difference. Not wishing to go too far along the road with this group though I asked the question on the second evening. I received the same clear response but this time without the "people like you" dismissal. The young group leader simply explained that Church Parade was a requirement. He also explained that there were similar Jewish Groups but that the nearest was at Stamford Hill as far as he was aware. I never did schlep up to Stamford Hill to join the Jewish Boys Brigade, but my sister did later go to the 'Hill' to join a Jewish youth club there. She actually got the opportunity to go to Israel with them. She even took the opportunity to visit our Aunt Pearl {Polly} in Bat Yam while she was there. I remember being quite envious of that. Aunt Pearl was a resilient character. She had lost her first husband with whom she was married in 1934 in an orthodox Jewish marriage. That husband Mark was a merchant seaman who was lost at sea early in WW2 during relief convoys in the North Sea to Russia.

Under these circumstances the death of my Aunt's husband could be assumed but not proved; which is the requirement of Jewish Law. She was thereby classified under Jewish Law to be 'Agunah' which means 'chained' as close as not, in Yiddish. Chained is indeed what it means in practice for a woman under all circumstances in which she can be classified as Agunah. There are other such circumstances that are beyond the scope of this story. First and foremost, it means that she cannot marry again in Jewish Law and if she were to marry outside of Jewish Law any resulting children would be classifies as Mamzerim {bastards}. Such children would be Jewish, as having a Jewish mother, but would never be able to participate in Jewish society. They would never be able to marry as Jews for example.

After the war my Aunt Pearl moved to Israel where she met a man whose whole family had been murdered by the Germans under the Nazi regime. Pearl and her new man, also named Mark as had been her first husband. They wanted to get married which was not possible at that time for her in Israel. They decided to cross the Mediterranean on that short trip to Cyprus. They married there in a registry office ceremony and went back to Israel where they metaphorically 'stuck two fingers up' to the religious authorities.

"Well Tony" she explained to me years later when I finally met her. "They could do nothing to us. We were well past the point of wanting children or even of having any and after all was said and done, we couldn't be declared as Mamzerim, could we?"

I also recall my first public rejection of the then seemingly global assumption that we were all tied to Christ. I was eight or nine, no more, and it came to bear on the assumptions by the majority that we all have a Christian name. It was during an afternoon role-call by the teacher. It had been irritating me for ages! She came to my name. "Kreit" she called "Yes Miss" I replied. "Christian name?" was the expected continuation… silence….I kept my silence for just a few tense seconds. Again, it came but with an embellishment and quite terse…"Christian name Boy?" I needed to break the ice…"I don't have one miss." "You don't have one what?" "I do not have a Christian name miss…" "Are you deliberately trying to make me angry?" "No miss I don't have a Christian name because I'm not a Christian…I'm Jewish." My given name is Anthony or Tony whichever you please." I had spotted the erstwhile unknown to me expression of 'given' name in an American comic. I liked it then and still prefer it to 'first name'. I gathered from her frozen silence that she was not keen on either, not just at that moment anyway.

This is not to be just the story of one boy though. It is a compilation of boys' stories rolled into one story. It is about me and my friends and just how I remember them, and how they remind me of stories as concerning how we played and lived and survived during and after WW2. It is set on and around Edmonton Green, north London. The times were, and had been, hard for many years but we were not aware of it being so because that was just the way it was and always had been for all of us. I did sometimes go to bed hungry because I had eaten the one last piece of the bread, with dripping, for my tea. That, however, was the measure of it for me. I was a young boy, the sole member of my generation to be born before the war. I lived in a house occupied by my Mum, my Nan, my Aunt Joan and my Aunt Rose and frequented, off and on, by many other members of the family mostly Aunts sometimes Uncles as well and I was the only child in the house. There was no way on this earth that I was going to be allowed to suffer real hunger!

Houses were not warm in the 1940s and 50s; they were not built for warmth then, as they are more and more these days. We had all-coal fires, one in each room in our house, except for the kitchen and the scullery. In the kitchen was a large black kitchen range and, in the scullery, we had a brick-built copper, constructed as a quarter circle into the immediate right-hand corner of the room as you entered from the kitchen. Into the top of the copper was set a large bucket which held the clothing whilst it was being boiled. The water in the bucket was heated by a coal fire from below. I do not actually remember this myself but there were family tales that young children had been known to have their early bathes in that copper. On reflection it occurs to me that the necessary judgement of the equilibrium between adequate heat and boiling alive could have proven very tricky indeed. I can testify moreover that I was never boiled alive!!

My very best friend was a boy called Trevor; he was the same age as me. I was convinced that he was the very best runner in the world. I once saw him run to catch-up a cyclist who had offended him while riding past. He clearly thought that he was fire-proof on his bike. He looked quite surprised when 'Our Trev' caught him up and held the boy's saddle in a firm grip during the ensuing interview.

 Another good friend was Brian. He was the eldest son of my Mum's good tea drinking and smoking friend Phil – Phyllis. They lived directly opposite. Mum and Aunty Phil often had one of their girls-together sessions on Friday evening in the kitchen when I was in the bath, in the kitchen.

 Bath-night chez Kreit was always Friday night. Dad had his bath first and I followed him with the addition of a scanty top-up with hot water. Mum and Aunty Phil's chat session would seem to begin right after Dad had finished his turn. It was the convention in those days and for decades after for children to refer to close neighbours as Aunty and Uncle. It is a good convention which adds its weight to the general pot of good manners in society in my view. If it still exists, then long may it do so!

We possessed just the one Tin bath that hung on a hook in the scullery during the week when it was not in use. On Friday night it came off the hook to be placed in front of the kitchen range for warmth. Warmth was a precious commodity in the house in those days. True enough there was a fireplace in every room, but coal was on ration just like all other commodities and stayed so for longer than others too. Windows were single glazed and the move towards heat insulation of houses was not even yet in its infancy. Coal did not come off ration until June 23rd, 1958, a full four years after the last of the food items in June 1954. Even when it came off of compulsory rationing it, like many other 'luxuries', remained firmly rationed by price.

I have to add here 'a propos' the situation of Mum and Aunty Phil using the kitchen for their mutual Friendship meeting while I was in the bath just a few feet away from them; it was Ok as far as I was concerned for quite a long while. That was until I got to my pre-teens and began to grow both pubic hair and a sense of masculine dignity. We did not have a bathroom and the front-room was always kept locked and virtually used only 'for best' until we achieved 'telly' status in or about 1951.To coin a phrase I quickly became peed-off early in my puberty that my Mum and her smoking mate should be so close while I was naked in the bath. At the point of maxi 'peeing off-dom' I made the decision that enough was enough and I asked – no demanded, money so that I could take myself off to the Town Hall baths to luxuriate in the privacy of a hot bath where, after a while, you could shout "More Hot water in No. 4 please" and a respectable quantity of the necessary was delivered to you without you having to get out of the bath in full view if two lady 'smokers' and schlep the stuff for yourself. I often chose to stay in that bath until the water became cold in the hope that the 'foggy pair would depart. It never happened, hence the escape to the Town Hall! In all this discussion of my own problems I cannot remember when my Mum and sister had their baths. This is due either to the selfishness of youth or the frailty of aged memory. Beg Pardon!

All this also happened about the time Dad bought his first car; a brand-new Ford Anglia of which I can still remember the registration number [NXY 705]. Dad was very proud of his little car and quite rightly too for it was a lovely little car for its time. It also served him well for years; as well as me for Dad himself taught me to drive in it when I was about 19 ½ . I passed first time when I was just 20.Dad was as pleased as Punch and so was I because it was one really good thing that he and I achieved together during that period of my life. Dad loved his little car. I can understand this love for a car because I have experienced that very feeling a number of times over the years with different cars.

NXY-705 was, however, a car of its age beloved as it was. It had no internal heater until the engine itself was hot enough to spare some heat through a flap in the engine compartment. In lieu of heat we had blankets over our knees. Dad even became used to a method of driving successfully with a knee blanket. He must have done OK; nobody died!

I am now going to try to describe the method of starting the car. This was achieved with the use of a simple piece of apparatus called, simply, the starting handle. This is a crank that is inserted, usually through a hole strategically provided in the front bumper. The end of the crank thereby becomes inserted into the front of the engine so that the engine can be turned manually. In cold weather this operation was often combined with the use of the choke.

A choke valve is present in carburetted engines. One of the fundamentals of combustion of fuel is that the fuel needs to be atomised and vaporised before supplying it to the combustion chamber. Now during cold winter days, the temperature is low so the fuel may be supplied into the cylinder in liquid form; as a result, there is a problem in the initiation of combustion. The choke valve solves the problem of the demand of more and more fuel in the form of a richer air-fuel mixture.

The combination of a starting handle with the choke on cold days was not always a friendly one for the poor unsuspecting or inexperienced user. The first rule of procedure was to keep the thumb of the hand destined to turn the handle Well Out of The Way by tucking it under the fingers of the hand gripping the handle and doing the work! Many a thumb has been damaged or even broken by a starting handle that has been violently kicked back by an uncooperative engine. For a more expert explanation of this painful phenomenon please consult Mr Google.

Dad joined the AA immediately; he wouldn't consider the RAC because the name smacked of "Upper Class Snobbishness" Mum and Dad both enjoyed a trip in the car out of London. T'was a joy indeed to get away from the close and often foggy environment of the biggest city in Europe.

As far as I can remember we were never able to have a fire in every room. I should know; I was the one for the most part whose job it was to lay and set the fires from my early years. I was about eight years old when I took the job away from my Mum. This was down to my earnest desire to save the house from unnecessary conflagration at the hands of my mater. She never got the idea of laying the kindling or of cleaning the grate out before setting the fire and then when the fire would not draw properly, she tried to compensate by holding a sheet of newspaper over the whole of the open fireplace. This was not a bad idea in principle because it can help to draw more air into the would-be fire from below and thereby give it the extra energy it needed. My Mum however would overcompensate more often than not for her failure to lay the fire properly in the first place by holding the paper in position for just those few seconds too long or that special distance just too close. In this way she often did create a fire in the very newspaper she was holding. Newspaper in this situation fairly flares up with a vengeance. More than once she singed her amply long hair to the chorus of a series of angry words containing the expletive "bugger" or "bugger it". That was the extent of her 'street language' range. I never heard her swear in other circumstances. I took on the mantle of chief firelighter chez Kreit both because I could and because I was by far and away the safer option.

It just occurs to me that I have not yet mentioned the loo. That may have been a Freudian slip, I'm not sure. The fact is that I would rather not have to mention that toilet at all. The memory of it has played such profound and lasting havoc with my 'loo psychology' throughout all the years since. It was an outside toilet, as favoured it is said by the Victorians, and as being the healthier option. All I would say to that is NUTS!! I remember only that it was bloody cold in winter. The door had a six-inch gap both top and bottom. We used to have very cold, often snowy winters in those days. You could be sitting on the loo in January with snow blowing in on you from above and below. If there happened to be any moisture on the seat when you sat down, then your bum would freeze to the seat whilst you did what you had to do. I got into the habit of always wiping round the loo seat with a sheet of newspaper before I sat down for fear of having the seat stuck to me when I went to get up. I am now over eighty I have only recently forced myself out of the inclination to do that. Newspaper was not my tool of choice by the way. Newspaper was the tool of necessity for all loo needs in those days. Manufactured toilet paper came into general use only fairly slowly after the war. Paper was far too important a commodity for it to be allowed to be used for base cosmetic needs of that sort.

Chapter Seven

Ways to Earn Money

Paper conservation and collection was a feature of public duty during and for years after the war. In fact, paper collection became an opening for me at a very young age to earn some money in the years after the war. There was a paper collection centre at the Edmonton Green end of Balham Road where they paid out money for wastepaper against a tariff of charges according to weight. One only had to construct a suitable means of carrying reasonable amounts of the stuff. It became quite socially acceptable in my area of society for young boys and sometimes girls to knock on doors to ask the householder if they had any wastepaper that one could take off their hands. That meant, of course, that you could be in business with a bit of get-up-and-go and an old set of pram wheels allied to whatever construction you had the patience to make. My own preference was always a steerable wagon because that meant that, after business was done fun could be had by using the wagon as a racing car in which to tear down Bury Street Hill. I managed to de-construct several promising wagons in that way. Several different sets and combinations of wheels came into service over time, for a number of such chariots. There were other ways to earn money though…

In the following pages I take a brief look at food rationing which will bring me to the national campaign to 'grow your own' in gardens and, above all allotments. That brought my entrepreneurial mind straight to the universal availability of horse dung. There were very few motor vehicles around in those days. Those that were available were strictly restricted in their movement by petrol rationing. It was still, for some years to come, the day of the horse and horse-drawn traffic. In my street alone all deliveries, coal, bread, milk and vegetables were delivered by horse-drawn vehicles. One only needed a small shovel and a bucket to be in the fertilizer business! It would have been wasteful to miss such an opportunity. There was many a time when I was able to collect a couple of buckets of 'prime fresh' horse poo from right outside our front door; load them onto my trusty multi-use cart and tout the merchandise straight to the allotments beside Bury Street hill just two minutes away. I don't remember ever having to bring any home unsold. In those long-lost sweet days of youth, I always had spending money in my pocket as well as in the top drawer of the chest of drawers in my bedroom. My problem though was there were many more ways to spend money than there were to earn it. I was good at that too!

During the war and right up to 1954 many foodstuffs were on strict ration. This certainly included sugar. During the summer months, though, when summer fruits were ripening, families were allocated extra sugar rations so that 'women' [almost 100% women]could bottle the fruit for use throughout the year. The essential reason for mentioning that now though is that glass jars were in high demand for those women who were engaged in fruit preservation. The preferred jar for this was the Kilner Jar. This is a jar with a rubber-sealed, screw-top, and is used for preserving (bottling) food. It was invented by the Kilner family and produced by the factory in Yorkshire that had been established there by John

Kilner in the 19th century. Hot fruit is put into the jar for preservation and the jar sealed. As the fruit cools and contracts inside the rubber seal tightens and a partial vacuum prevents the fruit from deterioration. It can also prevent you from ever gaining access to the fruit; that however is another story. Collection of unwanted glass jars was another profitable business for young boys and girls, for many years. The same collection point as for paper was good for a variety of glass jars, a further popular venue for youngsters and their pram wheel conveyance facilities. Business was good for those kids willing and able to get up and get busy!

Water and Sun

When we were quite young my friends, usually Trevor or Brian and I felt very confident to travel quite widely in North London. We used all forms of public transport, bus, train and tube. North London was our home territory but south London, somehow, was always a different place! From Epping Forest to the River Lea, to Tower Bridge and mud larking, to Hampstead and its ponds and the great London Parks we travelled and enjoyed.

I was not ever a boy for staying indoors, and one of my very favourite occupations centred upon playing about in water, all forms of the stuff that were available to us in those days. We played in Salmon's brook because that was on the way to and from school and we had all so often been told not to play there when on the way to, or from the place for that matter. Once home your eagle-eyed Mum would often challenge you; "have you been playing in that brook?" "No Mum," Was the automatic response and you would then remember to look down at your feet to see the incriminating evidence of wet socks and shoes amid a growing puddle of incriminating evidence staring up at you. What was so galling was that one's Mum clearly knew the answer to her question before the inquisition began.

I learned to swim on my own in the sea at Folkestone when I was on holiday there with my parents. I had had the luxury of being on holiday with my Nan the previous summer in Ramsgate. I was eight. I remember that because it was the first summer after my sister was born. It had been a long hard winter that year. The snow began to fall just after Christmas and seemed to continue without pause until well into March. Denise was born in March just three days before my birthday. Mum had had a difficult confinement. As was usual in those days she had her new baby at home. I remember that she was so bored that the sight of snow falling on the rooves opposite became her main entertainment. The word confinement' was particularly apposite for my Mum during those long days.

Yes, the winter had been hard. There had been power cuts due to poor fuel supplies to power stations. There were also greater demands on power as industry tooled up and powered up after the War and they had priority. I had had to go with Dad to try to scrape up some coal from the ground of an old wartime fuel dump at the corner of Church Street and Haselbury Road. That was a miserable adventure. It was the winter of 1947, one of the worst on record. Dad and I were both on our bikes and hoping to carry back as much fuel as we could manage, each with two shopping bags held dangling from the handlebars. I was going-on eight and my hands were so cold, even inside my woolly gloves. I remember being in tears of pain from being so cold from half-way home. There was little comfort for me at the time, that we had managed to scrape together some much needed fuel….I digress.

Getting back to my achievement in the field of swimming I am reminded that Dad had decided that we needed a break by way of a good holiday the summer of 1948, and so he booked us into a hotel on the front in Folkestone. The weather was kind for us that summer. Mum and Dad had a year-old baby, my sister Denise, born during the winter of 1947, and so were not too mobile but I was quite happy to go off on my own to explore the town. Mum and Dad were always surprisingly relaxed about my wanderings. I remember clearly my first visit to the large outdoor pool near the rotunda. I was only nine years old but was allowed in on my own. Regulations were not so tightly guided by health and safety considerations in those days. It was a hot day and after a good play in the water. [I could not swim yet] I settled down to rest for a while in a corner formed by two walls. It was warm and I fell asleep. When I woke up, I felt a bit groggy and quite dizzy. A kind lady helped me get back to the hotel. I seem to remember a lot of steps to climb to get back to the level of the hotel. I would not have made it without her help. I was ill with a dose of sunstroke for nearly two days. That was a good lesson that I learned the hard way!

After my experiences in the swimming pool though, I decided that I needed to be able to swim if I was going to enjoy my holiday properly. We had a family room at the hotel with, yet a sea view! On the third morning after my losing battle with the sun and after breakfast, I began to stare wistfully out at the sea. My Mum knew that I was thinking about going down to the beach to try my hand at swimming in the sea. I had been muttering about it on and off during the time since my experience in the swimming pool. It had cropped up at breakfast that morning. I just wanted so desperately to become, not just a swimmer but a competent one. To my surprise Mum had my swimming things in her hand as she approached me. "Go on boy get yourself down there." She pointed towards a section of the beach that she could see from the window. "We know you won't be satisfied until you've swum your first few strokes." She paused for a few moments. As I remember it, I gave her little chance to change her mind or to impose any rules for this sudden and unexpected period of release after my too close encounter with the sun. I grabbed my swimming trunks and towel and made a quick exit with a simple "Thanks Mum". "Back for lunch, and don't be late!" were all the instructions she managed to impart before I disappeared through the door and down the stairs to the street.

I changed into my trunks on the beach just using a towel. One becomes quite skilled at that particular method on British beaches. I made it slowly into the water. It's usually a cold entry into the sea from a beach anywhere on these islands. As I have grown older, I have come to realise that the 'quick dash entry system' is by far the best. On that occasion, though, I could not take the chance that I would not end up in water that was too deep for me. Slow entry, however, has its drawbacks. The slow entry is fine up to the knees; once past there however the cold waves begin to hit the parts that you don't want the cold shock waves to reach. The only way to avoid the drip, drip of slow entry after that is to quickly bend your knees and so dip your tender nether regions into British waters. In this way you avoid the 'depth' considerations as mentioned above and you also get the thing over without the slow torture of the persistently slow entry system.

I had a swimming acclimatisation plan that had begun to ferment, the previous year, during the second of two annual holidays at Ramsgate with my Nan. I had noticed that as the waves approach you, they lift you off your feet. I had long- since concluded, in my now nine-year-old wisdom, that once off your feet you could take advantage of those few seconds to swim a few strokes. I realised that, for me, the most difficult part of learning to swim in a pool was to keep your feet from touching the floor. In the sea the incoming waves did that part for you. I had reasoned that, once you had achieved that, you could say that you could swim, just not very far, not yet anyway.

Once I had persuaded my private parts safely into the water, I proceeded to put my swimming acquaintance and familiarisation plan into practice. It went far better than I could have hoped. Swimming parallel to the beach and making a bandwidth of noises not usually associated with the gentle art of swimming I was able to swim about 16 strokes on one breath before I decided to quit whilst I was ahead and leave the beach. Even as I went back to the hotel to give my parents the proud news, I realised that any future progress would depend on my learning how to breathe and swim at the same time. There were practical limits to what even I would ever be able to achieve on one breath.

I returned to the hotel and made my parents aware of both my morning's success and the limitations to my 'glory'. Dad was very pleased at my news and said that he would help me with the next stage. He agreed with me, with a huge grin on his face, that in the swimming world sixteen strokes would never cut the mustard! Nonetheless he said that I had done really well to work out my own self-teach swimmers guide. Dad turned out to be quite a good swimmer and teacher. It appeared that he had learned to swim in a local in-door swimming pool in the East End while still at school. I do still, in fact, have some of his school swimming certificates at home. By the end of the next day I could both breathe and swim at the same time. It was much more fun to be able to do both!

Together with my friends I later fished and swam, whilst dodging horses pulling barges along the towpath in either direction, on the River Lee near Ponders End lock and near Pickets Lock too, as well as along the reach between the two. The adult population of my ken had long been hesitant about allowing us to swim in the Lee because it was not deemed clean enough. They didn't seem worried about the notion that we might get steamrollered by a barge! Our counter arguments to the swimming objections were twofold. Firstly, we didn't plan to drink it. Secondly there were fish actually living in it so a mere swim could do us no harm. There was a third argument that we didn't care to voice out loud; it was "How then are you going to stop us?"

I have to say here that being on and about the river was very much like living through the War. You had to grow up quickly. It made you canny. You needed to be smart at avoiding being run-down both by rampant barges that could not stop on a sixpence as well as the huge Carthorses that were their sole source of propulsion. Any equipment like fishing gear or disrobed clothing needed to be carefully positioned so as to avoid it being chucked into the river by a fleeting but powerful towline. Remember Rule one; the first and main – the barge does not stop when the horse stops! Rule two; get out of the water well before the barge comes close! The Good news: no-one died!

We played and fished for anything including, beneficially for me, daphnia in the 'blue lakes' where the Olympic site later became a famous tourist attraction, in long to be experienced time, as in many a decade to come. In those days of youth however access was gained to the lakes and the surrounding marshland via a 'road' that sloped upwards, next to the Cart Overthrown Pub in Montagu Road before descending towards that treasured land of "Who knows where?"

Live daphnia were a speciality income for yours-truly; yet another of my several means of earning 'a few bob'. My parents had bought me a tropical fish aquarium for my 8th birthday. Those fish really enjoyed catching and eating live daphnia when I was able to find somewhere to buy them. It so happened though that I made two discoveries at almost the same time that 'sorted' two problems for me in one go. A few weeks after my birthday I discovered that a small pet shop on Edmonton Green, almost opposite Woolworths. They actually sold live daphnia when they could get it. Later that spring my friends and I discovered the Blue Lakes behind the Cart Overthrown pub. What did I spy there in those lakes that meant nothing to my friends? Live red daphnia were there in abundance and swimming around as if they had few natural enemies. Well, they were about to learn that those days of freedom were over. They were just about to acquire one, though unnatural enemy, me!

At the first opportunity I went back to that little shop on the Green and struck a financial deal with the owner. It was not the deal of the Century, but it suited me well enough. I later developed a further minor side-line with the owner of that little shop. My aquarium happened to be particularly 'fecund' in the matter of producing a water plant called vallisneria. This is a long grass-like plant that was in demand in those early post-war days of aquarist-based activity. From my own tank I helped in my own small way to ease that demand via an arrangement with my friendly local aquarist centre.

Trevor and I, sometimes with Brian, frequently played in the brook that snaked its way from the culvert under both Winchester Road and the long culvert below the Green. We eyed and stared and giggled through the 'eye' of the manhole cover, at the underwear, those who had any on and those who didn't, of the ladies on Fridays, queuing for vegetables at the end of the Green near the Railway crossing, just by the War Memorial there. Fridays were good days for that particular activity because Fridays were food shopping days, and the queues were longer and more often reached well past the manhole cover. We lived in times when the Cole Porter song 'Anything Goes' from the 1932 Broadway Show, also 'Anything Goes' was popular. "In olden days a glimpse of stocking was thought of as something shocking"…Well then, our activity at our some-time eyehole caught more than a glimpse of stocking and we certainly would not have been popular had we ever been caught, and so no regrets! The full lyrics of the song are apposite to this sentiment and can be obtained via the simple act of 'Googling'.

We also swam in the local Lidos when parents could afford the money, and when they were not closed due to a declaration of a polio outbreak, this most often during the summer holidays when the lidos were at their most popular. The big open-air public swimming pools were a feature of London that no longer exists in the numbers that could be visited in those days, more's the pity! They were major havens away from the comparative utilitarian boredom of the Town Hall indoor baths. On a warm day one could have a swim then bathe in the sunshine for a while, have a pic-nick then rest a while before having another swim then perhaps another while in the sun and a chinwag with friends before going home. If the weather were good enough one could spend the whole day at the local lido. The indoor baths served a purpose, i.e., as a place to practice swimming but not, in realty, for socialising.

I have just mentioned the polio epidemics that imposed regular restrictions on one's activities in those days. The word polio is short for poliomyelitis. It manifests itself as a highly contagious disease that is caused by the poliovirus, while myelitis refers to an infection or inflammation of the grey matter of the spinal cord, which is part of the central nervous system. If you were to mention polio to almost anyone born before 1960, they would instantly recall the reign of horror that held the country hostage for over a decade. Thousands of children and adults who had full, active, and healthy lives were almost instantly crippled by the horrible disease known as polio.

Small polio epidemics began in the early nineteen hundreds, but it wasn't until the late nineteen forties and early nineteen fifties that the disease expanded to reach epidemic proportions. In fact, the polio outbreak in nineteen fifty-two became the worst epidemic in the history of G.B. Some 58,000 cases were reported that year. Of those, 3,200 died and 21,000 were left with mild to very to extremely disabling paralyses.

In the dreadful year of nineteen fifty-seven in Northern Ireland the epidemic brought the worst ever outbreak of polio to her shores and it was when children became quite used to keeping themselves in social isolation.

Polio is a cruel disease, often known as creeping paralysis and it targets children and teenagers. Survivors were often left unable to walk or move their limbs. In all the summers that I can remember it was a virile and widespread epidemic and parents warned children to stay away from swimming pools and cinemas. My own parents forbade me to use swimming pools when outbreaks had been notified by the good old B.B.C.

My own younger cousin David very sadly was stricken and died during one of the frequent outbreaks of the disease in the late nineteen forties. He was only six years old, and he and I played together from time to time. He was about two years my junior and lived in Woolwich together with his younger sister and his parents who could never speak about David not even to me who was quite close to all of them. In fact, it was David's Dad, my Uncle Bill, and his older brother Bert, another Uncle and both brothers to my Mum, who took me to my first Spurs game at White Hart Lane. I was quite young, but I can still remember the spectacular antics of the Spurs then goalkeeper Ted Ditchburn. Of all the famous and truly great players I have watched over the years at the famous Tottenham ground the name Ted Ditchburn is the name that most resonates with me; just because it was those two of my Uncles who first took me there.

As we have seen, water featured quite strongly in the menu of activities that my friends and I enjoyed. Salmon's brook was one natural and local stretch of water that was relished by the whole crowd of us. Access was easy and familiarity was a given because we all passed by one access point at least twice a day on the way to and fro from school. On the way to school I walked, often with one or more of my friends, along Winchester Road into Glastonbury Road from where we would turn right into and along Chichester Road as far as the culvert over that section of Salmon's brook. From here we had to turn left along and on that culvert towards the Iron Bridge over the railway. In those days, because of war needs for food, there were allotments alongside the railway. There was also easy access to the brook at that point because the culvert opened up briefly for ten yards or so before the brook disappeared again under the arches supporting the railway.

The brook ran eastwards and opened, gurgling softly to the air for a short distance, once through the railway arches it then turned right to run parallel to Balham Road for well over 200 yards until it disappeared under the long culvert that began at the railway junction close to the Green, next to the Cross Keys Pub. I remember clearly that the next covered section was truly a very long one because the brook did not reappear until it emerged just a few feet or so past Plevna Road. There was then a long open section that ran down to Montagu Road alongside, on the right, the Jewish Cemetery that I now know to be a cemetery for the Federation of Synagogues. Some of my forebears are indeed buried there. I visited that same cemetery some years ago with my cousin Shimon. Shimon knew at that time that he was suffering from stomach cancer. He wanted to Pay His Last Respects, both there and in several cemeteries in Manchester. Joyce and I both accompanied Shimmon and his wife by then, Hedvah, on that trip.

Shimon was working in those days as the Chazzan (The Cantor) of the beautiful Synagogue in Cologne Germany. In fact, there are two synagogues in one in the cathedral-like building. There is the main synagogue on two floors: the ground floor for men only plus a first floor, a large balcony for women. To the side on the first floor is a smaller but very adequate synagogue, also for men, so that the dedicated can complete their morning prayers (Shacharit) in a space that is sensible for the smaller numbers. It is still of a size that would suit very well many communities in this country. By the time of my last visit the Cologne Jewish community was just over 3000 and rising due to the evacuation from the Communist countries that took place during the late 1980s and early 1990s.

We were quite young when we began to explore the brook more thoroughly which we did, over time and often, from just past Montagu Road in the east to Church Street in the west. The flow of the water runs roughly west to east between these points. These trips always included culverted sections because that was more than half the fun, exploring in the dark with the aid of the poor-quality torches that were available to us in those days. The longest culverted section in our territory was, as I say, the one from the Green, with its very educational manhole cover, to where it opened out again at Plevna Road.

 Most of the other culverted sections either showed a light continually from the other end of the tunnel, as it were, or very quickly did so once the first bend was negotiated. This was not the case with the section from the Green to Plevna Road, however. It was a longer section with several twists and turns. There were long sections where there was no light other than that from whatever torches we could scrounge to take with us on our underground adventures. Candles were of no use because the culverts behaved like wind tunnels and blew them out as soon as they were lit. There were, of course, rats scurrying about in the dark. It's strange though, they do not seem to bother you at eight or nine years of age as much as they do when you are older and more civilised.

There were also dangers that were inherent from playing in the brook. These arose almost entirely from playing in and investigating the culverts. They were dark and mysterious places and very interesting when you are young, and your imagination is whirring away in your head and competing with those of a group of like-minded adventurers. There were rats, of course, but as already stated they did not really bother us when all is said and done. Sometimes a dead dog or cat would float downstream, particularly after a flood and more particularly after a flash flood. That then brings me to the greatest danger for young 'watermen' investigating a long culvert where you have no knowledge of what the weather is doing in the real world, for you are still in the world of "Who knows where!"

Trevor and I were in the Green in the Plevna Road culvert one Saturday morning after kids' cinema. We had both been warned heavily about not playing in the culverts because they were dangerous places according to some. We also needed to be home in time for dinner although we had each just bought a penny baked potato, with vinegar, from the old chap who plied his trade at the end of the Green near the level crossing; made famous in the Chas and Dave song about Edmonton Green. Dinner to us in those days was what is called lunch today. Anyway, we were in the culvert, and it must have started to rain fast and furious on the outside because we quickly began to feel the rising force of the water against our wellies. I should have been more aware because although I did not usually go to the 'pictures' in my wellies my Mum had warned me that rain was expected. She said that she "felt it in her water". Well then, her 'water' was often wrong but, this time she had apparently heard it on the radio which had guided her water on this occasion and in the person of the BBC weatherman. His 'water' was often more reliable than Mum's! Luckily although he rarely wore wellies Trevor's Mum's 'water' must have been functioning well that morning because he was also sporting his welly boots.

Anyway, the water was rising quite fast. We tried desperately to get back to the Green, but the water flow was really slowing us down and in grave danger of filling those poor old wellies as it rose in depth. We quickly realised that we were in a bit of a pickle. There is no doubt about it we were both becoming very nervous (for nervous read bloody worried) We grabbed each other's wrists to gain some mutual support against the brook that, in the confines of the culvert was taking on the proportions of a fast-flowing river. Then Trevor, who had the torch, had noticed that the water seemed to be flowing less fiercely close to the culvert wall. We edged over to the wall very gratefully because we did gain some support from that move, on the downside, however, we had to let go each other's wrist so losing that element of personal support.

Then, after some more worrying minutes the doom and gloom lifted just a bit, as we neared a bend the atmosphere seemed to become slightly lighter. As we rounded the bend, we were able to see light at the end of the culvert where it opened up next to the Cross Keys Pub. It was still about 50 feet or more away but psychologically it gave us a big lift. We were also very well aware on the other hand that, even when we got as far as the pub, we still had a way to go before we would come to somewhere where we could get ourselves easily out of the water.

Reaching the end of the tunnel at the entrance to the culvert helped more than psychologically moreover because the water seemed to flow just a little easier once out of the confines of the culvert. Maybe it was simply the noise reduction, but the apparent easing of the flow gave us heart to move more easily to the point past the railway bridge where we could make an easy exit from the water and begin to breath more easily once again. Our next and perhaps more fearsome challenge was that of facing our parents. There were several issues that would present themselves during that conversation; wet clothing, being late for lunch, playing in the brook when we had been told repeatedly not to do so. Sure enough, as we approached my house, we could see Trevor's Mum leaning on our front garden gate in animated conversation with my Mum. That, in itself, did not bode well for us, and so it proved……

There was, however, no keeping us from the pleasure of exploring the mysteries of the brook, our closest waterway. There was moreover another direction completely that needed to be explored from Edmonton Green; we had explored the brook as it dived into the long culvert under the Green, there was however the lack of knowing where it came from. One Saturday morning after the pictures and the usual menu of brash 'B' flics and fortified by our habitual baked spud with vinegar Trevor and I decided to find out. It meant after all starting out in the general direction of home. Just to set the scene more clearly, I would mention here that all of these explorations too place for us between the ages of 7 to 11 years. They were preparation for things to come I suppose.

The brook flows in a general west to east direction towards the River Lee. We then were aiming to walk upstream in a roughly westward direction. Entry by the Cross Keys pub was both too obvious to the public eye and quite difficult because there was a road in front of the pub that ran over the brook. The public were protected by a fence of railings from falling into the brook. Discretion in this case being much the better part of valour we decided to take a longer route to a much safer entry spot.

We set out towards and up the length of Balham Road to Croyland Road, turning left into Croyland Road we quickly made the easy distance to the short alleyway next to the little general shop on the corner there. Fifty yards or so along the alleyway came the Iron Bridge over the Railway tracks. Just another short distance along beside the allotments there and we were back to the brook; we were perhaps a mere 300 yards from where we started but out of the prying eyes of nosy adults who might have wanted to stop us from climbing down into and wading in the brook. We did not see it as a dangerous exploit; no rain was forecast after all.

We slithered carefully down the bank, so as not to attract the notice of allotment keepers, in that way then when we hit the water there would not be too much splash. Before I go any further, I must admit to my reader that Trevor and I were exploring the brook way back in 1946-1950 or so; from the time we first went to school and began passing that intriguing waterway. As I say we were about 7 or11 or so years old. In doing some much more recent research about the brook I see that it has changed quite a bit during the intervening time. I fully admit that my memory may have played a few mischievous tricks on me, but I am certain that the body of my story hereto laid out is true. If there are any errors, they are due to memory failures and not at all deliberate. Please forgive!

With our poor torches showing but weak light we made our way into the culvert and through it under first Chichester Road and then Winchester Road and out into the open stream shortly after that. I note from some of my reading that there is talk of rubbish dumping as one moves towards St Joan's between it and Marlborough Road and westward towards Latymer Road. Rubbish dumping was known in those days, but mass dumping is a thing of today. We were kids who had lived through the war and were still playing in bomb sites. Indeed, Trevor and I competed fiercely for the accolade as to which of us had the best collection of the schrapnel we had collected on and in such places; which were also theoretically forbidden playgrounds on several grounds; firstly, they were intrinsically unstable but secondly and far more importantly, unexploded bombs were a distinct possibility.

My research tells me that the Chichester/Winchester Road culvert was probably constructed in 1915. We had worked this out for ourselves because by the age of ten because we had tried in vain to lift one or two of the manhole-covers in order to investigate the culvert via one of them. They were dated 1915. I admit that it was only impish curiosity that led us to try the 'manhole' route. That route never worked for us and would probably have been quite dangerous.

As I read about rubbish dumping, I remember that one of the fruit and veg. merchants on the Green I think that it was a man by the name of Jiggins, but I apologise if I have misremembered the name. As I remember it Mr Jiggins lived nearby the entrance of the culvert at the western end of St Joan's Road; he took a personal interest in both the tidiness of that section as well as the safety aspect of the entrance of the stream into the culvert there. If one chose to inspect the brook on a quiet summer day the impression in those days would have been of a pleasantly trickling and not unpleasant stream. That impression would have been a disarming one, even dangerous, compared with that of the fierce and raging torrent of water that would have confronted you after heavy rains. Mr Jiggins won a campaign to have a safety grill fitted to the entrance of the culvert; thus, preventing adventurous souls like Trevor and me from risking life and limb on adventures into the culvert. Culvert exploration was not a form of collective behaviour that held major popularity among my age group but, of course, there are always the occasional idiots who can be relied upon to challenge common sense norms. I readily acknowledge that Trevor and I were paid up members of that group! We enjoyed the crack of doing something that others did not care to try or had been forbidden to do.

Winchester Road was in fact where I lived for all of my life up to the age of 18. It held some interesting features for me as a child and a teenager. Firstly, Mr Rounce's general shop was one of a small parade of shops in Winchester Road but next to its junction with Glastonbury Road. It was not a huge shop, but Mr Rounce seemed able to produce anything for his customers from a bag of nails to a pound of rice.

It is in fact rice that immediately springs to mind. Mum nearly always tried to send me on the frequent missions to undertake 'top up' shopping missions; that is when she could catch me. Her reason for sending me I now feel certain was due to the interminable democracy and mind-bending boredom of the queuing that had become embedded into the way of life in Britain during those war years. It wasn't the queuing per- se that 'tacked' me off; it was the endless long-winded chatting that went with it. It was always the person being served who hogged this particular stage. There seemed to be a rule that she had such interesting stories to tell that old Rounce's day would not be complete until he had heard them to the full. I have to say that it was nearly always a woman, although men were quite capable and willing to succumb if they were entrapped into doing a bit of shopping. This happened very rarely in those days. I, on the other hand, simply wanted to get in, get served and get out. That though was seldom a piece of good fortune to come my way. It seemed that Mr Rounce had endless amounts of time to spend shooting the breeze with anyone who cared to chew the fat over subjects from a cat's sore leg to grandma's outstanding pension claim. If you were just third in the queue you could almost guarantee that meant a minimum of a twenty-minute wait.

Then there was the incident of the large sack of rice! You have to remember that much of what Mr. Rounce had for sale was on ration. I cannot remember the full list of rationed items but from July 1941 - Coal was rationed because more and more miners were called up to serve in the forces. Coal was, I believe just about the last commodity to come off ration and that was in 1958. In January 1942 Rice and dried fruit were added to the seemingly endless list of rationed foods. February 1942- Soap was rationed so that oils and fats could be saved for food. Tinned tomatoes and peas were added to the list of rationed food.

I was waiting in the shop one day when a lady came into the shop and joined the queue behind me. I took no notice of her at first. I was too busy hopping from one foot to the other from impatience. It took me a short while to realise that she had a small dog with her, a small dog, a terrier perhaps. More important though and endlessly more interesting in my otherwise pit of boredom was the fact that the dog was not on a lead. This was a crime in Rounce's shop on several levels, the first that there was a sign on the door banning all dogs except guide dogs on a lead from entry. Now of course the dog could not read but surely his owner could? I say 'his' because evidence of his sex became immediately indisputable when he cocked his led to pee on a bag of rice that had been placed by the door to Rounce's storeroom. Some of those who had noticed the dog's wanderings gasped in disgust others in anger. I could do nothing but grin and resolve to tell my Mum not to buy rice from Rounce for a while. That embargo became permanent once I had described the dog and his toilet activities. As I say rice was on ration and for that reason neither Mum nor I could envisage that Rounce would throw away the contents of that rice sack. Rice, after all, was a precious commodity, even with the additional dog flavouring!

Winchester Road was well served with sources of alcohol. It had a pub at either end, the Rose-and-Crown in Church Street opposite the end of Winchester Road and almost on the corner of Victoria Road. At the other end, right opposite the bottom of Bury Street Hill was the Rising Sun. As a teenager of sixteen plus I made several successful attempts to obtain alcohol illegally in pubs but never in either of those two. They were, after all, in my own street as near as maybe. As far as I can remember I never did drink in the Rose-and -Crown but, for my twenty first birthday my Uncle Ted took me into the Rising Sun for a celebratory drink. I was fond of all my Aunts and Uncles but Ted was the one I had the most contact within those years. He did in fact ask me to leave out the 'Uncle' on the occasion of my twenty first, which was the coming-of-age date in those days. I had moreover a real soft spot for my Uncle Ted because I used to work for him on his bread round on Saturday mornings in Stamford Hill. He treated me very well as is indicated by his wish to celebrate my significant birthday with me.

Winchester Road had one further source of alcohol which was of particular interest to my Nan. Now Nan was not a big drinker just as were none of my family, but she did like her jug of Guinness on a Sunday morning. On the other side of Glastonbury Road from Rounce's shop was an off-licence but was one that was licenced to 'pull' pints of draught beer into customers' own jugs, for consumption off the premises of course. Mrs Ball was the proprietor, and she obviously had a very liberal attitude to the licencing laws. My Nan would often send me on a Sunday morning with her jug for a pint of her favourite, Guinness,

Mrs Ball did not bat an eye when I went into her premises and asked for my Nan's pint of her favourite tipple. I was about eight years old when this first happened. I got into the habit of always taking a sip or two as I sauntered the two hundred and fifty yards or so back to Nan's house. The first time was in the cold winter of 1947/48. It was bitter cold, and I was still in short trousers of course. Nan grinned when she spotted the tell-tale Guinness stains around my mouth. I'm not a big beer drinker but Guinness is still my favourite beer and reminds me of my Nan and her favourite trick that materialised as soon as the jug was in her hand. She stuck a red-hot poker into the jug of dark. Grinning she would say, "Mulls it, gives it an extra bit of bite".

And now back to Salmon's Brook and my memory tells me that we were able to wade against the stream all the way from the end of the culvert under Chichester and Winchester Road all the way to the culvert under the Great Cambridge Road and then on as far as Church Street where it curves north easterly towards Ridge Avenue and on the way passes Bury Lodge Park. We had had enough by the time we got to Church Street. We had moreover spotted Bury Lodge Park from the waters of Salmon's brook which discovery moved our interest in that direction…

Chapter Eight

Land based entertainment. Days of Guilt

Bury Lodge Park as it was called in the 1940s/50s is apparently on the site previously occupied by Bury Lodge, which was probably a timber-framed house dating from late medieval or early Tudor times. The house may well have been linked to Salisbury House next door, because as children it was almost certainly the big, abandoned house to the left of the park in which we played and thought of as Bury Lodge.

 Salisbury House is still apparently in use as a Community Centre. Although I have not visited the park since I was a child it seems that the layout of the gardens and award-winning rose-beds, as established by Enfield Council in the 1930's, is much the same as when I and my friends played there in the 1940s.

One of the most attractive features of the park were the long-established rose beds, plus many other smaller flower beds, there is also a lily pond with very decent sized goldfish as well as frogs and toads. There was also a large field, a walled garden which would be particularly acceptable in today's mores as wildlife friendly. There was moreover a very popular children's play area with a large sandpit, a water feature, a slide, swings, etc.

There was moreover a large paddling pool in which I often played despite repeated instructions from my Mum not to do so because there was often broken glass hidden in its less than crystal clear depths. I was repeatedly in trouble with my Mum because she invariably spotted the very slim line of wet trouser at the bottom of my short trouser legs. Very unfair is the inherent spottifying power of the average Mum.

I got into real trouble though with Mum on one afternoon in particular when she had warned me very seriously not to go anywhere near Bury Lodge Park with specific reference to the paddling pool. I was dressed in my best clothes because Odette, the friend from Normandy, was on a week's visit to us and we were all due to go to Haringey race track that evening to see either the motor bike races, or the roller skating races. I cannot remember which, but the certainty was that I did go to the park, I did try the pond and I did cut one of my feet, not badly but the surprise was enough to make be fall over into the less than crystal clear water thus rending fruitless my Mums efforts to 'clean me up' for the evening out. Useless were my pleas to get her to look at my poor foot. Instead, she banned me from the treat of that evening, the visit to Haringey. She was totally unmoved at my constant pleading for mercy. She came so close to frustration at my constant nagging that she actually threatened me, in front of Odette, with physical violence.

There was one further escapade I need to mention; it is also one that I would rather be confined to the depths of a mysterious and hidden history. I have however committed myself to telling the truth as far as I can remember it. I must admit here that the big house, probably a very dilapidated Salisbury House was subject to several episodes of illicit intrusion by two eight- or nine-year-old boys. These were not crimes of the century you understand but they were all of illegal entry, one of which resulted in me purloining a couple of lengths of electric lead-shielded wire. As a boy I suffered years of guilt and worry over this lead. I had cut it up into short lengths and placed it in a huge glass jar under a loose floorboard in my bedroom. The guilt that I suffered would, I am convinced, be regarded as punishment enough by any court in the land. Served me right! Trevor and I had many invasive sessions totally unchallenged into the old house. We pretended that it was haunted and if ever a place could have been haunted that would have been the one! It had many gloomy; some quite dark, corners even during daylight such that the pretence of being scared was often overtaken by reality. Nonetheless we had some tremendous episodes of exciting fun such that only small boys can achieve when they know that they are doing wrong. I cannot remember what ever did happen to the jar of lead pieces. They may still be under the floor of the upstairs back bedroom of 180 Winchester Road Edmonton N9 London; for all I know!

<u>More Days of Guilt</u>

Some of the more pleasant times for me and for my sister Denise as she grew older were when we all went on holiday together. If I am going to be really cynical for just one moment I might say that Mum and Dad could not argue so much when we were on holiday; because we were in such close proximity to them even at bedtime; in the sort of holiday accommodation that was available to us in those days, the 1950s, such as Holiday camp chalets or hotels in a family room where they did not have the false security of feeling that they were alone. There was no 'out of sight, out of mind' situation for them to take cover in. Their arguments were often so bitter at home that they apparently needed to have that heightened level of feeling hidden from view. There were of course some moments of icy frigidity between them but overall, they did seem to enjoy the experience of being on holiday. A week's holiday or a fortnight even, which we sometimes enjoyed was a thing of some rarity for working class families in the 1950s.

I have also to admit some guilt regarding my own sniffy attitude towards the type of holidays and day breaks that my parents enjoyed. For day breaks we would usually go in the car to Frinton-on-Sea, on the coast of Essex. I have not been there for many years. My memory however has it as a very quiet sea-side retirement town full of residents who seemed then to me to be very ancient. It offered the benefit of having a nice beach, a couple of decent cafes and a quiet atmosphere which my parents enjoyed. From the age of twelve to sixteen I attended a private school in Hampstead. I made friends there with some young people who have become well known public figures in my adulthood. They went on holidays, yes! Often though they went abroad to France or Austria, or they owned canal boats or yachts. That was a far cry from us and from a day out at Frinton, the last resting place for the senile as it seemed to me, or an asbestos walled cabin in a holiday camp. I was therefore quite a young snob and very unkind with it as I all too frequently expressed very uncharitable opinions. I was never slow to express contemptuous, even arrogant, views mocking some of their choices. That is behaviour of which I really cannot be proud. Our parents provided us with holidays and day trips that many of our peers never did have.

Up to the age of about eleven some of my peers had never even seen the sea! I am certainly not proud of my attitude towards our holidays.

I had some real issues with my parents, but I did love each of them as individuals. As I re-read this, I realise that I have repeated this expression of separated love from time to time throughout this work. For me their relationship remains a mystery, an unfinished story. They did nonetheless provide well materially for both me and Denise and we did go on an annual holiday with our parents every year. It must have been a hard financial stretch for them too; what with our regular holidays together with not infrequent days out to Frinton and the London Zoo and Whipsnade as well as a variety of other places. All this is admitted without mention of the cost of my schooling. Therein lays for me the base of one of my major seats of guilt and is thereby installed by me at the head of a list of such guilty admissions. My schooling sucked out much of the disposable income of the family.

At this point I must comment on the different environments that Denise and I encountered during our early years. I grew up to the age of six in an environment of kind protective adult women. There were hardships certainly the first on the list of which was the Nazi War machine in the form of the Luftwaffe. There were general shortages of nearly all commodities but there was plenty of love and care. These are things that you don't notice when they are always present. You do though, sure as maybe, notice them when they are absent even just at night-time as was my later experience. Denise would have to comment on this for herself. There was though the reality of a very different experience during the first eight years of life for my little sister and me. To my shame I hadn't realised it until I began to think about it more fully through my various episodes of writing.

Denise and the Mucky Ditch

Then there came the incident of Denise in the mucky ditch. For the life of me I just cannot remember where this happened, it may have been at Butlin's Seaton, but as certain as today is Sunday it was my fault. [I am writing this on Sunday 31st January 2021 amid a vaccine dispute in Europe which truly is not my fault!].

We had just arrived on a Holiday Camp site somewhere on the South Coast. Both Denise and I were restless after a lengthy journey in the car. We jointly expressed the wish to stretch our legs. Denise was 4 which meant that I was 12. I am quite certain about those details because her birthday is just three days before mine in March and, just as we were rushing out through the chalet door Mum shouted at me "You make sure you look after her Tony, remember she's only four". Well, I knew that right enough! I was told it often enough. It was all Denise's fault, the poor demented girl did like being with me, her big brother. I must admit moreover that I liked the role of big brother and Denise was a lovely kid.

Not ten minutes passed before I was carrying her back to the chalet, she was crying and covered from head to foot in mucky, muddy, slimy water. There was a small field right next to our line of chalets and we had taken a small plastic football with us…well… I kicked the ball, Denise cried with delight and chased the ball seconds later she had disappeared into a ditch and suddenly I could hear her crying out, not with delight this time. I was trying to manufacture my excuses for this eventuality just as I was rushing over to investigate what calamity had befallen my little sister.

Denise stared up at me from the depths of a previously unnoticed ditch. As I stared down at my poor little sister, I realised with doom laden certainty that this would be classified as my fault. Even as my mind raced through the list of authorities, I might be able to blame for this calamity, from the Holiday Camp Owners to the local council I realised that the burden of guilt would certainly fall right flat, bang at my door. What was also certain in my mind was the realisation that the accusation would certainly be correct. I did moreover feel a real sense of 'responsibility failed' as I scrambled down to pull her from the bottom of that dammed ditch and the foot or so of muddy water that she had plunged into. Denise was crying genuine tears of fright and discomfort as I carried her back to the chalet. Just as I had correctly assumed the blame fell smack down at my feet. In all the turmoil of which I was the centre I never did get the chance to apologise to my little sister - Sorry Den!

A Ceiling Too Far

I may have mentioned that my Dad was a member of the communist party. He was in fact a founder member of the Edmonton branch and had a lot of friends from within the membership of the branch. Many of these were tradesmen. There were skilled men from all branches of the building profession, there was one poor guy who was a television repair man and who lived in Chichester Road less than two minutes running time from our house. We just happened to be one of the first families in our road to have a telly. This was in the days where the body of the set was about the size of a modern fridge with a ten-inch screen. That box was filled with vacuum tubes and other unimaginables that were a total mystery to all except those strange beings like Matt who knew just how to shout at them. It seemed that our brand-new telly needed shouting at more than most. As Dad had bought it from the 'friend of a friend' he could not call on the guarantee for support. Thus, it became Matt's call-in life to be required, regularly, to do my Dad a 'favour' and my job to run round to Chichester Road, usually on a Sunday afternoon to issue the request for the favour. Luckily Matt was a truly amiable man.

Another of Dad's group of trade friends was yet another very amiable guy called Frank Phillips. Frank and his wife had two children a boy, Geoffrey, about my age and a daughter, Barbara about two years younger. B later married one of my friends from the RAF who she met at my wedding party in 1962.

One year when I was about fourteen Dad and Frank thought that it would be a great idea for the two families to go on holiday together. To give my Mum some credit she felt from the start that it might not be one of the best ideas of the season.

They found a four-bedroom bungalow in a place called Felpham, not far from Bognor Regis on the Sussex Coast. The adults' decision was they would have a bedroom each as the adult couples. Denise and Frank's daughter Barbara would share one of the remaining rooms and that Geoffrey and I would share the fourth room.

I must admit that I was not too happy myself at this holiday proposal nor, particularly, about the sleeping arrangements. Geoff and I were friends through our parents, but I think that we both felt awkward at the thought of sharing a room. Nonetheless the decisions were made, and the arrangements all tucked away Bristol-Fashion and suddenly we were there. We arrived at the bungalow in our two, family cars within minutes of each other. I have to say that my first day of that holiday passes just about as successfully as my first day of the holiday camp episode a couple of years earlier.

We had begun to settle into our rooms and become familiar with the interior of the bungalow itself. There was a very decent sized front room or lounge. To the rear of the house was another comfortable room that gave out onto a good-sized garden. I was about to open the French windows to go out into the garden when the strident voice of my mother almost pinned me to the glass door from the other side of the room! "Tony – Don't you dare touch that door." There was a pause as she explained that they needed to do some shopping. Apparently, she and Mrs Phillips had looked for the makings of a desperately needed cup of tea and had discovered that the cupboard was bare despite having been advised by the owner that certain basic provisions would be supplied in the bungalow.

"We're all going out shopping. There's nothing in the kitchen cupboards so we need to get some basics. We're taking the girls so you two can behave yourselves and get to know the place."

Those final few words would prove to be dramatically fateful within a very short time. The four adults and the two girls went off to some nearby shops crammed together into Frank's large estate car. The two girls protested strongly when it became clear that they were going to have to sit in the space behind the rear passenger seats. Mrs P had the foresight to provide some pillows from the settee in the living room so that they would be a little more comfortable. No seat belts were available for anyone in those days remember! Mum also was not too pleased when it became clear that the two men had jumped into the front seats and that she had to sit in a rear passenger seat next to Mrs. P. Mum could find a problem in most situations.

"Be good!" Mrs P shouted in our direction as they drove off.

Geoff and I both, almost in unison breathed a heavy sigh of relief as we watched the car as it disappeared around a nearby corner. We had a second quick look around the bungalow and then I noticed the hatch; that is the loft hatch in the kitchen ceiling.

We looked at each other and grinned, again in near unison.

"Looks interesting." I muttered, grinning at my soon-to-be accomplice in crime. He nodded and it was a simple jump onto the kitchen table and an easy haul up into the loft space. Geoff was just behind me as I tried hard to balance myself on two beams. I only took one successful step from start to finish. The fatal step was the first and my foot missed the next cross beam which meant that I stepped onto the asbestos ceiling of the kitchen below. I landed painfully back onto the kitchen table via a now huge new hole in the kitchen ceiling. "Sodding Hell!" I howled at the sight of the new loft ventilation.

"Well, yes…." Geoff whispered as he lowered himself onto the table whilst staring up at the gaping black hole in the ceiling.

It was a huge disappointment to me that the court of enquiry that was set up immediately upon the return of my parents took absolutely no account of the injuries I had suffered as a result of my falling through the ceiling. No mitigation was applicable apparently in the case of this near capital crime.

"Why do you always have to ruin the first days of our holidays?" Mum shouted at me with a clear reference to the mucky ditch affair that was fully two years old. The statute of limitations on that 'innocent' mishap should have run out long-since. Apparently not! Unfair though because one previous incident in a whole lifetime of holidays should not, in decent English, allow for the use of the word 'always'. One look at my Mum's gritted teeth though forbade me from arguing any case of mitigation. I just sat still in a huge protective armchair and took all that was hurled at me. It was good old Frank Phillips who finally took pity on me.

"Look here Mick, Jessie, it wasn't just Tony. There were two of them up there in the loft. Tony just happened to be the one to fall through. It could have been either of them!" That kind man held his hand up sharply to stifle completely the impending protest from his own son Geoffrey.

I heaved a huge but inconspicuous sigh of relief as I saw my parents beginning to come off the boil.

"Yes, but it was Tony who caused that!" Mum just had to have the last accusatory injection of spleen in the glance she threw at poor old me, pointing aggressively at my accidental air conditioning for the loft.

Frank persuaded my parents that he and Dad could fix the hole and repaint the ceiling in a morning and that was the way the matter was resolved. It was a long time though before my Mum let the matter go entirely. She frequently managed to mention my holiday wrecking capacity in casual conversations with her friends. After a while though the - retelling of the episode took on more of the nature of a joke than an accusation. In that manner some sense of justice came to be restored.

………………………………………..

<u>Chapter Nine</u>

<u>In which I discuss; Bury Street Hill, the Henry Barrass Ground - Jubilee Park
as well as Bury Street Hill as a representing variety of local playgrounds.</u>

There was never any excuse for us kids to complain that we were bored except perhaps
when it began to rain, and we had to stay indoors. Otherwise on weekends or holidays or
evenings in the summer, there were plenty of places to play very close to home. As we got
older, near to our teens or in our teens our area for exploration and play widened
considerably.

The closest place of real interest was Bury Street Hill. This was a hill that carried Bury
Street over the Railway from the end of Chichester Road to where the bridge meets
Galliard Road and Falman Close at the bottom of its Eastern and before continuing on its
journey from The Great Cambridge Road to the Hertford Road.

To the casual observer that hill was just a hill over the railway, but it was far more than
that to us. Firstly, the slopes of the hill were not huge, but they provided the venue for all
sorts of 'sliding' games. In the summer on the grass, one could 'ski 'on strips of wood tied
precariously to the feet. Tin trays as improvised sledges held their own fascination for
those of us who could manage to purloin one from the domestic supplies at home.
Tobogganing in either summer on grass or in winter on snow or icy grass both provided
the same level of topsy-turvy fun as well as the excitement and medium level danger
element encompassed by the necessity to avoid the wire fencing around the allotments that
began right at the bottom of the slope. The trick was that the slope was not a long one but
quite steep. Stopping without hitting the wire fence at the bottom meant a quite skilful and
very necessary sharp half turn at the correct spot near the bottom. The alternative was
either to 'chicken out' or make an entry into some poor bloke's allotment as a series of
bloody sections sliced horizontally.

The Hill had other slopes that could be used as go cart-slopes for the 'pram-wheel' mock-
ups that many of us had made, usually with some help from one or other of the adult male
members of the family when and if they became available and willing for the task. Those
carts were, it must be admitted, usually more 'up' to the various stresses that we out them
to than the 100% self-made version. The slopes in question were the four pedestrian
pavements as defined from the top of the hill over the rail line.

There were four of these go-cart slopes available and they were graded 1-4 in recognition
of their difficulty. Grade 1 of course both the easiest and the safest, albeit the longest. That
was the long slope on the North-western pavement. That slope was great fun and quite
safe because it had a long gradual curve downwards in the direction of the Great
Cambridge Road and alongside more allotments on that side of the railway. It was for
beginners and casual runs. This was definitely the 'green' slope.

The next two ratings were of the 'suck it and see' variety'. Nos 2 & three were both on the Southern side of the road. The Southwestern Pavement was shorter and so slightly steeper than the South-eastern but the bend at the bottom, near the Rising Sun Pub, was not quite as tight as the bend at the bottom of that on the Western side and so was rated No2 the 'blue slope'.

No 3 was the slope that had caused the destruction and mayhem for the most of our trolleys in the course of time. It most definitely rated the colour code 'red'. The run down was not too bad, nice and long was the bend to the right but the very sharp turn at the bottom into Falman Close was such as to test the ardour of all but the hardiest. The main element of the cart that had to be saved at all costs in case of a crash was that of the wheels. Spare pram wheels were a rarity in and after the War and they were the wheel of choice particularly for the rear wheels for most aficionados of 'wheeling'. Front wheels could be obtained with some difficulty from a variety of sources such as discarded toy bikes or toy prams. Very little of the likes were discarded either during or for many years after the war. Items of that type were generally repaired and re-cycled in their original form.

Slope number 4 was one that was only attempted by the foolhardiest. In modern ski slope parlance, it was most certainly the 'black' run. This was because at the bottom of quite a steep slope you had to make the very difficult choice between going straight off the end of the slope into the junction between Galliard Road and Bury Street and the extreme left hand turn into Hickory Close. My own near-real crash there involved damage both to myself and my cart and was on only my second attempt at No4.

It was a Saturday afternoon in the summer when I was about eight years old. It was my second attempt at the slope and one that I had been engineered into making through huge and insulting provocative remarks like "chicken" and "Cowardy Custard" by some of my 'friends' who sought to egg me on after watching my first slow and very careful trip down slope No4. In the end I just had to go and without any reservation. "Cowardy Custard" being the provocation that most often provoked idiot boys in those days into the most profound stupidity.

One of the most important of all safety precautions that we had imposed on ourselves was to take care not to begin a descent when pedestrians were in sight below. On this notable occasion I set off at full lick and with no civilians in sight when suddenly a young woman with a baby in a pram came out of no-where around the corner from Hickory Close. What bad luck! What truly bad luck! Of all the times I had played on the hill I had never seen anyone come out of Hickory Close; it was such a short road of relatively few houses and a consequent tiny population. I began to shout at her from the second she put in an appearance. She did fortunately stop wheeling her poor endangered child further round the bend and so did give me one single option for missing her and the baby.

I made no attempt to turn the corner for fear of hitting the woman and her pram. I simply careered across the road, dissecting exactly the junction between Bury Street and Galliard

Road. Heart in mouth I escaped the jaws of death by narrowly missing both a startled young man on a motor bike; a Norton motor bike and another startled man in a three wheeled milk delivery vehicle. I just cannot say how on earth I remember that it was a Norton. Luckily both were slowed down as each was approaching the junction from a different direction. I seemed to hurtle across the road; I hit the curb on the other side at a speed too great for the small front wheels to mount with aplomb. The wooden cross beam that I like to refer to as the 'front axle' broke off in its entirety together with the now much buckled front wheels. By some miracle the precious rear wheels were undamaged because they had separated from the cart as we struck the curb. I hit a wall at a thankfully reduced speed, but the rear wheels struck me in the back as they followed me faithfully towards the brick wall that presented itself very firmly to me on the other side of the pedestrian pathway.

My friends, heavily chastened at having goaded me into the challenge helped me to carry the various bits and pieces of my cart home. Mum patched up my wounds together with weighty threats that there would be no more 'carting' for me. Dad though, as calm, and kindly as ever with me, waited a few days and mended my precious cart in the back garden. I was hugely grateful because that cart was the centre of my business enterprises.

....

Among the many exciting places for play were, high on the list, disused public air raid shelters. There were many of these that remained abandoned for years after the war. There was one on the allotments that ran alongside Latymer Road near where we all lived in Winchester Road. We were able to gain access to it via Lancing Gardens there; entrance to the allotments was directly opposite the end of Lancing Gardens. I see from my current London A-Z that the land that was occupied by the allotments is now occupied by Churchfield Primary School and its playground. On the allotment though was one of the unused air raid shelters. We used these places as ideal 'camps. They were dark they were dank, and they were dingy which were all characteristics that we enjoyed hugely. There was another of these abandoned shelters under the side of Bury Street Hill. It was built into the hill next to the allotments; just below and to the side of cart run No4 the 'black' run. Before I continue, I would like to say a few words more about the allotments that were created during and remained for many years after. They were a very substantial element of the Government's "Dig for Victory" campaign.

Allotments abounded during the War Years and for years afterwards. I remember that my Uncle Ted had an allotment for a while after he was de-mobbed after the War. It was in the area that is now marked on the London A-Z as King George's Field on the Western side of the Great Cambridge Road close to where Bury Street meets the A10. I seem to remember that I did go with him to his allotment on the pretext of helping him. I have memories of allotments having been established on every possible vacant site that could be used in the National Dig for Victory Campaign.

Britain of course is an island state. Our nearest sources of supplies of all sorts were then as they are now our neighbour countries in Europe. That source was not available to us for all of the war years due to the conflict as well as for some years afterwards due to general scarcities. These existed both in Europe as well as in much of the rest of the world. As the importation and shipping of food was very significant for Britain during these times, enemy states discovered this to be a weak spot for the country and that cutting off any imports could have led to inhumane, mass starvation across the nation — meaning Britain needed to act — immediately.

Food Rationing became a necessity for Britain throughout the war. So much so, that in the early stages of 1940, the government initiated a rationing system for the public to ensure that there was a fair distribution of food and commodities for the wider community.

A typical weekly food ration for an adult was quite sparse by today's standards but it is calculated by some authorities that it was also quite healthy compared with what the British adult will consume in a week in the second half of the 20th century to the present time. It might have included:

4oz margarine -.1 fresh egg and a dried egg allowance.-2oz butter.-4oz bacon and ham. The equivalent of two chops (monetary value of one shilling and two pence).-Three pints of milk. - 4oz cooking fat.2oz tea.-12oz of sweets every four weeks. 8oz sugar. 2oz cheese. Plus, 1lb of preserves every two months.

This may seem like a long list, but it wasn't a lot. We had to live like that to well beyond the end of the Second World War which ended in 1945. Rationing was eased gradually over the years but did not end until1958 with the de-rationing of coal.

These were all good reasons why the Government instituted The National GROW-YOUR-OWN CAMPAIGN.

Professor John Raeburn, an agricultural economist who was recruited by the Ministry of Food led the campaign until the end of the war. The aim of the campaign was to encourage Brits to transform their gardens into vegetable plots, removing some of the need to be reliant on imports during the tough times. Not only this, as communities could now use some local produce, shipping space was thereby available for more valuable war materials and could also potentially replace some food items that were sunken during previous transportation attempts.

It was calculated that Germany was responsible for Britain losing 728,000 tonnes of food by 1940.

Green spaces across cities, including public parks, were transformed into allotments. Even the lawn outside of the Tower of London was made into a vegetable patch. The idea was a success, nationwide estimates clearly showed that home gardens were producing over one million tonnes of food annually by 1943.

The Royal Horticultural Society found that by the end of the Second World War, there were almost 1.4 million allotments in the country. During the same year, 75% of food consumed in Britain was locally produced. Pig Clubs (6,000 pigs were kept in gardens that year); chicken coops and rabbit-keeping became a bigger trend for homeowners too; allowing them to add more protein to their diet. We became a population of small farmers!

Today, 'growing your own' is becoming a more popular trend. Although more homeowners are laying down decking boards and creating a cosier outdoor space, they're also adapting some of their green space to create their own vegetable patch — realising perhaps that both the cost and health benefits of home-grown produce can deliver are real. As a result, the government has urged Britain to return to the Dig for Victory campaign in recent years to combat food shortages! I heavily recommend the activity of producing your own fresh food in your garden if you have a spot you can use; even better if you can rent an allotment from the local council. They are though becoming more popular these days and a bit of a rarity as many previous allotment sections have been built-on during the intervening years.

I did hold an allotment myself for a few years in the 1970s. My younger son at the age of about 14 had expressed the wish to have an allotment. I spoke to the council amenities officer and very easily procured the use of a 10-rod plot which I held for several years. My son did help on the plot sometimes but as a teenager he had other uses for his time. Later though, when he moved to a village in Derbyshire and began to have a family of his own, he ventured into holding an allotment himself at the end of the village. He held that plot for a good number of years. Looking back on that period I guess that I probably helped him on his allotment over the years equally as much as he had for me on mine. It was moreover a very nice piece of land which produced some good cropping for those years until it began to be subject to flooding from the nearby road.

Back to the story though

Just a hop and a step from Bury Street Hill was and still is the Jubilee Park which now comprises an area of about 52 acres, including the Henry Barrass Sports Ground. There was a number of public tennis courts available for use by local residents as well as other Londoners. The Henry Barrass Sports ground could be accessed by a simple gate at the Bury Street end of Galliard Road. The Henry Barrass section included a large field on which several football pitches provided space for decent quality amateur football teams on Sunday mornings. The rest of the week we played football in the winter and cricket in the summer. I'm afraid that I acted like a young despot in both seasons. In the summer I was the only one in our group who possessed a real cricket bat. It was a bat which had belonged to my maternal Grandad. I gave out the story that he had played for Glamorgan. That story paraded as the truth all the time that we were young enough to still be playing together and presenting the single wicket we used as a pile of random clothing. The bat itself had suffered a small injury to one of its shoulders so I added the convincing story that Grandad had needed to put the bat aside in favour of a new bat when 'my' one had suffered the injury when Grandad was batting against Larwood in the early 1930s. It was not that I deliberately wanted to over-egg that particular pudding it was that when I was suddenly challenged as to the authenticity of my Grandad story Larwood's was the only name that I could drag out of my cricketing memory of famous bowlers of the era. I had claimed that the 'injury' to my bat had in fact been caused by the great man.

I was sorely chastened some years later when relating my story of Grandad's 'prowess' to my Aunt Joan, his youngest daughter when she roared with laughter." Well dear you really got away with a big whopper there. Your Grandad never did play county cricket. He was for a while working as a groundsman. It was at Glamorgan I believe but, in those days, ordinary folk like your Grandad could not get into a county side. There was too much snobbery going around for that". "In fact," she added; "the bat was only given to your Grandad by one of the 'gentlemen' players because it had been damaged in a match." Yes, there it was the explanation for the damage to the shoulder of my bat.

Yes indeed, what my Aunt told me was very true. Players were segregated into distinct groups as 'Gentlemen' and 'Players' up until 1962. If Grandad had ever risen to the dizzy heights of actually playing for Glamorgan he would have been classed as a player and as such would have been accommodated in poorer dressing rooms and lower quality hotels than the "Gentlemen", if on tour or playing away.

Yes, moreover the term "Gentlemen and Players" is a reference to long-term class differences and snobbery both in sport and in society. In cricket, the Gentlemen v Players game was a first-class cricket match regularly played from 1806 until 1962 between a team made up of elite amateurs, the "Gentlemen" were young sportsmen of independent means mostly from the Universities and the other made up of professionals who were the "Players". Until the Sixties, Gentlemen and Players had separate changing rooms and entered the grounds through separate gates; these different gates can still be seen I believe at Lord's cricket ground.

My 'wounded' cricket bat was not my only claim to fame as a provider of sporting equipment in the park, for our two National Games. We played cricket in the summer but switched to football as soon as that season had begun. In the 1940s and 50s the two seasons were much more clearly differentiated than nowadays. In the football season a present from my ever-present Uncle Ted came into play. During his journey home to 'Blighty' it was after the cessation of hostilities in the Far East. He fought in Burma but, I believe, returned home via India. Whatever the case may be on the way home he found an opportunity to buy me a beautiful, hand-made, size three leather football. I do not have to add that that ball promoted me to the top of the one-upmanship stakes in the winter. Boy! Times really were good!

<u>The Henry Barrass Ground and Jubilee Park -Some History</u>.

Edmonton UDC acquired 37 acres of land west of Hertford Road in order to provide recreational facilities for the growing population as the area became increasingly built up.

The site was previously used for brickworks, a major local industry until the 1970s, and many of the surrounding houses were probably built from local bricks. Jubilee Park was planned in commemoration of George V's Silver Jubilee in 1935 but as it turns out the park did not open until 1939, sadly after the King's death.

Jubilee Park now comprises an area of about 52 acres, and this includes the Henry Barrass Sports Ground. There are six public tennis courts available for use by local residents and other Londoners. At the time of writing all six of the Jubilee Park tennis courts are completely free to use and do not require advanced booking or payment. Just turn up and play!

In the days when I played with my friends in the park there was a stadium in the Henry Barrass which had a good class football pitch but also a cinder running track. The running track could be used by members of the public for training purposes for a small fee.

There was and still is, a decent sized pitch-and -putt course as well as a bowling green. My friends and I played some rounds on that nine-hole course as we grew into our teens. By the time I was in my older teens though and had met Joyce, now my wife and best friend of nearly sixty years, my interests had developed in a different direction. No! Not that – Behave!

I had developed an interest in constructing model aircraft and the pitch and putt course was an ideal venue for flying my latest creations- far safer than risking them against the larger and more powerful flying danger of either cricket balls or footballs. I'm afraid that I all too often roped poor old Joy into the role of model aircraft 'launch assistant'. This was a particularly onerous task in the case of model gliders where bags of forward propulsion were needed in the form of a forwardly mobile 'launch assistant'. It remains a miracle that our early courtship survived that model aircraft phase. I did delve into the world of model aircraft later in our relationship; after we were married and when our children came along in fact. This time though it was the more sedate version of constructing model replicas of specific aircraft. The ceiling of the boys' bedroom steadily became the 'hanging' ground for replica airplanes, mostly WW2 favourites. .

At the rear of the park, close to Hounsfield Road, Edmonton Lido was situated. Like many of its kind though that particular facility has suffered closure in the intervening years. It may be that the polio epidemics had played a part but, in my opinion, public lido type pools went the same way as holidays in Britain. I would be inclined to say that they suffered muchly from the Brits being lured towards foreign holidays and the heated swimming pools in warmer climes.

The Edmonton Lido was particularly good; it was also very close to home for our group of kids. It had a big raft in the middle on which you could sunbathe as long as you didn't get chucked off by someone a size or two bigger. There was also a cafeteria where you could get a hot drink and a snack if you had any spare money; that would be a rarity for most of us although we were always willing to share; money was always tight even for those of us with one or two or even more money-making ventures on the side.

One of the major differences between both indoor and outside pools of those days compared with modern pools was that the diving facilities were almost invariably sited within the swimming pool. That is not the case with modern pools where there has been a strong movement towards the much safer option of separate diving pools. The fashion of having the diving element sited within the main swimming area never did seem to be a major danger to most of us; wherein the act of 'dive-bombing' innocent swimmers always seemed like great fun to the 'dive-bomber'. That is until the reforms were made whereupon the erstwhile foolhardy nature of that activity became more widely understood.

<u>Epping Forest</u>

The forest too was fu**n**, Epping Forest, where you could still catch sight of dear in dappled glimpses in the sun and in the stippled sunlight of the trees and bushes of the forest. We gained access close to Chingford where the buses stopped, and you could see the forest and walk to it easily from the bus stop there. We could pretend to get lost in the magic of that place but no, in reality we knew it far too well. The magic, however, never let us down; it far outlasted our long familiarity with the place. We did however, one Bank Holiday Monday manage to lose Billie Jameson's young sister Doris in the forest and the holiday crowd for a long, long, and worrisome while…

It was just as we realised it was time to go home that we noticed the absence of young Doris. We shouted for her and searched as hard as we could. Billy didn't dare go home without his little sister. He began to cry, not so much afraid for losing his sister but at the thought of having to explain it to his Mum and Dad. He knew only too well that his Mum would have fair 'killed' him if he were to arrive home without young Doris. We searched and continued calling for 'our' Doris every inch of the way as we edged towards the part where the forest ends, and rough grassland begins. Smaller bushes indicate the end of forest. Billy shouted and roared for his young sister. He was rapidly becoming so distraught at the thought of going home without her that he was beginning to make threats about not going home.

"I mean it Tone." He whispered to me as we reached the forest's edge. "I Can't, I just can't go home without her. Oh God I'm dead meat!"

I began to pray, for in those few well-chosen words it became clear that there was not to be a gentle brotherly meeting by our Billy towards his young sister if and when they finally did meet. Johnny G. it was who eventually spotted her, away in the distance, deep in the holiday crowd; with a lady with the dogs and playing yet! with the dogs, all the while that we were searching, and Billy increasingly convinced that he was looking at close to a death penalty if he turned up at home 'sans' Doris. Neither did he calm down at that moment when Doris was finally spotted. He gazed ferociously at the infuriating picture before his eyes. The girl sublimely unaware of the trouble she was causing. Strolling and chatting with the lady and petting the dogs as she was walking, all the way up the slope towards the bus stop. We had all stayed later than we should but only because we had been so worried at the thought of explaining to Doris's Mum that we had lost her little girl.

By the time that the dawdling girl finally arrived close to the bus stop Billie had worked himself into a frenzy of frustration and plain anger at her apparent carefree and totally unconcerned attitude. Three of us, his true friends had to insert ourselves into the very speedily closing gap between brother and sister. Billie was so angry that we had seen warnings of imminent danger for and to Doris. We all felt quite strongly that Mrs Jameson would not have been much better pleased if Billie had arrived home with a sister badly damaged at his own hand, rather than no sister at all. Billie calmed down quickly when the situation was explained to him in that way. And so, both brother and sister arrived home safe and sound and softly singing the praises of a quiet and happy day spent in the beautiful setting of London's own forest!

Apart from some evening favourites on the 'wireless' the Saturday morning film show for kids was the entertainment highlight of our week. Serial heroes like Hoppalong Cassidy, the Cisco Kid, Roy Rogers as well as the Lone Ranger and Tonto, all held us spellbound from week to week. There would also be a very popular, all too short, session of cartoon characters from the 'Looney Tunes' stable.

The ancient Empire cinema on Empire Hill Edmonton was not the only game in town but it was the closest. There was also the 'Regal' cinema in 'Upper' Edmonton, sited in what was then called Silver Street and was said to be the largest cinema building in Europe. It also held a kids' show on Saturday mornings and in nicer surroundings than the Empire, but the walk was longer, and that argument usually won the day. In any case the Regal was more secure than the Empire cinema against 'free-entry' initiatives.

Each Saturday morning a more or less orderly queue would form down the hill and alongside the outer wall of the Edmonton Empire cinema. Thus, we youngsters were there all awaiting the opening for the regular dose of 'B' picture serialisation of popular film characters, mostly American, the like of those indicated above. The site of the queue was unfortunate as far as the cinema management was concerned because the only place possible for queuing ran alongside the building and right past the doors to two fire exits. It was sometimes possible for the first few boys to enter the building to run round to the fire doors and open them from the inside. In this way it was, on occasions, possible to gain free entry for a few friends and thereby share a cheap Saturday morning's entertainment for all.

The cinema staff were of course aware of this possibility but there were two fire exits along the wall some ten yards or so apart. The sole commissionaire whose job it was to keep an eye on them was a slow tubby guy who simply could not keep an eye on both doors at once. His technique was to walk up and down between them and, thereby, to make people wary and disinclined to take the risk of attempting to use the 'free' route into his picture house. And so he imagined but, in the real world, his attempts at prevention were not 100% successful! A system of coded knocks between those inside and outside the doors, gained from a long and beloved diet of war-based escape films, often allowed clandestine entry of one or two people each time the 'guard's' attention was elsewhere. I hereby must admit to having both used and enabled the use of this criminal network a number of times. It was at least as entertaining as many of the films we turned up to watch.

After the show there came a very popular end to the morning. For a penny it was possible to purchase a hot potato, baked in its jacket, from the old chap who had established his trade at the end of the Green near the level crossing. For a penny you got a beautiful hot potato, with vinegar, wrapped in a piece of salvaged newspaper. It was so good that you didn't care about the newspaper. In fact, I never gave it a thought until later decades came up with ideas about germs and contamination and suchlike. Germs cost no extra and our stomachs had long since learned to behave themselves and mind their own business! We enjoyed our spuds. Fish and chips in 'chippies' were served in the same style. As long as there was salt and vinegar we didn't care.

It was during the period after the end of The War and up to this time that I began to wonder more and more about my Jewishness. The classroom incident during the first days at school and the comparative silences that dwelled on the matter at home after Dad came home after the War had led me to make enquiries elsewhere. My Aunt Joan was always prepared to go against the grain of congealed family opinion and on the quiet helped a lot to fill in some important gaps for me. It was Aunt Joan who gave me the most information about the structure of my paternal family other than my Uncles Harry and Ruben who I already knew. It was largely she who had informed me of the early history of Dad and his two non-Jewish relationships: the second being that of my Mum. My Aunt Joan was and still is a committed Christian, but she was good enough to give me background information that I couldn't get from my parents.

<u>Chapter Ten</u>

The Good Fight.

"Whoever tries to bring you down is already below you."

This story is about an eight-year-old schoolboy, John Pearson, and what I learned from him and what he learned about himself.

For an adult it is easy to accept the concept that all bullies are cowards. When you are only eight years old, as John was at the time, and have only just entered into junior school a few months ago, that thought is not one that even crosses your mind. John was being bullied. He could not tell his parents because his father was an ex regular soldier who preached a maxim that his son should be prepared to stick up for himself, and not act like a 'cry baby'. John was, thereby, being bullied both home and away. John lived in Rugby Avenue, Edmonton, in North London just around the corner from Winchester Road, where most of his friends lived. I believe that they even had indoor toilets in Rugby Avenue.

The times were very different, in many ways, from what we see today. The term Political Correctness would not enter the common vocabulary for decades. John had red hair and wore glasses. He suffered daily persecution by ribald remark, with regard to both of these aspects of his appearance. "Ginger nut", "strawberry bonce" and "carrot top" were common epithets that John had to endure on the first count. "Four eyes", "Specky" and "Window face" were just a few of the insults, sometimes delivered as ponderous jokes, related to the second. Thus, John was an easy target for verbal character assassination on several fronts. He was, moreover, a medium size boy who had never seemed inclined to assert himself in the jungle that opened up for him once he found himself within the school bounds.

The situation would not have been so bad had John not also had two dedicated persecutors who, it seemed, had decided to make it their personal business to make John's life a misery. Their names were Leonard 'Len' Pearson and Brian Hall. These two were the bullies of the junior school. They lost no opportunity to persecute John whenever they could catch him on his own. This was not as frequent as it might otherwise have been because John had many friends to mix with, to and from school, as well as for most of the time at school. His one major downfall, as far as these two sleaze balls were concerned, was that he was in the same school class as those two caitiffs. None of his immediate friends happened to have been grouped with him in that class and so those two had free reign to make hay with their bullying tactics during class time. That included out of school experiences like weekly trips to the local indoor swimming pool at the Town Hall where the opportunities for a pair of cowards were almost endless.

The trip to the swimming pool usually took place for John's class group at the beginning of the afternoon on Fridays. The 'walking crocodile' left the school dead on time at the end of the lunch break: there was a short walk along Croyland Road to Balham Road, down Balham Road for a few minutes took you to the old Green. The crocodile usually turned right to pass in front of the Cross Keys pub and past Salmons Brook where the brook entered the long culvert under the Green to Plevna Road. A further short section took the group to Edmonton Broadway and the Town Hall where the baths were located. The whole journey might take about twenty minutes of uninterrupted walking time.

It was late November in the winter of 1948. The previous winter had been the worst that anyone could remember. The tar-soaked wooden blocks forming the base structure of the road, the Broadway, at the beginning of the 'Fore Street' Edmonton, had swollen and erupted so that the road itself was unusable. The blocks however were very usable, they disappeared in short shrift into many of the fireplaces of the town. Coal was in short supply and rationed, those blocks made a useful addition, albeit a smoky and smelly one, to the better warmth of the citizenry.

The boys of junior school, form 2C, were on their way to the Town Hall swimming baths. Some of these boys had, indeed, been active in the wooden blocks 'evacuation' movement the previous winter. Among the group were John, Len Pearson, and Brian Hall. The two bullies had already been active on the persecution front all the way down Balham Road. They were, of course, clever enough to make their moves unseen by the two accompanying teachers. The usual teasing chants were accompanied by the occasional 'chicka'; a swift upward, slicing, movement by the flat of a hand to the back of the head of a vulnerable or unsuspecting victim, not particularly dangerous but very unpleasant.

John tried desperately to keep within the sight of one or other of the teachers but they, as usual, had their hands full due to the task of keeping control of the group as a whole. Form 2C was not an easy group! It was early afternoon, but the day was gloomy and inclined to be foggy. Visibility was poor. The two young tormentors aimed to take full advantage of the opportunity that this gave them. Tension had been building for John all the way down Balham Road. The swimming group had just turned the corner into the Green. Just as they passed the frontage of the Cross Keys pub Len gave John a nasty 'Heely': that is he brought his foot down the back of John's left leg with sufficient force to take his shoe off at the heel. John was forced to stop in order to replace the shoe.

As John bent down Brian snatched his rolled-up swimming towel and bathing trunks and, in one swift movement, threw the whole bundle over the railings into Salmons Brook, just where it disappeared into the culvert. John could not tell either of the teachers what had happened for fear of even greater reprisals. In tears of worry and frustration by the time they reached the baths he was forced to stutter a feeble excuse that he had 'lost' his bundle on the way to the Town Hall. He could not remember, he Mumbled, where this had come to pass. A report of John's 'poor' behaviour was sent home to his parents. His father gave him 'the belt' when he read the report. This was both for the report and for John's attempt to explain the truth of what had occurred, for, in his eyes John was a 'cry baby' coward who would not stand up for himself, 'like a man'. This was just one example of the school of hard knocks that John had been enduring both at home and in the class group, 2C, since the beginning of that autumn term.

Croyland Road School Edmonton was neither a warm nor an inviting school. In the 1940s it still had gas lighting. It was, in fact, three schools on one site. The playground was a large hard uncompromising rectangular slab of tarmac behind the school building, or one should say buildings. As one looked at them from the road the central building was the infants' school, to the left was the senior school and to the right the junior school was situated.

Each school had its own playground and children were not permitted to enter any playground other than their own, although there was no actual physical barrier between them. The walls between the three playgrounds gave way to gaps of several feet between the ends of the walls and the buildings themselves. These gaps allowed staff and other permitted persons to pass from playground to playground as necessary.

The junior school was positioned on the right as you look at the schools from Croyland Road. The children's toilets were outside toilets and positioned in the far-left hand corner of the playground. They were cold and draughty, particularly in the winter. The girls' and boys' toilets had been constructed as part of the same brick building but separated by a further brick wall across the middle of the building. The boys' and the girls' amenity each contained a number of cabins constructed along the back wall, which also doubled as the wall separating the junior from the infants' playground. The boys' toilet block had the additional facility of a urinal trough that ran the whole length of the wall opposite the cabins. This trough disappeared mysteriously into the depths, just as it reached the central wall separating the two sets of toilets. Entrance to each of the two facilities consisted of a simple gap in the wall at opposite ends of the whole construction. The cabins had rooves but the rest of the whole construction was 'en plein air' so to speak.

Alongside the toilet block and separated by about four feet from it was another, larger, brick building. This had been constructed to serve as an air raid shelter and had been used all through the recent World War 2. Many of the children in the junior school at Croyland Road School had, in fact, had had lessons in that shelter towards the end of the war when the Germans had been directing rockets at London. All the children in John's class were very familiar with the shelter. The entrance to the shelter had been placed in the side wall that ran alongside the toilet block. It was, in fact, almost opposite the entrance to the boys' toilet section. The entrance itself consisted of a short corridor about six feet long into the building. The door into the well of the shelter was set into the far end of the right-hand wall of that short corridor, thus reducing any blast impact that might have occurred from a nearby explosion. At the point of time in question the door was always locked. There was some talk of the shelter being converted into a workshop.

It is a sad fact that boys of John's age could not simply go into the toilet to do their business quietly and leave. At that age a boy knows that his penis is useful for other things than simply peeing. His problem is that he has not yet quite worked out what those other things might be. He frequently puts his equipment to other uses whilst in an inviting loo like the one at Croyland Road School.

The main attraction for boys there was the wall by the urinal itself. It was at a decent height to provide a competition site. Boys would compete with each other to see who could pee the highest. This was not an intellectual game, it must be admitted, but it provided many moments of fun, much more interesting than simply doing the business into the urinal. There were even some stalwarts, who could reach the top of the wall and, better, over the wall. Boys of that distinction sometimes transferred their attention to the wall between the girls' and boys' blocks. Orders to desist the practice were issued after very reasonable complaints by the girls. The order was, though, difficult to police. Like any order that cannot be supervised properly, that one fell into a level of disrepute; so much so that many of the girls refused to use the cabin closest to the dividing wall. It was a simple solution but not an ideal one.

On the afternoon in question John was in the toilet block, with a few other boys, for the simple purpose of having a 'Jimmy'. To his horror he suddenly felt his feet becoming very warm ant wet. He turned to see his two nemeses and the grinning face of Brian who had just peed on his feet. Boys present stated afterwards that they thought at first that John was finally going to burst into tears at the continued abuse from those two bullies. His face reddened but it was in pent up and previously controlled anger. Just as Brian stepped towards him, with the intention of goading him further, John turned and swung a terrible punch. The combined effects of John turning and Brian stepping forward gave the punch that ferocious kinetic impact that professional boxers dream about. John's fist connected with Brian's face just at the point between nose and mouth. The nose was crushed, and front teeth were shattered. Brian apparently rallied quickly in shocked anger.

John ran out of the Loo with the two bullies hard on his heels. To everyone's surprise however he ran straight into the entrance to the old air raid shelter. Other boys thought that he had gone mad. They fully expected him to rush out into the playground where he might attract the attention of a concerned teacher. None of that though; John had other plans. The two erstwhile tormentors followed him, gleefully at first, into the entrance. Their glee very quickly turned to concern, however, because they quickly discovered that they were getting in each other's way in the confined space of the entrance. John, on the other hand, could strike out at anything that he saw moving. He took full advantage of his sudden and welcome advantage. He punched and kicked everything and anything that he could reach. The fight lasted only a minute or so, but it must have seemed much longer to John's battered former tormentors. He really vented all his pent-up feelings of anger and frustration on his erstwhile nemeses. It all only ended finally when John had become so exhausted by his efforts that he could inflict no more punishment. Our friend then stopped to lean against the wall so that he could rest and taste the victory that he had just experienced. He told friends afterwards that, even if the two had rallied sufficiently to finally win the battle, he would have regarded the time well spent. He had shown them that he could and would fight back. In his own mind, and mine, 'he had fought the good fight'.

<u>Chapter Eleven</u>

<u>Burgess Hill School</u>

In 1950 I took and failed the 11 plus exam which, had I passed, would have taken me to Grammar school without passing Go. I was so disappointed not simply for myself but also for my Mum and Dad. They had pinned many high hopes on me. Even at that stage they were clearly hoping that I would pass enough exams at a sufficiently high level to enable me to get into a college to study Medicine. At that age and stage of my life that also seemed very attractive to me and so there was little argument between us on that score at that time.

I remained at Croyland Road Senior School for the next year during which Dad began to explore other routes towards a better education for me. I was allocated a second attempt at the 11plus in the February of 1951 but again I did not gain a place at a Grammar School. Dad then mustered his full mental effort into seeking out different options for me.

A friend of Dad's from the local Communist Party mentioned the name of A.S. Neill who was apparently the recognised leader in the field of progressive education at the time. That was all the information that Dad was given to work on. He discovered that A.S. Neill ran a School called Summerhill which was founded in the year 1921. Dad's research gained the information that the school had a good and well-known education standard but somewhat unconventional. It was however situated in the village of Leiston, in Suffolk, England, and that that was about one hundred miles from London. This information alone meant that it was impossible for my parents to pursue that option. I would have needed to be a border which would have been out of the question financially. Nonetheless the Summerhill reputation seemed to be sound and so Dad began to investigate the possibility of 'Progressive' Education options closer to home.

The name of the King Alfred's School Golder's Green was given to Dad by yet another local Communist Party member. He was told simply that the school had a good ambience and a well-deserved reputation. He contacted the school and we arrived there for a pre-arranged visit. The school was and is situated on the edge of Hampstead Heath.

On the day of the interview the meeting began very well but finished as a serious disappointment. We were shown around the school by one of the older pupils and it all looked very agreeable, very nice open grounds and good facilities both educational and for sports activities. Then came the bummer! We were shown in to meet with the Head teacher who took no time to advise us that there were of course no vacancies for the next intake in September 1951. That intake was full. He did though, after some discussion and an expression of our disappointment, give us the name of another school, The Burgess Hill Progressive School in Hampstead. In an effort to be even more helpful the Head actually made a telephone call and Spoke to his opposite number in the aforementioned school, a Mr. Geoffrey Thorpe. He explained that his school had some sporting contacts with The Burgess Hill School and that he knew Mr. Thorpe quite well. It appeared that Mr. Thorpe was available that morning for an interview if we so wished. Dad thanked the man for his help.

That useful further piece of information took us up the North End Road onto the North End Way and Whitestone Pond from where we had a journey of about two minutes to the road in which Burgess Hill School was situated.

I was somewhat disappointed when I first caught sight of the school. It was nothing like The King Alfred School. That school was laid out in a very open and attractive fashion. Burgess Hill on the other hand was simply a group of three three-story houses with basements. These were only noticed during the subsequent tour that was quickly offered and gratefully received.

We were met in the corridor near the front door of the building one saw first when driving up the hill to the school. We were met there by an elderly gentleman dressed in a grey suit that had seen better days, but which was, even so, clean and in good condition. I had an annoying habit of noticing such things due to the strong family connections with the clothing 'rag' trade. The elderly gent introduced himself as Geoffrey Thorpe. Just as he did so a dark shadow appeared to dim the daylight coming through the open door. The shadow swept past the three of us and offered a reluctant grunt of greeting as it did so. The light via the front door and the world outside made a re-appearance. Mr. Thorpe grinned at our looks of slight astonishment and named the sweeping shadow as Peter Vansittart the famous writer of historical novels and currently the English teacher at the school.

"We're very lucky to have him here." He added, "He just enjoys teaching." Peter was not, by any means the only famous person that I would meet and sometimes become friends with, during my forthcoming four years at Burgess Hill School…

I waited impatiently for the beginning of the autumn school term of 1951 and my first day at Burgess Hill School. I had lived in total envy of my boyhood friends who had managed to pass the 11 plus exam and thereby gain places at Grammar school. Much to my surprise I had begun to realise that what I envied them was the fact that they were all able to begin learning a foreign language. During that year after my own failure to get into Grammar School I had actually purchased an EUP Teach Yourself Portuguese book so that I could maintain some level of credibility with my mates. That realisation was the very first inkling that my own long-term interests might be at variance with the aspirations of my parents.

The term began at the beginning of September 1951. I had hoped that I could persuade Dad to drop me off at Whitestone Pond so that I could then walk the short distance to the school. No Chance! Dad insisted that he wanted to see me into the school himself on the first day. My Mum and Dad had supplied me with a monthly season ticket for the tube. I also had my lovely second hand but beautifully hand-made Claude Butler bike that I intended to use as soon as my parents could be convinced that I would be up-to the daily return trip. I have to say that convincing them did not take long. For Dad the journey to and fro would have to be a 'seldom thing' because he worked long and difficult hours. After the first month of travelling by bus and tube my dear old C.B. was pushed into service; along with my legs and lungs I have to say. It was only during the first few weeks of initiation into that task that I fully realised that Edmonton sits on a level with the Lee basin whereas the endpoint of my ride was just about one minute's ride from Whitestone Pond the highest point in London.

Whitestone Pond is a roughly triangular pond; it is centrally located on the heath's south side. The pond was originally a small dew pond called the Horse Pond; it was renamed after a waypoint stone and is artificially fed. Whitestone Pond lies 135 metres above the London Basin, and at the summit of Hampstead Heath marks it the highest point in London. This area is the source of one of London's "lost" rivers, the River Westbourne whose headwaters gathered to form the pond before heading off in a south -westerly direction.

The pond takes its name from an old milestone which is located at the top of Hampstead Grove; it can be seen just to the south and bears mileage inscriptions in two numeric styles i.e., "IV miles from St Giles, 4.5 miles 29 yards from Holborn Bars".

Whitestone pond was originally known as a Horse Pond; it was fed solely by rain and dew, slopes were later added at each end of the pond to allow horses with their carriages an easy entry and exit for a short resting opportunity in the cooling waters of the pond as well as for them to drink and wash their hooves as well as to gather their breath after the inevitable uphill struggle up the hill to that point. Over time the pond became known affectionately as Hampstead-on-Sea as the usage of the pond expanded as it was used for paddling, floating model boats and skating in winter; the latter function becomes less and less available these days because the winters only rarely become cold enough to freeze water sufficiently that the ice is thick enough to bear weight. It is a shallow pond however and so would be far less dangerous than many natural ponds or lakes should an accident occur. A water fountain that was once located at the top of West Heath Road, became known as a local speaker's corner and was the scene of angry fights between fascist groups and their opponents in the 1930s. For a period, it became a popular spot for donkey rides.

The first few days at BHS were a very pleasant and welcome surprise as the atmosphere at the school was a happy one; not totally peace and calm of course but nothing like the pictures of mayhem that I have seen painted in some sections of the press in later years. I had after all left BHS with huge sadness in 1955 and hated to see it pictured in less than positive terms. One can only hope and suppose that the pictures were being painted by members of the press on a 'cold-news' day.

The journey to the school had made Dad late for work and so there was only time for him to see me into the main building before he was off again in his recently purchased black Ford Anglia; purchased new even!

My entry into the school regime was the 'school meeting' of which there was one every week. This meeting came as a complete surprise to me. Its purpose was apparently for the airing of grievances and to settle disputes. I had formerly become used to a more 'animal' environ in which disputes were settled. The 'meeting' in those cases was usually very short but not so sweet. The school meeting at BHS was a real eye opener as well as a culture shift. I was introduced to the group, about twenty-five young people all in their teens and mixed boys and girls. I managed to respond with some remark like;" HI there good to be with you...." I noticed a few grins, chuckles even as I came out with this.

Uniform was neither required nor available at BHS. Swearing and smoking were allowed but discouraged. My memory is that lessons were compulsory, and games were available. I learned in time that BHS played 'mixed' hockey from time to time against a similarly 'mixed' team from King Alfred's. In a mood of determination to ensure that 'we' would win as many of those games as possible I managed to work up a pretty decent game of hockey. I was never as fast on my feet as some, but my stick-ability and ruthless determination were second to none.

We played all our games on Hampstead Heath. My four years at that school were a real education to me as to the value of the heath as well as others of the many open green spaces as real community assets for London. I had long enjoyed the activity of wild swimming and the selections of ponds on the heath are, and were, ideal places for anyone to begin. I of course had become used to swimming in the River Lee which was not as salubrious an environment as Hampstead Heath and its swimming ponds. In London the Serpentine is another place where one can swim with like- minded bathers. Joyce and I have also swum together in the River Thames near Kingston when we were courting. The river Medway was yet another venue for me when I was working in a Children's home in Maidstone in the 1980s; until I eventually heard of Weile's disease that is! That did not fully end my enjoyment of wild swimming; it did though make me more cautious, sometimes.

After the school meeting Geoffrey Thorpe called me into his office which was positioned at the end of the corridor directly opposite and about twenty feet from the front door.

It was a large and quite comfortable room with plenty of light coming through a pair of large French Doors. They were open as the early autumn sun sent its morning message that all was well with the world. That was just a reflection of my own emotions at that moment. Mr. Thorpe began to ask me a few simple questions but stopped me in the full flood of my embryo responses. I had apparently and unknowingly broken rule No one of the school mores. I had called him 'Sir'. His preference was to be called by his first name which was the general rule and practice adopted by all the staff of the establishment. "Geoffrey, he insisted, not Geoff, nor Geffers, nor Thorpie just Geoffrey is what you should call me". I nodded and grinned as I suppressed the urge to respond… "Yes just-Geoffrey!"

I learned quite a lot from that meeting with Geoffrey. I learned that I would be able to study Latin with him and that Peter Vansittart used the room next door to the office that we were in and that Ruth R. taught French whilst her husband Glyn taught Science and Maths. A chap called Ken taught woodwork as well as other craft skills.

The door of Geoffrey's room was situated at the bottom of a set of stairs leading to the first-floor rooms which were used as classrooms as I found out immediately following my meeting with Geoffrey when one of the boys showed me around the school buildings. The stairs continued up to the top floor and bedrooms used by boarders or staff members. From the hallway a set of stairs led down to the large basement from which even at that time of day drifted both the remains of the aromas of recent breakfasts together with the noises and early smells of lunch being prepared.

The boy had introduced himself; - "I'm Mario, Mario Dubsky. When we get down into the basement, I'm going to introduce you to the most important of all he members of staff." "Mrs. Burns" he responded at my quizzical expression. "Mrs. Burns is our cook," he began "And she doesn't put up with any of this first name stuff. She's Mrs. Burns and no nonsense."

In fact, as I discovered in pretty short order Mrs. Burns [Helen] was a lovely lady, very kind and helpful but that she simply demanded to be treated as she treated others. I grew to both admire and like her intensely. She had a son Mike who was a great guy and a very decent hockey player.

As we continued the tour of the buildings my mind began to whirl at the apparent complexity of the place. Buildings two and three were actually the single building of two semi-detached dwellings that had been developed to make one large joint building of some classrooms and some bedrooms for borders as well as staff members. The basement contained a couple of classrooms as well as a workshop which was the domain of Ken, the young and very amenable craft teacher.

On the way round we met what seemed a host of new faces but were in reality just about a dozen students and teachers. Then we strolled into the garden. It was large, somewhat unkempt but certainly very interesting. It was in sections; less by design than by accident it seemed to me.

As we nattered our way down the garden, we passed to our left a large fruit tree with a rope swing dangling quietly from one of the longer, stronger branches. "Much used that!" Mario grinned as he saw my interest in the object. I believe that the tree was an older cooking apple tree but there is a risk here that I am trying to exercise my long-term memory too far. There certainly was a tree and it certainly had a very decent single rope hanging from it whose only use as I saw it for that first time was as a swing. I got to test it as such many times over the next four years.

Mario was a very friendly boy, and we became quite good friends over the next four years. He was a really accomplished artist who, during his life exhibited at many well-known venues and in a number of countries. He became very well known as an accomplished artist. He was born in the same year as me 1939 but, tragically, died in 1985 of an aids-related illness. It was in fact through my friendship with Mario that my years at Burgess Hill School saw my French language studies move forward much faster and more meaningfully than all my other subjects put together. We studied and competed in a very friendly rivalry.

As we reached the end of the garden, we came to a rather tired tennis court with no central net. Mario smiled at me and essayed that the court was used more for cricket than for tennis but that he did not play either. Nicky B. is our cricket star "he added. "You'll meet him later. He was in the school meeting this morning, but you probably won't have put names to faces yet." He was certainly right on that score!

We began to make our way back to the buildings. I noticed a line of small trees and bushes to our right beyond which there appeared to be a semi hidden garden that extended from the French windows of Geoffrey's office and Peter Vansittart's room. "All in good time"! My guide added at my obvious interest in everything. It was all so new to me; the idea of first names for staff, even the headmaster, and a large garden instead of a bare tarmacked playground and a school meeting where the students do most of the talking. "There's something else you might like to see before lunch". He led me back to the front of the buildings and turned left onto the narrow road. We then walked a few yards until we came to what looked like a quiet country pathway that ran alongside the school grounds. The pathway was shaded by a line of huge trees that stood within the school grounds right next to the side of a 'semi-detached' building. Mario smiled and pointed up at one huge tree. I have no idea what type it was. "That my friend is the Skylon Tree" The smile widened into a veritable grin. "You have to climb that tree in order to graduate to membership of the Skylon Club, I haven't made it yet."

 As we stood gazing up at the monster, I have to say that it piqued my interest, I had always regarded myself as a bit of a tree climbing buff. 'Skylon' however needs explaining!

The Skylon was a futuristic-looking, structure. It was slender; it was vertical and was a cigar-shaped steel tensional integrity structure which was located by the Thames in London. It gave the illusion of 'floating' above the ground and was built in 1951 for the Festival of Britain.

A popular joke of the period was that, like the British economy of 1951, "It had no visible means of support" The object and test of the ascent of the Skylon Tree was that the 'derring do' merchant going up there had to climb far enough to be able to see the Skylon over the building next to it. Mario added that the would-be adventurer would be judged from below by a team of judges made up of 'maniacs' who had already achieved membership of that particular club for the insane; by achieving the dizzy heights themselves they knew from experience just which of the upper branches had to be reached in order to be able to see the object of that particular lunacy.

English Lessons @ Burgess Hill School

I began my English language studies at Burgess Hill School totally in awe of the established teacher of the subject, Peter Vansittart. I first 'met' him when he had brushed passed me and Geoffrey Thorpe in the main entrance of No 11 during my first few minutes at the school. In reality he flourished past us with a somewhat disdainful glance at me in the passing; seemingly blocking out the daylight as he did so.

I was only twelve years old when I first entered into Peter's world and my early impression of him was that of a large and austere man. In the process of twelve becoming sixteen however both his size and the impression of austerity reduced. I guess that I might say that we grew on each other. After my parents took me away from the school at the age of sixteen, I visited Peter a couple of times at his home, not much more than a stone's throw from Belsize Park tube station. It is to my lasting regret that I failed to keep in contact with the man. It was he who did much to give me my love of the English Language.

I think that Peter's first impression of me was clouded from the moment that he heard my 'cor-blimey' accent. The cloud lifted somewhat however when he finally realised that I could spell. I say finally because it took him some time to get used to reading my execrable handwriting. I became certain that Peter felt that the Good Lord had fed him the challenge of a consistent flow of students who did not understand the principle that written thoughts became more comprehensible if we all spell to the same standard; but that it didn't matter too much because their handwriting could not be read anyway. With me on the other hand he did have one out of two. Spelling was a subject that my previous school, a lowly council school, had taken very seriously.

At Croyland Road School one had to stand in the class from time to time to be publicly examined verbally against a list of pre-arranged words. It was easier to learn the words than to face the public retribution that would follow a failure. Under that regime my spelling improved dramatically. On the other hand, I had always attributed my wretched handwriting to natural ability until my mother informed me that I had shown signs of being left-handed as a young child but that at school I had been forced to write right-handed. I have no personal memory of that happening; just that my Mum had told me so.

Even Peter's best friends would never have thought of him as a dapper, smart man; in fact, he often came to class quite unkempt in both his clothing as well as unwashed and unshaved. Nonetheless I came to know him as both generous and kindly. He introduced many young people to the Everyman cinema not far from Hampstead tube station. As my French improved, I began to enjoy the slapstick humour of Jacques Tatti. He took a group of us one summer's evening to an open-air concert at Kenwood House where one listened to the beauty of the music; enhanced as it was by its journey across the lake; Peter's generosity also took some of us to a concert by the great Italian tenor Gigli singing in The Requiem by Verdi at the wonderful Albert Hall. We stood, a group of eight or so, in the 'Gods', the round gallery, about a mile above the great man's head!

I never did learn much actual English Grammar from Peter. That negative aspect of his teaching led to disappointment for my parents following results of the first set of GCE exams I took after four years at BHS. What I did learn from Peter however was an enduring love of the English Language and its literature; his readings from chosen authors of our national literature were clearly those of a man in love with his work. To this observation I would add that Peter set assignments for us from which he would select a few of those that he regarded as worth the effort and read them to us. His deep, booming, and enthusiastic reading style encouraged one to hope sincerely that your own masterpiece would be one of those selected.

Peter was not a man to foster false self-pride. I remember one specific lunchtime when several of us were sitting at a table with Peter. He had arrived for the meal in a particularly scruffy, unwashed state. Suddenly one of our number cried out, it seems that he had been suffering in silence for some while.

" For God's sake Peter, your breath smells really awful".

Peter put his utensils quietly down on his plate and said with an uncharacteristic soft hiss.

"Tell your ungodly nose to mind its own damned business".

With that he continued with his meal smiling but saying no more.

Peter Vansittart was generous with his time. He could be moody and maybe we gave him cause but the man organised games with us and for us all in his own time. Assignments were always appraised and marked at good speed. Peter never ridiculed assignments; criticism was always constructive. After knowing the man for upwards of four years I can say that I both liked and admired him. I am deeply conscious that it was very remiss of me to have allowed myself to lose touch with Peter Vansittart after I left Burgess Hill School. I have just ordered a copy of his novel 'Broken Canes' which I intend to read as one connection to an old friend.

Peter Vansittart was the main English teacher at the school but there was one incident that was particularly offensive to me during a period when Peter was away from the school for a while.

A locum teacher who I will not name here other than by referring to him as John came and stood in for Peter during his absence.

"That sounds very much like anti-Semitism to me;"

John was glaring at me with that intense glare, of the proud defender of the meek against injustice. He was clearly wishing to put me down; firmly that is, in my place. I then trumped his premature triumphant ace.

I replied in reasonable terms as I thought they were at the time but well; it was a progressive school.

"You clearly wouldn't know anti-Semitism if it were to bite you in the arse."

I had come to class that day well prepared for a solidly antagonistic reception. The grounds for the antagonism had been set by a Liberal Jewish girl Sue W {name changed} with whom I had discussed my most recent essay, set by John but with a subject to be chosen by the writer.

I had only very recently experienced the 'Shabbos Goy' incident while working in Stamford Hill with my Uncle Ted. The injustice I felt still rankled. My chosen subject was intended to make a strong point…it was entitled.

"The hypocrisy of orthodox Jews who use gentiles to avoid breaking the Sabbath laws."

I had discussed this essay with Sue during the morning break just before the English lesson with John. I was in truth, quite surprised at her really hostile reaction to me but had prepared for a strong criticism from John. Then I saw Sue in heated discussion with John just before the lesson was due to begin. I went into that room doubly prepared for firm exchange of views.

I rose to my feet at John's charge of anti-Semitism. I could not, would not stand still for that.

"You know John, one should think before he speaks."

Suddenly the room hushed; all gossip stopped to focus on John's reaction. It followed quickly and noisily. John gripped the table's edge as if trying not to fall over.

"Who do you think you're talking to boy?"

"I think that I am talking to some person who has just charged me with fascism without knowing a thing about me."

"I didn't mention fascism."

"Anti-Semitism - fascism – same thing – both the same colour – swastika black."

"I didn't mention any of those words."

John had begun to scream. I decided that enough was enough. I needed to interject an explanation. In the years before I came to that school, I would never have dared to argue publicly like that with a teacher.

"You need to know John, and this is something that I have never discussed with anyone at this school because there's been no reason to before this. I am Jewish myself. I just don't believe in God."

"You don't believe in God…? How can you be…?

"Listen, that's all my business. My claim and Jewish status give me the 'Right of Return' to Israel and that's a civil status not a religious one."

"But…?"

"No John, no buts, I do not believe in God but I sure as hell know Jewish Law pretty well. I don't believe in God but the lady in my story does, and she breaks the fourth Commandment, in my view, every time she calls for a Shabbos Goy. She's not on her own either and I don't by the way, like the expression Shabbos Goy. It's not nice."

I then handed him and Sue each a copy of a slip of paper that I had prepared earlier. On those slips were the words of the Fourth Commandment.

Remember the Sabbath day, to keep it holy. Six days you shall Labour and do all your work, but the seventh day is the Sabbath of the Lord your God. In it you shall do no work: you, nor your son, nor your daughter, nor your male servant, nor your female servant, nor your cattle, nor your stranger who is within your gates. For in six days the Lord made the heavens and the earth, the sea, and all that is in them, and rested the seventh day. Therefore, the Lord blessed the Sabbath day and hallowed it.

In retrospect I realise well enough that all religions and indeed all human associations are guilty of such pieces of relatively harmless hypocrisy. It's simply I guess that the twin charges of "Shabbos Goy" and "Anti-Semitism" had rattled my cage. Many years later I was staying with my cousin Shimon and his wife Hedvah in their apartment in the Cologne Synagogue. He was the Cantor and Cheder Teacher there at the time. They were both religious people of course. At the beginning of the first Sabbath of my visit the trip switch tripped, the one governing the electric power in their apartment. This meant that they would have been without power for the full day until the end of the Sabbath. Hedvah came softly into the lounge where Shimon and I were preparing ourselves for the evening service.

"I know that I shouldn't ask."

She spoke quietly and without looking at me, but I knew where it was, and she knew very well that I would not mind. I made my way quietly to the cupboard in the hall and switched the switch back on. In the way that Hedvah acted she clearly acknowledged that she was breaking the commandment but in my view she did it in such a nice way that only a very surly G'd would object.

One other factor that the neither the teacher, John nor Sue W. had known at that time was that some weeks earlier I had made contact with a Jewish Youth Club in Finchley Road and had joined because they were a very friendly group: not ultra-religious but 'simpatico'. I had not told them because it was none of their business at the time although Sue W. found out when I introduced her to the group there a couple of weeks later. John was a locum and temporary stand-in for Peter and so his opinion meant nothing to me. The youth club was simply a step on my way towards my own understanding of my path.

<u>Studying Languages at Burgess Hill School</u>

Geoffrey: Geoffrey Thorpe was the Latin Teacher at BHS. My efforts to gain some insight into the language of ancient Rome hove into being from my very first sit-down interview with 'just' Geoffrey after lunch on my first day at Burgess Hill. He asked me the question.

"What are the subjects that you would most like to study while you are at this school Tony?

Geoffrey was smoking a cigarette which did not cause me any problem or any negative thought at the time because I came from and had lived with a family for much of my life in which most of the adults smoked cigarettes. I only mention it now because society has moved on in strides since that time. It is inconceivable that a modern schoolchild would be exposed to such a situation.

I have to say that I had been very nervous at the thought of being interviewed by the headmaster. The only occasions when that had happened at Croyland Road were on the rare instances when I had been guilty of misdemeanours sufficiently serious to warrant the 'Cane'. Such corporal punishment was not an element of the regime at Geoffrey's school. When one is on first name terms with all of the staff corporal punishment becomes a much less likely option in my experience.

I was actually slightly surprised at the first few words that came from my mouth at question Geoffrey had just asked.

"Well…I've always wanted to learn another language…hmm…perhaps I believe that I can learn French here" I opined.

"Well, yes, of course. Ruth Richards is our French teacher; you'll like her and her style of teaching. There's also a bonus for you if you're up to taking advantage of it… you see hmm... in the summer term each year we have a group of French students here come over for most of the term. They're here to improve their English of course but there's nothing in the rules that says you cannot improve your French at the same time."

He sat back in his chair, a comfortable armchair, lit another cigarette and produced a very self-satisfied grin before going onto another very favourite topic from his own teaching 'box'

"You might also want to take Latin, you might enjoy it, and I'm the Latin teacher…"

He said this as if I really ought to jump at the chance, which in fact I was inclined to do. A couple of puffs later rom his rather pungent fag; I later discovered that it was a Gauloise bleu; a rather cheap French nicotine selection whose scent was not designed to take prisoners. He regaled the merits of learning Latin with any 'Latin' language of which French was one He assured me with the pride of a man who had assumed 'ownership' of the subject. As my newly acquired Head Teacher continued to expound the merits of 'family' language I began to lose interest in favour of the happenings in the garden about fifty feet through the French Windows behind him and which gave on to the garden. Boys and girls were playing, swinging, and jumping from, the rope on the 'rope' tree… He stretched again and gazed at me as a person awaiting a response to something. I came back to reality under the pressure of that gaze.

"Yes sir, I would love to…" He held up his hand, the palm facing me.

"What have I told you? No 'Sirs' please, just Geoffrey."

I smiled inwardly at my own previous 'just Geoffrey' thought.

"Yes Geoffrey, it takes some getting used to but…er yes, I would love to study Latin as well as French. He leaned forward and smiled in satisfaction.

"Right then, we'll begin tomorrow morning 9 to 10, one hour to begin your Latin career."

I breathed in a deep breath as we continued to build a weekly timetable; one that catered for all the other subjects that Mum and Dad would expect a budding doctor to absorb and in which to become proficient. Maths, English, Physics, Chemistry, Biology…I discovered with some nervousness that BHS could cater for all of those if only I would put in the effort. Thus, the responsibility was place firmly on my shoulders from the very beginning. That was in fact the raison d'etre of the school. You study and learn at you own pace; and that finally began to worry me after the end of my third year and the time for my first set of public exams began to come down the road at me at an ever-faster approach.

I began to study Latin with Geoffrey bang on time, 9am the next morning. His style was much looser than I had expected it to be. My parents were, very much to my surprise, quite animated at the news that I was going to study Latin. I had not thought it through you see; for them it was just another affirmation of my intention and ambition to qualify as a doctor in medicine. For me, of course, Latin had been proposed to me as being beneficial to my aim to study French.

Yes, indeed Geoffrey's method of teaching Latin surprised me. It was very much a 'learn by absorption route. We had a series of Latin primers which were graded by increasing level of difficulty. We read through those at a pace that pleased me because it looked like progress. I learned to understand the passages and to recognise them from memory. That is all very well on the face of it but I realised after a while that although I could recognise certain texts I was not being prepared to be able to compose Latin texts for myself. I was not being instructed in Latin grammar for a steadfastly and systematically growing vocabulary. I tried to discuss this limitation with Geoffrey but on each occasion, he insisted that that was the way it was done. To this day I have never believed that to be the case. I was being taught to 'daven' in Latin just as Jewish boys used to 'learn' Hebrew in Cheder. I was quite quickly 'reading' Caesar's wars but would have had no idea of how to write about them from my own knowledge of the language.

My studies of French with Ruth Richards were quite different. There were several differences in fact; firstly, I was the sole student of Latin with Geoffrey whereas French was more popular, and we had a group of about six in our age range. I was twelve at the time. I also 'teamed up' with Mario into a competitive group of two. We raced through the French primers which were quite different to the Latin readers that Geoffrey favoured. These primers were true study books. Each section had a uniformed structure of a short piece of writing in the French for translation into English using words previously encountered plus a selection of new vocab. There was also a grammar section which nurtured a growing and useful understanding of how the language 'worked'. Finally, there was a piece of English that was for translating into French to be marked and assessed by the teacher. Added to this structure moreover Mario and I came to engage in a friendly rivalry and so we fairly raced through our studies with Ruth Richards.

Then in the summer of 1953 came the arrival of the first batch of French students that I encountered. From memory I have to say that they seemed to be with us for most of the summer term. Whatever the case of that I had a firm resolve to use their presence to aid my French; an unannounced 'Entente Cordiale so to speak. I made friends with one of those boys. There were about six of them from different parts of France, so they were not a close bunch of friends before they came. In fact, the group that came in the summer of 1954 included a young lad from Algeria. The other French boys were clearly intending to give that boy a hard time right from the start. The period was fully in the middle of the worldwide de-colonisation movement that promoted very high emotions on both sides; that is within the colonised countries and the colonisers alike. The French boys seemed to be determined not to accept the presence of the young Algerian among them. The situation became so bad that they attacked him physically one night. The Police were called, and the riot act was delivered to the five bullies! The end-result however was that the young Algerian elected to go home.

What with the visits of French students in the summer terms together with the continuing friendly rivalry between Mario and me, my French was coming along nicely by the end of that summer term of 1954. And so came the school holidays and our regular two-week family holiday. Dad announced that we were going to try something slightly different. We were going to spend two weeks in a small private holiday camp at Brighstone on the south coast of the Isle of Wight. I decided to use some of the time to improve my French. I took with me a combined French Grammar and dictionary.

I had decided that I would use as much of the time as possible to think in French during the holiday. I did just that. My plan of action was to spend time walking around the camp with my dictionary-plus and making the effort to think in French. Words that I did not know I checked in the dictionary and so built up a very useful vocabulary just by walking and observing. During those two weeks of comparative piece and isolation I improved my ability with the language enormously.

I continued to use the visits of the French students shamelessly to the advantage of my French. In fact, I made friends with two boys: one in each of the last two years of my four at Burgess Hill School. Paul Bouilloud lived in Paris and Pierre St Martin was from Besançon in Eastern France. They both visited my home in Edmonton for a weekend during their respective sojourns in Hampstead. Paul, I remember was particularly enthralled by our telly and a comedy show involving Tommy Cooper. A sound choice that, Tommy has long been my favourite comedian even now that he is no longer with us!

I thoroughly enjoyed my French studies with Ruth Richards at BHS. I have to say though, that Geoffrey's assertion that studying Latin would help my French was a claim far too far. In recent years I have achieved my lifelong aim which was to study languages to degree level. I have gained experience and some understanding of the histories of the languages concerned from that degree "The Study of Modern Languages" I see only a remote relationship between French and Latin; with Spanish however, the relationship is much clearer in my view.

Climbing the Skylon Tree

I stood underneath the monster, looked up, and immediately wished that I were somewhere else. I had prided myself as been an enthusiastic tree climber for all the years that tree climbing had been an option for my physical and mental strength as they had improved and hardened. The beast before me though was of an order that I had never had either the opportunity or the incentive to tackle.

It was the spring term of 1952, and I was about to answer the challenge; the existence of which my new friend Mario had mentioned on my first day at the school. It was not just that it was a monster but that looking up from the ground below it seemed to have a distinct dislike of the building, No 13, situated not far away, because it leaned away from it so that the upper part of the tree appeared to hover above the narrow tree-lined road that ran right and left from the very end of the road just where the school buildings Nos. 11, 12 and 13 were situated. I tried to console myself, to very little avail, that a tree that size had to be at least a hundred years old and so there was very little likelihood that it would collapse into the road below in the next thirty minutes or so.

As I write about this episode, I am reading from an article on the net that although tree climbing is a risky activity it also has many benefits for childhood development and that young people, apparently, love the challenge of climbing trees; that the physical effort involved creates a boost to self-esteem and the feeling of accomplishment. As I stared up at the sky-bound behemoth I felt not one of those emotions. Yes, indeed I was wishing that I could be somewhere, anywhere, else. Retreating, however, was not an option and one that I would never have taken. Pride it is said goes before a fall or, as in the original Biblical version "Pride goeth before destruction and haughty spirit before a fall." I have never liked that narrative. The Bible has its points, but it is too full of 'Death and Destruction' for my liking.

Trying to hide my base emotions on the subject and casting any negative thoughts aside I began to plan my ascent. The lower climbable branches were above my reach and the girth of the lower bole of the tree was too big to provide me with the shimmy-up option. There was, however, a hurdle nearby which would provide a handy step-up to that handy lower branch. I glanced in the direction of the small group of adjudicators who had gathered in order to give approval or otherwise of my efforts.

Attaining the lower branch was still a stretch even with my approved step-up but once I was there and had made to first few moves of the upward climb I began to realise, as was always the case that the dangers were in the mind just as much as they were in reality. It was indeed a big tree and the effort needed to climb it was real but as each move upwards was achieved my initial anxiety at the size of the 'big' boy waned and I began to think of it as climbing several smaller trees that had been piled one on top of the other. I had long been used to climbing trees and so I knew in my heart that each climb accomplished would give me a true sense of achievement but would never remove the early butterflies.

As I slowly made my way up the tree it dawned on me that I had little idea where I might find the Skylon amid the vast panorama of London that was beginning to unfold around the corner of No. 13. I had been told that I would not be able to actually see the object of the exercise until I could see over the building.

Nervousness began to creep back as I realised that I could not yet peek over the top of the building and that I was very close, all too close, to the slim, even thin, branches near the very top of the tree. Was this whole mission an elaborate and dangerous hoax? I asked myself. Damn! My foot, my right foot just slipped, and my heart raced more than before the climb began. Three more branches up just three more forks and I would stop and bedamned the challenge! Two more branches onwards and upwards and that would be it then, suddenly a cheer from below and a very welcome "well done Tone!" "Great effort mate" as well as other raucous but less printable exultations drifted up from below. Members of the assessment committee below from experience had clearly identified that something laudable had been achieved but I didn't know what.

"Look over there, where I'm pointing!" It was Mike, Helen's, the cook that is, her son who had called on me to look down to see where he was pointing. I did so and instantly regretted it. I had done the one thing that you should be very careful about when at a dangerous height; I had looked down at the group to find out where I should be looking. I held on tight to the tree for a long while just to reassure my brain that I was not falling. They had seemed so tiny from the heights of my tree. My racing heart and my brain both began to calm down as I returned to reality to try to identify the object of my climb. After a while I could just make out, in the misty distance this nondescript, elongated stick-like cigar thing that I could only just identify from the rest of the London clutter for the sole reason that the Sun was shining on it, and it glistened.

Well, that was it. I had done what I had climbed tortuously up the tree to do; I had seen the Skylon and had received that accolade from my observers below. Now I had to get down alive. That would round the event off just nicely; I grinned inwardly. Some people maintain that the hardest part of climbing trees is the descent. I have never found it so. True you do have to look down, but the ground gets closer with each element of the journey down. The effort, particularly with the monstrosity I had just climbed, was less, much less than in the ascent; you have gravity on your side during the descent.

I am now happy, very happy, that I made that climb; it was not Everest, but it was my success in front of my friends. I did climb the tree several times after that; at least twice after the Skylon was dismantled later in 1952 but none of those latter occasions held the same sweet taste as the first.

<u>The Great Smog of 1952</u>

It was a fog so thick and polluted it left thousands dead, as it wreaked havoc on London in 1952. The smoke-like pollution was so toxic it was even reported to have choked cows to death in the fields. It was so thick that it brought road, air and rail transport to a virtual and frequently to an absolute standstill. This was certainly an event to remember, but not the first smog of its kind to hit the capital; nor sadly the last.

Smog had become a recurrent even persistent part of London life, but nothing quite compared to the smoke-laden and intense canopy of smog that shrouded the capital from Friday 5 December to Tuesday 9 December 1952. While it heavily affected the population of London, causing a huge death toll and inconveniencing millions of people, the people that it affected were also largely to blame for the existence of that smog.

Up until 1956 the main source of heating was to burn coal in fireplaces in domestic homes as well as by many industrial concerns for both heating and power. The Clean Air Act of 1956 was enacted in the UK Parliament and was passed in response to London's Great Smog of 1952. The Act was in effect until 1964. It was sponsored by the Ministry of Housing and Local Government in England as well as the Department of Health for Scotland.

The Act introduced a variety of important measures aimed at reducing the very serious air pollution of the time. In particular it introduced "smoke control areas" in some larger conurbations, in which only smokeless fuels could be burned. By shifting the main culprits' sources of heat towards cleaner coals, to electricity, and gas, it reduced the amount of smoke pollution and Sulphur dioxide from household fires. In order to reinforce these changes, the Act also included measures to relocate power stations away from cities, and for the height of some chimneys to be increased. The 1956 Act was a belated but immensely important milestone in the development of a legal framework to protect the environment.

During the day on 5 December, the fog was not especially dense and generally possessed a dry, smoky character. When nightfall came, however, the fog thickened. Visibility dropped to a few metres. The following day, the sun was too low in the sky to burn the fog away and, more importantly, there was very little wind. That night and on the Sunday and Monday nights, the fog again thickened. In many parts of London, it was impossible at night for pedestrians to find their way, even in familiar districts. In The Isle of Dogs area, the fog there was so thick people could not see their feet!

In those days I was going to school, a private school, in Hampstead. I had, in fact only begun to attend Burgess Hill School at the beginning of the 1951 autumn term. The distance of about nine miles from home did not worry me at all. I was very used to making my way around London on my own, with friends and, sometimes, with my little sister Denise. Her favourite visit at that age, five years, was the London Zoo. We had tried one of the Kensington Museums, but they were not very child-friendly in those days, plain and boring boxed and stale exhibits in fact, and not interactive like nowadays.

I say that I was used to travelling around London, but I have to define that to meaning North London. South London was another country! I did not venture there until much later, until I was in my twenties and in the RAF, in fact. Still, North London was quite big enough for me in 1952. I travelled by bus and tube for a short while then, as a huge surprise, Mum and Dad bought me an early Christmas present of a new bike. It was actually a secondhand bike but what a bike it was! It was a beautiful hand-built Claude Butler Special and was the envy of all my friends. The bike had a five-gear rear derailleur as well as a front two gear derailleur. It had Drop handlebars too, I loved it.

The ride to school though was all uphill and quite hard work for me at the beginning, when I was getting used to it. Whitestone Pond is the highest point in London. Edmonton, in the Lee Valley, is one of the very lowest. The pond itself had been a drinking stop for coach horses in the days before the motor car. It had a slope at each end so that the coach could enter and exit the refreshing pond with the minimum of delay to the company and the passengers. Mind you, many of these passengers might well have been intent at stopping for refreshment, or bed, or both, themselves at the nearby famous Spaniards Inn.

My school day effectively began at Whitestone Pond because I usually had a rest there before completing the short two-minute ride that was left of my journey to school. The ride to school was, as I say, a long uphill journey to where my mind now has me standing, by Whitestone Pond. From that pond I could see the heath on either side of the pond. I was often puffing as I stood there. A large percentage of the uphill struggle, for me, began at the bottom of Bishop's Avenue. It was all steeply uphill from there on up to Spaniard's Avenue near Kenwood House where I learned the beauty of hearing concerts in 'plein aire'. At Spaniard's Avenue I needed to turn right, away from Kenwood and on up past the Spaniard's Inn to the pond.

When I first began the ride to school, I could only make it up Bishop's to about halfway; before having to get off and walk myself back into breath. As the weeks went by, however, I completed a bit more each day, such are the determination and fitness potentials of youth until, just a few days prior to the Friday in question I had finally made it all the way up from the bottom of Bishop's Avenue right as far as the pond. It was a goal that I was both happy and proud to achieve.

On a clear day and standing at Whitestone Pond one can see magnificent views of the Heath and of London beyond the Heath. On that Friday morning, however, there was a mist everywhere. On the day in question, moreover, the 5th of December, my bike was securely locked away in the school's woodwork room. I had spent two nights sleeping at school which was something I really enjoyed when I could conjure up an argument strong enough to convince my parents. They were already paying more for my education than they could really afford. On this occasion, though, the school had allowed me to stay a couple of nights gratis, so that I could say a fond farewell to a French lad, Paul B who had been staying on an exchange scheme at the school. Paul had stayed over at our house one weekend during his visit. He left for the airport on the evening of the 4th of December. When I roused myself on the 5th it was as if a shroud was descending over London. We all knew the signs, and what was likely to be coming our way.

 For most of the years of my young life London had been synonymous with thick fogs. A person indeed has only to read the immortal works of one of this country's most famous authors, Charles Dickens, to read of the city's peasoupers. The smoke-laden fog that polluted London and choked her streets and killed people in their beds from 5-9 December 1952 was the worst-ever single incident of air pollution in the UK and was about to descend upon us. The school head had decided that I would not be allowed to cycle home that night. I pleaded with him, but he had already phoned my parents to advise them of his decision. In the event he had made a good one.

I knew the way home like the back of my hand by road or by tube and bus and so there would be no bother getting home, or so I thought. School staff were continuously reminding me during the afternoon that I ought to be getting on my way. One even took me to the top of one of the three-story houses to take a look over London. Hampstead was not so badly affected by the cloud of smog because of its height above the rest of London. For that reason, and my own renowned stubbornness, I kept delaying my departure even though I could clearly see the creeping veil of dark yellow that shrouded my beloved city. I remember that I was totally unreceptive to any idea that I might come to any harm on my way home.

The modus vivendi of the school was based on self-control and persuasion rather than any direct instruction by adults to children; until about 3.30 in the afternoon that is. Peter Vansittart, my illustrious English teacher for most of my four years at Burgess Hill

School, suddenly became totally fed up with my intransigent disregard for sensible argument. He approached me very quietly in the hallway of the main house of the three, he put his face down to mine and glared at me; "Am I going to keep having trouble with you over this?" Peter had a craggy 'lived in' face that could glare very efficiently. I began to feel that the argument for going home had been well made. I departed down the hill on the ten-minute walk to the tube station at Hampstead.

When I arrived at the station it became apparent that something was up. There was a much larger than usual crowd in the booking hall of the station. It seemed that one of the lifts was not working added to which people were attempting to do what I should have done much earlier in the afternoon, i.e., go home. Now Hampstead had the reputation for having the deepest platforms on the system, largely due, no doubt, to the fact that Hampstead was the highest part of London. There was a way down to the platforms via a spiral staircase. I decided, reluctantly on that occasion, to take that route. I was young after all and did not want to waste more time than I already had. I was beginning to feel a bit of a chump for my earlier stubbornness.

I puffed myself out by running down the long spiral staircase. Luckily there was a train coming in as I got to the platform. Six stations down to King's Cross on the northern line change to the Piccadilly line and then six more stations up to turnpike Lane and so came the biggest surprise of my young life. I came out of the station into what looked like a wall of swirling yellow snow. There were buses but they were hardly moving. They were ghostly red spectres in the deep yellow gloom. There were bus conductors walking slowly in front of each bus. They were holding fiery torches or flares in order to see street signs - and so that drivers could see them. Most of the buses though, were making their way back to their respective depots. I realised that the only way home was to walk home. I realised that it would take a while because there was no visibility to speak of. The statistics of that night were incredible.

One heard tales of great good nature developing from the adversity caused by the weather. Inhabitants of the Isle of Dogs, it was said, could not see their feet. That adversity led to an almost forgotten camaraderie such as was experienced during the all too recent war. Those struggling to find their way joined together to make their way through clouded streets. One motorcyclist, on his way to hospital to watch his wife give birth, found his way by tapping his wheels against the curb - when the wheels hit empty air, he knew he'd come to an intersection. Glancing over his shoulder en route, he saw a string of cars following behind him through the gloom, each one taking advantage of the lights of the vehicle immediately ahead.

The air that night was not only dark, it was also tainted a sickly yellow, it stank moreover of rotten eggs. Apparently, the fog had become a toxic mixture of the heavy smoke from millions of coal fires mixed with a poisonous combination of sulphur and other toxins. Those, like me, who were forced to venture out into the soot-choked air that night recall returning home with their faces and clothes - even petticoats - blackened. Some were brought to their knees, coughing uncontrollably. I remember well that, even when I eventually arrived home, there was no immediate relief of a welcome bath or shower to ease the filth from one's body and clothing. We had no such luxuries in Winchester Road in those days.

I was not really concerned as I sauntered cockily away from Turnpike Lane station. I was very confident that I knew the way 'like the back of my hand'. There was so little traffic that I was able to walk in the road following close to the kerb to make sure of my way. I began to pride myself that I was making really good progress by using this method. After twenty minutes or so, however, my pride in myself took a significant knock southward. Through the gloom I saw the lights of what had to be a shopping centre and then, alas, the lights of Wood Green tube station. In some inexplicable way I had taken the directly opposite wrong direction from the moment that I had left Turnpike Lane.

There was nothing for it but to retrace my steps and to get myself back to Turnpike Lane station and start out again for home. I have to admit that I set about this task with much less of the cock-sure attitude and a great deal more care. I did keep to my original plan of walking in the road when traffic permitted. This avoided the many obstacles that one can encounter on pavements. I did so, however, with much less bravado. I checked each and every road name as I passed road intersections. I wanted no repetition of what had happened before. I have thought and pondered over that error many times over the years. Even now, and allowing for the brashness of youth, I cannot think how I came to miss my way the first time I arrived at Turnpike Lane. I had travelled that way so many times that I did, really, feel confident. That alone is a marker of just how disorientating the smog was that night.

We knew then and we know now that the Great Smog was due to freak weather conditions and a build-up of years of pollution. An unusually chilly November meant that to keep warm, Londoners burnt record amounts of coal which added to the fumes belched out by factories, power stations and diesel buses. December had brought little wind and an inversion of an anticyclone, which combined to trap filthy air in a yellow grey blanket over the city.

It had become clear in those epic few days and nights that the national habit and necessity to burn cheap, dirty coal for heating had to be ended. It became an absolute certainty that coal deliveries were to become a thing of the past. That change came far too late however to save the thousands who fell prey to the poisonous air of those few days and nights. The smog of 1952 was thought to have killed at least 4,000 people - particularly the elderly and infirm - and the death rate remained above average up until Christmas

It was not, of course, only human beings that fell prey to this disaster. Animals, too, suffered; both wild and domestic. Birds were recorded as having crash-landed after losing their way in the thick smog, and although cattle at Smithfield market were fitted with smog masks many were reported to have asphyxiated.

Unlike the polluted air dangers that lurk dangerously in the air of our great cities nowadays the pollutants that caused the catastrophe of the great smogs of the fifties and sixties were only too visible. The catastrophic smog of 1952 was the first that brought firm parliamentary action, action that was centuries overdue. It led directly to the Clean Air Act of 1956 which regulated what could be burned in houses and created smoke free zones.

But as the whole population, both residents and industry needed time to take the necessary action to convert, choking fogs continued into the 1960s - 750 Londoners died as a result of a toxic fog in 1962. Joyce and I were married and at work in different areas of London at the time. We both had very difficult journeys home and tales to tell about our experiences!

In our great cities nowadays, we have yet another toxic killer luring in the air. The particulates from diesel fuel in cars, buses, and Lorries are silent and invisible killers and so the public can go about its daily business and hardly notice them while children fall ill and die, and so less direct pressure is applied to successive governments to organise an immediate plan of action. This is the great scandal of the beginning of the 21st century.

While the air, seemingly, has cleared, the effect of past smog laden events can still be understood today. Landmarks cloaked in soot can be cleaned; children's lungs cannot so easily be treated. The great populations of London, Birmingham Manchester Glasgow, and many others, I cannot name them all here, will not forgive lazy, incompetent, and downright disinterested politicians who swivel on their arses and do nothing whilst our children die from the colourless and silent killers that inhabit our streets today.

Three Easter Camping Holidays with Bill F.

Three Easter Camping Holidays with Bill F. 1952-1953-1954

I must admit to any reader that my memories of the details of these three camping holidays are somewhat vague as I write. For me, the author of this series of stories within a larger story is that the camping trips were made and were permitted to be made. The accuracy of the contents for me is of the least importance. They were the Easters of; 1952 during which we were away from Friday 11th April through to Tuesday 15th. Then we went away also both hitch-hiking and camping for the two subsequent Easters of 1953 and 1954. I am now 82 years old as I write these poor notes of which the circumstances are, therefore, almost 70 years in the past. I remember the trips of course very well. They were important occasions in my life; extensions to the freedom for outdoor activities that Mum, and Dad had always permitted. I had made such proposals previously, but the parents of my neighbourhood friends would not consider them. It was not until I moved school to Burgess Hill School that I came upon a friend whose parents were prepared to go along with our plans. I should say parent because Bill's parents were separated, and he lived with his Mum.

I am bound to say as I write this that I am still in awe of the parents of both of us that they allowed us to undertake these trips in the style that we presented it to them. It is for that reason that the details of each individual trip are not as important to me as the fact that we were able to make them. We had come up with the idea during a school meeting at BHS. These meetings were often a crescendo of noise as disparate groups held mini meetings and arguments with few resolutions taking place compared to the noise created and with which there was often very little comparison to be made with the agenda for the meeting. Bill and I somehow began chatting; out of which came our plan.

Our proposal which met with the total approval of our committee and body of two within the meeting was to take, in the first place, a five-day camping holiday of the forthcoming Easter Bank-holiday of 1952 which would be the April after my first winter at BHS and as it happened, not long after the great smog of 1952. We hoped to tour something of the home-counties by hitch-hiking whatever transport might be prepared to give us a lift. I cannot for the life of me remember how Bill and I came together to make this pact of intention. We became friends because of the three holidays we took together rather than before them. Between Easters, even, we were not stuck to one-another like bosom buddies but when Easter came along, we made our plans; a different destination each time, and off we went. It was to be an education for each of us.

Before parental agreement was received Bill and I each had to make a trip to visit the other's home. Bill's parents were separated and so I met just his Mum on that occasion. There was something of a mix-up about the meeting in the first place. I spoke to Bill on the 'phone to make the arrangements and could swear that he said he lived in Upton Park which is near East Ham. I was so confident in my knowledge of North London that I set off for Upton Park on my bike, my lovely Claud-Butler, thinking that I would simply ask for local directions when I got to the tube station at Upton Park.

You may know, as I did, that Upton Park is way off to the Far East in London terms and a reasonable bike ride through London from Edmonton. I got to Upton Park and asked several people including finally a police officer. He did me the courtesy of contacting his station, but no-one had heard of the address that I was offering up. I phoned Bill.

"Hi Bill, where the hell is your house? I'm at Upton Park tube station and no-one has heard of your road; including a policeman."

"Why on earth are you at Upton Park? I've never heard of it."

"But you told me Upton Park, near the tube station…" There was a short silence here…

"You silly sod… No-one here said anything about Upton bloody Park. I don't even know where that is…where is that anyway?"

"Near East Ham…East London."

"Well then, you've got a damn long ride back matey. This is Acton…West London…the other side of Shepheard's Bush from where you are."

I groaned. I knew well enough where that was from my wanderings around North London. I almost came to a decision to give it up for that day and try again another day. Stubbornness on the other hand will sometimes take you to places where a clear head would hesitate to go.

My best route across London for me at that time as I worked it out was to ride just North a bit to pick up the A124 and head West to Barking and connect to the A 13 and so head further West along the East India Dock Road, Smithfield, Lower Thames Street –Upper Thames Street, Oxford Street to Bayswater then onwards through White City and with a final stretch to Acton. In my mind I worked it out to be a fairly direct journey of about 18 miles across central London. I knew the route in my head but, for the life of me I wouldn't have been able to name the roads. I couldn't now either; I've just looked them up in a London A-Z!

The year was 1952 and the London traffic was not as formidable for a cyclist as the same journey would be nowadays. Nonetheless it was London, central London, and the best route for me, already quite tired, was simply to head ever westwards keeping to roads just north of the Thames. I had of course just completed the fruitless ride from Edmonton to Upton Park and so I was pretty fed up as I set off...

It took me over an hour! Bill's Mum had a nice pile of egg and tomato sandwiches {Bill knew these to be my favourite from my descriptions of day trips to the London Zoo} I still call them 'London Zoo Sandwiches'. There was also a jug of lovely cold apple juice ready for me as soon as I staggered through her front door. I needed though to let her know very speedily that what I needed most desperately and urgently was a Pee. There are few opportunities for casual needs of that variety across central London; especially if you have to protect your most valuable possession; your beautiful and much-loved Claude Butler bicycle.

In 1952 the only frost of the month of April occurred on the first night, for during that night the maximum temperature was just low enough. It then became milder with some rain but also with plenty of dry weather. Milder though is a relative term. It was milder weather than you get when the nights are frosty. Nonetheless it was Easter, and it was still April. English weather myths for April predict showers and that is what we got! Even so no heavy rain occurred during the month, nor did it snow! The nights were chilly, but we were well equipped for the level of cold that invades the Home Counties in April. I only ever met Bill's Mum the once, but she struck me as a kind and homely woman. Bill's Dad on the other hand proved to be a very different kettle of fish.

Bill hadn't seen his Dad for a while and so we agreed that we would stop and pay a visit on our first mission, on day one. I was told that Bill's Dad lived in Dorset, in a lovely country cottage with his new lady, and their two children, as I later discovered. So in fact she wasn't all that new!

Bill's Dad and new family lived apparently near or in the village of New Alresford in Hampshire. This is not far from the City of Winchester in Hampshire about sixty miles from Morden tube station in south London. We had decided that it would be too complicated to try to hitch rides in London and so we decided to meet up at Morden tube Station in south London. This meant a couple of changes but otherwise was the most straightforward way of getting close to a place where we could begin to hitch rides.

I had started out early that morning much to my Mum's annoyance. It was Friday 11th June, Good Friday and although we kept neither Jewish nor Christian festivals in our family Easter was nonetheless a Bank Holiday and an opportunity for hard working adults to have a lie-in. There was no chance for Mum that morning what with me clattering about! That was just me getting myself some breakfast; I had packed my gear the previous evening.

"What the bloody hell are you doing making a racket so early?"

"Morning Mum just getting some breakfast before I get going.

"So early, don't you know it's Bank Holiday today? Why so early, bloody early Tone?" My Mum had three ways of addressing me; my full given name 'Anthony' surfaced only if she was really cross with me and calling me to answer for some misdemeanour, 'Tony' was my daily familiar name and Tone was her 'pseudo-annoyed' option. She was irritated with me for waking her so early, but she didn't want me to go off, away from home for five days or so without seeing me off safely. You get tuned into these nuances within families. I was ready to go, and I didn't want the drama, so I gave her a hug and turned towards the front door. I had seen the beginning of a tear just before I hugged her.

"'Bye Mum." I said as I tried to shut the door behind me, but it would not close, I turned only to find that Mum had grabbed the door, face flushed with emotion that as a callow youth I had not anticipated… A big kiss on the cheek and a moment later…

"Bye son be good er be careful." "Bye Mum" I repeated and didn't know why.

I turned away quickly, heaved my rucksack firmly onto my back… through the nearby front gate and off down the road en-route for the Great Cambridge Road and the bus that would take me to Turnpike Lane tube station for the underground journey to Morden tube station where I was due to meet Bill. I was a month passed my 13th birthday and I was excited because I was going away from home for the first time and under my own steam.

We had decided to meet at the tube station at Morden at 10.30 that morning and Bill was already there when I puffed my way up from the platform. We had carefully checked on the route that we would try to follow to Alresford near Winchester in Hampshire.

Bill was grinning wildly as I walked towards him

"Nice of you to come." He took an exaggerated glance at his watch.

"You look a bit puffed, what's your problem?"

"For one thing I've got the tent as well as all the cooking gear; what you got, just your sleeping bag and a pair of jammies I suppose?"

"Yup, that's just about it." The grin remained.

He consulted our plan for a moment and so we began the journey by walking up towards the Martin Way the B286. The 'sharp' reader might suppose here that I have again consulted Mr. A-Z to remind myself of the names; correct! We stopped about a hundred yards or so into Martin Way for two reasons; firstly, so that I could distribute one half of the two-man tent to Bill, secondly because that was where we felt it to be a good place to begin hitching lifts. The tent by the way was an ex-US Army two-man tent that conveniently divided into two by way of a double row of very efficient press studs that ran from back to front along the centre of the tent. When erected, the front and rear of the tent each formed into a pointed, triangular shape, not a flat end, so that there was storage space at both ends; one each for the two person's equipment. A really well-designed piece of kit for two persons. My load was much lighter after I had divvied half of the tent to Bill.

That was to be the first of my many experiences of hitch-hiking. Over the years though you learn certain techniques that you hope will stand you in good stead. I never stand in hope near the exit to a roundabout because it can often be a difficult place for a motorist to stop safely. Traffic lights for me are a no-no partly for the same reason but also it can seem too much like a demand to a driver. Another one on my list of don'ts is not to walk and hitch at the same time. As a driver myself I prefer to see the face of strangers who are asking me for a lift. When I see a person walking away from me with his/her arm swinging in a lazy arc away from me I am not impressed.

We were standing on a grass verge between the pavement and the road so, on the one hand it was a safe and convenient place to stand on the other hand though and in retrospect it was no more than a shot in the dark place as far as our intended onward journey was concerned. We really needed to get to the Bushey Road and turn westwards towards the A3 so that we could head towards Aldershot and Farnham to pick up the A31 which would take us very close to our destination.

We must have been covered by the 'luck of the Gds.' on that journey because we had only been hitching for a few tentative minutes when a white Austin A35 5 cwt commercial van pulled over just a few yards ahead of us. I remember the colour and type of van so well because from friendly discussions with the driver we discovered that the van was the property of the travel firm 'Black & White Coaches' and that he was one of their inspectors.

The man actually laughed when we told him that we were heading for the A3 and the A31 towards a village near Winchester in Hampshire.

"You're in real luck today boys; I'm headed for Aldershot I've got to see to one of our coaches there that's in difficulties."

Bill and I looked gleefully at each other or, rather, Bill peered over the back of his seat to grin at me sitting on a scruffy plastic covered cushion that was my seat in the back of the van.

"I use that sometimes to kneel when I do my inspections." The man had explained as he opened the passenger door, then the rear door thus indicating that one of us would have to sit in the back of the van behind the passenger seat. It wasn't too bad, but I had gritted my teeth with determination that I would move faster next time!

One really interesting and pleasing aspect of hitch-hiking that I began to discover that day is that you frequently get into interesting discussions with the people who offer you lifts. Our raconteur for the next half hour or more was clearly very proud of his firm and after he had asked who we were and had satisfied himself that we were not vagrants or lost and that we were on route for a short camping holiday and that our first port-of-call was to be Bill's Dad he launched into the story of the history of his employer; 'Black and White Coaches'. For those who have no interest in this small corner of the transport history of this country please ignore the next two paragraphs.

The founders of Black and White Motorways, Ltd., commenced in the road-travel business in 1926, an early venture being the running of one coach a day to and from London. Since its inception the company had grown considerably according to our raconteur. The organisation 'Associated Motorways' which never owned or operated any coaches was formed as a result of the Road Traffic Act 1930, which encouraged competing coach operators to co-ordinate their services. The six coach operators came together in 1934 to form Associated Motorways, pooled their services between the Midlands and the south and west of England and between London and South Wales. Those founder members were: Black & White Motorways of Cheltenham, Red & White of Chepstow, Royal Blue, Greyhound (owned by Bristol Tramways), Midland Red and United Counties of Northampton.

 Each member company committed itself to providing an agreed mileage of coach journeys for Associated Motorways and took an agreed share of the profits. The pool mainly operated the hub and spoke model, the hub being Cheltenham where Black & White had opened a new coach station in 1931. The consortium had to suspend operations during World War II from 1942 to 1946 but prospered after the war. All the members except Black & White also operated their own coach services outside the consortium.

I cannot remember the first name of our charming driver, but he did give us his first name. Nonetheless that man goes down for me as the first person to offer me a lift in my future experience of hitch-hiking. He chatted enthusiastically about his work and finished by dropping us off on the A31 near a place called Badshot Lea just outside Aldershot.

Just along the road from where our 'Black and White' friend had dropped us we came across a refreshment van in a lay-by.

"Just about time for char and a wad." I heard Bill say to me over his shoulder.

He turned and winked at me; the fool liked mocking my sometimes-casual use of cockney expressions.

"Silly arse!" was all that I could think of by way of response.

There were a couple of tables with chairs by the van. We sat gratefully as the owner shouted us for our orders.

"Two Rosie Lees and two bacon sarnies." I shouted back in exaggerated cockney. It would be years from that moment when I would choose to avoid all things pork.

"Luvley grub." Was Bill's contribution to that short exchange.

  As we sat chatting and waiting for our brunch a weak sun brightened the morning. Then slowly a beautiful cream and red mirage appeared from behind a long curve in the road and swept wistfully towards us, glinting brightly in the eastern sunlight. Then as if by some magic the mirage pulled into the lay-by and stopped within a gnat's whisker from us, from me. I was never a boy to be interested in motor bikes. I never did catch that bug, but cars! Well, they were a different matter. The car that swirled up next to me that morning was for me a true 'cream dream machine'! It sat so close, a true cream, boy's toy, with red leather interior upholstery. I was in love at once with that beautiful apparition from out of the misty morning sunlight.

  My adoration of the car must have connected immediately with its owner, a fine-looking middle-aged gent in suave toff's gear. That was my immediate reaction, but first impressions are not always right. The first words out of the man's mouth told me exactly where he came from. He grinned hugely: -

"Like my old jam jar boychick?" He was a man who clearly liked to smile and, with that car and in my opinion, he had good reason.

The term 'jam jar' and his style of speech put him firmly in the East End region of London. The word boychick on the other hand is Yinglish word used by Jewish adults as an affectionate way to address boys and adolescents. It can also be used by East End adults who are not Jewish. In this case I felt certain that the owner of the car was not Jewish. Nonetheless he had a beautiful car. He walked away to the refreshment van and quickly returned with a steaming mug of tea and a Cornish pasty.

"Mind if I sit with you boys?" I raised a huge grin.

"Just leave your car there and you can sit where you like!" The man just laughed and sat down heavily on the bench seat whilst spilling some of his over-full mug of tea.

"Bloody hell!" "Look at me! People will think I've peed myself." That just deserved a response.

"Don't stand up and they won't see you." That – my cheeky response.

We had almost finished our tea and bacon sarnies and Bill was making motions as if to get back on the road. Why couldn't he see the possibilities in this situation? I was waiting on tender-hooks for the guy to ask the obvious question about what two youngsters were doing hitch-hiking and where were we going. Then, as if he read my mind.

"Where are you two off to and isn't it a bit dodgy hitch-hiking at your young ages?"

So, I didn't get the exact order of the questioning right- so sue me!" I ignored the question at first; instead, I wandered back to the car. I was determined to flatter him about his car but, if truth were told, all the flattery was absolutely genuine. It would have made my day and given me a trip in heaven to have a ride in that car. I moved away from the beauty with some reluctance…then without even getting an answer to his questions…

"I'm off to Winchester myself, when I've finished my elevenses." He added with a grin. "Any good to you"?

Now then, if that man had said Glasgow I would have been hard put not to say yes please – with nobs on! But Winchester? It couldn't have been better. The morning was turning out to be just a succession of birthdays. Bill suddenly ceased his restless fidgeting and rush to move on.

"Absolutely well done er I mean thanks er that would be great for us." He didn't usually stutter but this was an exception. "What d-yer think Tone?" "Yes Bill, I think so." I began to breathe again and forget the struggle I had been having mentally regarding the event that had just transpired of its own accord.

The journey to New Alresford passed all too quickly for me. Bill lounged away in the very sumptuous rear seats of the Beautiful Cream Armstrong Sidley Sapphire whist I had scrambled for the front passenger seat and sat devouring the opulence and wonder of the cars dashboard and enjoying the smell of the car's leather upholstery. Then I realised Mr. Franks was playing music in the car; IT HAD A RADIO! I did not really notice much of the journey after that.

My Dad's beloved Ford Anglia was standard black and had no heating for its occupants; let alone a RADIO! Then after a while in dreamland I realised that we had diverted from the A31 a few minutes or so ago and were now driving through a small village. "Next on the left!" I heard Bill say to our driver. Mr. Franks obediently took the turning indicated then; "that's it there, the one with the white front door and the dog yapping at the gate. That's Dad's place."

And thus, we had arrived. I had had an all too short a ride in what was now my favourite car and my ambition to one day own one. Well, now, I have to admit that I have owned some lovely cars over the years but never, sadly, a beautiful cream with red interior and fitted with a radio, Armstrong Sidley Sapphire.

Thus, we arrived at Bills Dad's house. And the dog was still yapping at us, but we were inside the gate now. I looked up and my dream car was quietly driving away and out of my world.

"Sod the dogs." I muttered quietly under my breath. I love dogs in general, but I had taken a dislike to those two. I also took a strong dislike to Bill's Dad almost from the first moment that he opened his mouth. He did very little that would be likely to change my opinion of the man from the moment of our first meeting to the moment after breakfast the next morning when we parted company. He was an uncouth loud mouthed misogynistic, bastard, if you'll pardon my language. Well even if you don't this is my story and if you're reading it then it got past the sensors!

Bill's step Mum was lovely. How she got teamed up with him I'll never understand. Her parents must have been driven mad with anguish when he walked into their lives. Bill's Mum got lucky that day, that's for sure, I thought as we made the journey into the kitchen. As I have travelled through my life, I have abhorred the phenomenon of adulation, or its reverse, on first impressions but on that day, I took an instant dislike…have I made my point here? Well then, I'll continue.

The cottage I remember was quite lovely; built as it was in Dorset stone blockwork with a side extension in the same blocks. It also had a small entrance porch with a pitched thatched roof that followed the style of both the main roof and the side extension. I remember the large front garden particularly because we at home had only a tiny front piece about four feet deep and the width of the terraced house. There were also a couple of bench seats, one on either side of the porch. It was a picture-card setting.

Jane, Bill's step Mum met us at the door as the beautiful Sapphire pulled away.

"Hello," She smiled "I'm Jane; Bill's step-mother." Her using the word 'mother' had somehow formalised the situation. We arrived in the kitchen to be greeted by two children: a boy about eight and a girl a year or so younger. They sat quietly at the table without the usual noise and chatter that I would have expected of children seeing two unknown teenagers suddenly arriving in their midst. Bill, of course, was their stepbrother but had hardly seen them since they were born. His Mum did not wish for any personal contact with any of them for herself.

"Who're these two then?" The words, unwelcoming as they were, emerged from a grumpy face belonging to a very big man seated between the two children on the far side of a large dining table.

"You know well enough Bill, who they are. Surely you recognise your own son?"
So, then it seemed that Bill junior had been named for his father Bill senior.

"I haven't seen him often enough to recognise him."

"And whose fault is that?" Bill sprung up from behind Jane. He was suddenly angry at his father. "It took me long enough to get you to agree this visit with you." The meeting was not going well right from the start. There was quite obviously a lot of mud to be disturbed for my friend in this, his first meeting with his father for a while.

"You come up to London often enough." Bill clearly wasn't in the mood to let it go yet. His Dad had pulled his chain and was likely going to reap the rewards of that if Jane hadn't stepped in as peacemaker.

"Actually, that's a good idea." She paused a moment for tensions to come slightly off the boil. "London would be a good place for you two to meet. You could even go to see his school, Bill. You've never been to see him there. He is your son after all" …
Bill senior lunged to his feet, his face red and twisted in sudden anger."
Bloody hell! I thought what sort of menagerie is this?

"I do know he's my bloody son woman" … Then as suddenly as he fired up, he became a different person. It was bewildering in the extreme… "Yes, you're right of course; I could meet up with Bill junior when I go to London. Yes…I should see his school…yes." That was where he left it and I'm absolutely certain that everyone in the room felt the relief of that.

"And who are you?" He turned towards me and as he did, so he pushed a smile onto his face.

"I'm Tony Sir; Bill's friend from school." I had absolutely no idea why the 'Sir' escaped but it did and seemed to placate him further.

"Well, they do at least seem to teach some manners at that school. It may be worth the money after all." Bill and I sneaked and exchange of grins at this. If only he knew…

"Time for a bit of lunch!" Bill senior turned on his heels and strode towards the kitchen. He turned and glared at Jane and growled…" Well then woman, are you coming or not?" a pause… "I'll need some help."

Jane followed obediently to help with the lunch. It turned out to be a reasonable meal but not great considering that he hadn't seen his son for several years. It was also a lunch when I managed to make a blunder that completely negated all the brownie points, I had earned with the unintended "Sir" earlier. I cut the bread! Yes, indeed I crossed some unforeseen red-line and cut the bread!

"Anyone want the shpitzle?" I had asked as I leaned towards the centre of the table where there lurked a farmhouse loaf next to a lovely crispy bloomer. I had cut off, very neatly, the end knobby i.e., the shpitzle in Yiddish, although to me at that time it was just a term my Dad used so that's what I called it. Anyway, it was no longer the shpitzle by then but merely the end of the bloomer loaf lying next to several further neatly cut slices of the loaf that I had cut for other people thinking that I was doing a 'good thing'. Wrong! I had used a bread knife very expertly since I was about eight, but I had evidently crossed a line as far as Bill senior was concerned.

"Who asked you to cut bread?" Bill senior demanded, face reddened in anger that was totally unexpected by me and possibly by Bill junior too, by the startled look on his face. Jane, though, and the two children had clearly heard those tones before. Faces whitened, they all three stared at me as if I were one of the condemned and already found guilty. I on the other hand could not understand what on earth had happened to change the atmosphere so suddenly.

"Well, I'm sorry. I didn't mean to step out of line. I always cut bread at home, just trying to help a bit, that's all. I've been using a bread knife since I was eight." I added the latter by way of explanation. I just could not understand what all the fuss and anger were about.

Bill senior continued to stare at me, still in anger as the red face gradually toned down to the normal beer-fed rosy blotches. He clearly did not know how to deal with the situation. The man gave out all the signals of one deciding perhaps reluctantly, that death would be too severe a punishment. I tried a slow smile and followed my earlier "Sorry" with an additional apology; still without understanding why I should need to do so. I sat down. The atmosphere gradually eased, it did not mellow, however. Bill senior continued to growl at me but failed to explain how I had offended. I had though begun to understand that the range of personal freedom of action in that family was limited strictly according to the whims of Bill senior.

We finished the meal more or less in silence. The next morning when we were due to be on our way began to seem so far off. For the first time for a very long while I realised that I was beginning to feel depressed and, quite simply, angry, at that thought. The Bill senior centered misery did not end there though.

After the meal I helped to clear the table with Bill junior. I also offered to help with washing the dishes. This offer was politely refused by Jane. She did mention politely that the children might like to play a game. At this point I realised that I did not know their names. The boy perked up straight away.

"I'm Bill too." He chanted "After my Dad." Was there no end to this man's sense of self-importance? Three 'Bills' in that family set-up was one Bill too many. One man with two sons both called Bill; for goodness' sake I muttered as I turned to the girl half expecting her to be called 'Wilhelmina' also after her Dad but she spoke up sprightly and with a clear sense of her 'self' that was distinctly in discord with that of her brother and, in particular, her mother.

"No" she continued, "I'd rather not play an indoor game. I'm going into the garden to clean and feed the rabbits."

Bill junior No. 2 piped up. "They're her rabbits. She was told she was in charge of cleaning and feeding before Dad said she could have them." He paused; "she's got hundreds of them now, there were only two at first!"

"There's not hundreds you little liar, troublemaker too there's only ten of them and that includes the Mum and Dad." And looking at me again- "Just call me Willy; everybody does."

I had become bored with the name game by that time and returned my attention to junior Bill 2. "What are we going to play?" I asked him.

"Draughts!" The response came very quickly and with a grin. "I like draughts."

"Oh good "I mumbled to myself; thinking that here was someone that I might be able to beat at last. My Dad had taught me to play both draughts and chess. He had never beaten me at chess after the age of about 11 and that was two whole years ago, but at draughts Dad reigned supreme. I could not recall ever beating him at that game. Now comes along an eight-year-old Bill junior 2 who would be easy meat I thought. Again! Wrong!

The youngster won the first game and ended with a loud "Yes!" and rose, almost jumped, to his feet in clear triumph.

"Beginner's luck." I barely breathed the words but Bill junior 2 heard them well enough.

"No, it wasn't so; beginner's luck." He retorted. "We'll see!" I grumbled.

That boy beat me time after time. For four or five games I didn't get a look in. Then came the moment when Bill senior entered the room on his way to the kitchen where Jane was finishing the washing and tidying-up.

"Hello." He stopped behind his son's chair. "How's it going then?" Almost civil…

Junior Bill 2 turned his head towards his father, grinning hugely. I'm winning Dad, I've won every game so far."

With that Bill senior struck his son a blow with the flat of his hand, a big hand on a large bully of a man. "Don't lie and if you don't lie don't boast!" The slap was not a playful slap and because the boy's head was turned slightly towards his Dad, he struck the boy full in the face.

Bill junior 2 screamed with fright and sudden pain. I jumped to my feet indignant; red faced and fists clenched. "He's not lying he has beaten me and fair and square at that."

"Then you must be more stupid than you look, more stupid than him." He looked at the boy very un-tenderly. "He never beats me." "Perhaps he wouldn't dare!" I said it as a statement not as a question. "And what do you think you're going to do with those?" The lousy coward was looking at my still clenched fists. I relaxed them immediately; there was no way that that line of action or thought could go any further. He would have pulverised me without breaking sweat. The oppressive sod just walked away smiling to himself as if he'd just won some great battle. I held the little boy Bill double junior to my chest and gave him a hug. He continued to cry for some while; at first in pain and then in anguish.

I told my friend Bill shortly afterwards what had transpired. I suggested that it might be prudent for the two of us to leave earlier than the next morning – after tea perhaps?

"Can't do that Tone - sorry. I'd like to leave early. I haven't seen him for years. My Mum told me he was a bully, but I had to see for myself. I don't want to leave early 'cos he'll see that as a victory, over my Mum even, oh- no I can't leave early. ""OK then, that's fine by me when you put it like that." That was all that I could think to say. What a family, what a bloody family! I thought as I stood looking at my friend and mentally comparing families.

The outright bullying incident was not the end of the outlandish, even downright evil, behaviour evinced by that man that day, however. It was a visit that my friend Bill had been looking forward to with some anticipation in the hope that his Mum might have over egged the pudding as far as Bill senior's failings were concerned. It was a visit moreover that was destined to dash his hopes more fundamentally than either of us had thought possible even after the draughts incident.

On Bill senior's instructions Jane had not made up a bed or beds for Bill and I. We were to use our sleeping bags and sleep on the floor of the sitting room. That was in fact completely fine for us. We would not have wanted to put Jane to that much trouble for just one night anyway. We settled down for the night on the floor when the door to the stairs opened suddenly.

The stairs to the first floor opened into the end of the sitting room through a door and suddenly in the frame of the door stood Bill senior. It was a nervous moment for both of us when the man suddenly burst out laughing, opened his fly and pulled out his 'dick'. I call it that because he was too coarse a man to have possession of a penis.

"Look at this!" he balled with the pride of a man with no pride. "I'm just going upstairs to put this where it belongs." Stated with lascivious gleam and intent. I have never, thankfully, either before or since, witnessed such behaviour from anyone, man or boy. It was shameful, degrading both to himself and much more importantly, to Jane who was the obvious object of his design.

That incident took place some seventy years ago. It did not affect me personally, but it did have lasting effect as only this story will tell. I have often thought of Jane and her two children over the years, innocently incarcerated as they were with that evil beast. One can only hope that they found some way of getting shot of him.

Bill and I had our breakfast and took our leave of his step-Mum and her lovely children just after breakfast. I could not get away fast enough, but it was, after all, Bill's family and so I did not enquire as to his thoughts or feelings as we made our way away from that unfortunate house…

The day was bright unlike our mood as we made our way slowly down the road in the direction that the lovely sapphire had taken less than a day before. It had been a long-awaited foreshortened day at that. We walked a hundred yards or so in silence until I turned my head to speak to my friend. I noticed however the smudge marks of tears that had been quietly scuffed away by the wrist of a pullover sleeve. He had been silently shedding a few tears as we came away from the house. I said nothing and walked along with him in quiet companionship. We both knew why he had shed his silent tears.

There was no need to speak. There are truly times in one's life when the old saying "silence is golden reigns supreme. We walked out of that lovely village in silence and quietly came back to the A31 and the need to make decisions as to where to go next. The beauty of the three trips that Bill and I made together was that we did not draw up firm itineraries. We had arrived back at the A31 with the world or southern England at least, as our oyster. Southwest, towards the New Forest seemed like a good idea…

We had been so lucky regarding lifts on the day before. That Saturday however 'hitcher's reality' kicked in big time for a while. As we walked and chatted alongside the A31 we had made no firm decisions as to our destination. We were walking in the direction of Winchester, but it emerged that the New Forest was more attractive to both of us than the city of Winchester, interesting as it might be we both lived in a great city and the country-side appealed more to us. Having explained all that, we were getting no help; either from passing cars nor Lorries nor even, I remember, from a guy driving a horse and cart. Bill did try cheekily to beg a lift…

"How about a lift mate, for two weary travelers?"

"Sorry Lad I'd like to but this old bugger (pointing to his beautiful shire) he knows just where he's going and if I stop now, he'll be the very devil to get moving again."

The man grinned at us and finished his friendly refusal by pointing out that he was about to turn off the road quite soon anyway. Sure enough he did turn off but not that much before us because the "old bugger" was not plodding that much quicker that we were. He was not, as it turned out, the last shire-horse we were to meet that weekend.

There was a chill, biting, wind blowing in our faces as we continued to chat and hitch unsuccessfully beside the A31. We hitched and walked and continued to hitch but with our backs to the oncoming traffic. Over a quite short period of time, I began to think that it was not a good idea to have our backs to drivers…

"Look Bill." I began "Let's stop for a while and hitch when we can see what's coming. More important perhaps, they can see us, what we look like and so on?"

"Suits me." Was the near breathless reply. "I'm puffed anyway".

And so it was that my first rule of hitch-hiking came about. We turned to face our field of possibilities and lo! Although some cars did pass us by it was not too long a time that one kind fellow did stop.

"Sorry lads, one of you'll have to sit in the back." He pointed with a huge smile to the rear of his low-loader. "You can make yourself comfortable with a couple of those bales."

I turned towards the back of the truck…

"Hold on a minute! Where are you headed?" That was a good point. That's my problem sometimes – too hasty!

Bill chimed in; he had stayed close to the warmer option, the cabin.

"We're looking at the New Forest. We thought we might stay there for a couple of nights before beginning the trip back to London."

"Well, I'm taking those bales to a friend who runs a farm near Romsey. I supply Hay especially for his horses. He's got a few of those and cattle and grows some mixed arable. Not sure what actually; good chap though."

That seemed to be it. Bill and I looked at each other shrugged our shoulders and agreed that it was the best offer on the table for us at the time. Bill heaved his rucksack into the back of the low loader on the instructions of the driver.

"It'll save room in the cab." The man explained. I started to climb into the back. It seemed only fair as I had had the best seat in the lovely 'sapphire'.

"By the way." He said to me as Bill climbed into the warm cab. "I'm going through Winchester on to the road south towards Romsey. I'm planning to stop for lunch at a greasy spoon in Winchester. You're welcome to join me but be told; I'm not paying for you. If that's understood we're OK."

With that all said I settled myself down among the bales while my grinning companion finished his own climb into the cab. I settled myself down among the hay bales and, in spite of the rickety ride I actually dropped off for a while. I hadn't had much sleep during the night after Freshwater senior's disgusting curtain call.

I woke up to the sound of nearby traffic and of the squeaky brakes of the low loader. Looking around I noticed that we were in the small parking lot of a transport style café.

Our new friend 'Don' called it a 'greasy spoon' but I had seen much worse than this in London.

Over lunch Don and Bill relayed the gist of their en-route discussions the main feature of which was to get my opinion to what amounted to an agreement that they had already arrived at between the two of them. The suggested 'agreement' was that we should stay with Don all the way to his delivery point, his friend's farm near the village of Wellow in Hampshire. Bill had already all-but agreed to the idea which did aggravate me a bit but as they explained it the plan seemed a good one.

It appeared that Adam and Jane Mason {names changed in case the family still live in the district} apparently ran a mixed farm just outside of the village of Wellow a few miles south-west of Romsey in Hampshire. The farm was in reality situated on the edge of the New Forest National Park but was situated in a beautiful location in its own right. I didn't need much persuading in order to agree to the 'plot' that Don and my friend had cooked up between them. My single condition was Bill should take a turn in the back of the low-loader!

We finished our meal and true to the terms Don had indicated we each paid for our own meals. That was not in question as far as we were concerned in any case. Our families had not allowed us to go off without a decent provision of the 'necessaries'…

I knew nothing of the village of Wellow but have done some reading on the subject over the years on and off as I contemplated putting some of my experiences to paper. It appears that, see the following: -

The history books tell us that King Alfred magnanimously left "the toune of Welewe" in his will to his eldest daughter Ethelgifu. Royalty could do that sort of thing in those days. The peasants themselves probably came as a part of the gift. Thirteen households at "Welue" are apparently mentioned in the Domesday Book although I have never consulted that document. Only the name "Wellow" appears on Saxton's 1575 map of Hampshire; it is spelt "Wellew" in various later maps. East and West Wellow appear separately by the time of John Harrison's 1788 map. They are separated by the River Blackwater. Until 1895 when the county boundary was realigned, West Wellow was in Wiltshire and East Wellow in Hampshire.

Wellow is a village and civil parish in Hampshire, England. It lies within the Test Valley district. My memory of it is that it was a beautiful English village with a pub, naturally, as well as the parish church 'St Margaret of Antioch' which, together with some small shops and of course the houses of the village some of which are thatched and created for me a vision of the typical English village. Wellow itself lies just outside the New Forest which was our destination at the beginning of the day; until we met Mr. and Mrs. Mason; Don's farmer friends.

We had driven for a couple of minutes past the signs for Romsey when we turned off the road towards the signs for East and West Willow; through what seemed like one village over a small river and towards a place called Canada when Don turned into a sudden driveway and then to the left along an unmade but neat road on either side of which lay the picture of a quintessential English country farm. [Remember please that I was your typical London teenage boy and that almost every patch of land, unbuilt-on, was emblematic of English countryside.] I didn't know what Bill felt, he was out of sight in the back, but I fell in love with the place long before we reached the farmhouse and came to a halt in the courtyard just across from the house itself.

I jumped out of the cab and pounced upon Bill before he could catch his breath.

"It looks really great here Bill. Why don't we ask the farmer if we can pitch tent here for the night? We're real close to the New Forest anyway."

 Bill looked at me as if I'd gone mad, I was about to find out how Bill felt at that moment.

 "Don't rush me, Tone. I'm bloody freezing, back of that truck, and I'm covered in straw." My friend looked really grumpy just at that moment. Nonetheless I was about to try to persuade him while he was still quite unwilling to talk. Fortunately, however the farmer emerged from the farmhouse together with Don.

"Come on you two. Give us a hand to shift these bales. Bit of pay-back for Don."

With that he dropped that back flap of the low loader and grabbed one of the bales onto his broad left shoulder and marched towards the nearby barn door; opening the weighty door as he entered as if it were nothing. It was in fact a large heavy wooden barn door and the bales themselves were a good weight as I had just found out when trying to lift one from the back of the truck. I staggered towards the barn with my first bale just as 'grumpy' Bill grabbed his first bale and mimicked my stagger as he made his way the few yards to the barn. Don followed Bill, making each bale seem to be an easy-peasy lift as he completed the taskforce of four.

There were about twenty bales of hay on the truck but, between the four of us the unloading was completed in under fifteen minutes; all bales shifted and stacked neatly in the barn. The only casualties were two flushed and gasping thirteen-year-old boys. The bales were heavier than they looked.

"Well done boys." Mr. Mason followed us out of the barn. His first name apparently was Mark but neither of us even dreamed of calling him by his first name.

"Yes sir." Bill began… "They made us work up a bit of a sweat. We needed a bit of that after riding in cars and trucks all day."

Mr. Mason was a big heavy powerfully built man. He bore a thick crop of wild, red, hair. He smiled as he turned towards us again from moving off towards the farmhouse.

"Follow me lads! The misses has made us all some tea and sandwiches. And don't be shy!" he added.

The four of us walked through an out-house into a beautifully warm and friendly kitchen…Mrs. Mason was busy preparing mugs of tea and a huge pile of sandwiches. Strangely for a farmer's wife I thought at the time, none of them appeared to contain meat. Still, cheese and pickle and egg and cress with side jars of home pickled onions – lovely grub!

"Tuck in all of you. I hope you don't mind vegetarian sarnies boys. I must explain though. We raise animals of course but they're for market. As Don well knows I can't abide eating meat. Mark eats meat at the local pub when he needs a carnivorous top-up." She laughed out loud at this.

"They look lovely Mrs. Mason." I managed to stumble. We hadn't thought for one moment that there would be food at the end of this rainbow. It was truly an unexpected bonus.

"Nonsense!" she laughed again. "You've helped unloading Don's truck." "But…"- "But me no buts and get down to some eating!" The cheery command was clear. Eating was the current and very welcome order of the moment.

The five of us sat around the large wooden kitchen table and began to enjoy Mrs. M's kindness. She then took us further by surprise... "Look boys Don heard you talking about the possibility of pitching your tent in one of our fields overnight…is that right? Do you want to pitch tent here?"

I looked hopefully at Bill. He still had not made any comment to me on the subject. He turned his head from the plate of sandwiches to me but couldn't speak for a moment. His face was full of food. He was eating like someone who hadn't eaten for a week; whereas we had had lunch in Winchester after all and that wasn't eons ago. He wasn't a pretty sight.

Bill nodded back at me somewhat enthusiastically. He didn't dare try to speak. I grinned at Mrs. M. "It appears that the answer is yes Mrs. Mason, we would appreciate that very much."

"Hold on young man…" Her tone suddenly became a bit more serious. "How old are you two?" That was one out of the blue.

"We're both thirteen." This admission was produced with more than a little pride.

"Hmm, just what I thought." Her response was more serious, thoughtful. "Well then, you're both very young…do your parents know that you're hitch-hiking and seeking camp sites from strangers?"

"Of course!!" We both chimed at once, indignant to the core.

"In that case you won't mind me phoning your parents just to make sure, to set my mind at rest." She added this in response to our instant reaction of indignation. She was not phased in the least at our indignation. "Do you have telephones at home?"

This question about telephones was not anywhere near as strange in those days as it might seem nowadays when even young children often have their own mobile phones in their pockets. Landline phones were all that was available in the 1950s and there was often a six month wait after ordering before installation. More than that what was on offer was often a 'Party' line i.e., one that was shared with a neighbour. Our line at home was a sole line at least. We both nodded sullenly at her last question. I groaned inwardly because Dad wouldn't be home by that time, not for hours. That meant that Mum would be answering, and she was of a nervous disposition to say the least. No telling how she would react to a telephone call from a stranger out of the blue. I explained this nervously to a determined Mrs. Mason.

"Don't be silly young man. I'm not a fool. She'll be glad to know that you're O.K. and that you're staying where someone cares. Now then, what's the number, we'll begin with your Mum." It took me a few attempts before she seemed to 'get' my surname fixed in her head.

I reeled off the number and sat there with my fingers tightly crossed.

She dialed. It only took a few moments before I heard my Mum's voice. She always spoke loudly on the phone. It was as if she were trying to communicate long-distance without a phone.

"Is that Mrs. Krate?" I groaned again but Mum rallied quickly to the mispronunciation; she was well used to that.

"Do you have a son called Tony?" Oh God! I thought. Mum'll have a fit. Please get on with the 'he's O.K.' bit or she'll be coming through the phone....

"No, no, please Mrs. Kreit there's nothing for you to worry about. Your boy has just pitched up at our farm with a friend and they've asked us for permission to camp in one of our fields. They seemed quite young, so I took it upon myself just to check with a parent that everything was on the up and up. Would you like to speak to your boy?"

"Hello Mum, yes everything's OK Mrs. Mason just wanted to set her mind at rest." The conversation continued in that vein for a few moments. Mum had panicked a bit at first, but Mrs. M. had calmed her down and, as it transpired, Mum was glad that she had taken the trouble to phone. I assured her that things were going well and that we were really enjoying our first day. And so, it was settled, both Mum and Mrs. M. were satisfied; although the indefatigable farmer's wife was not satisfied until she had gone through the same process with Bill's Mum.

I have thought about that incident many times over the passing years. Mrs. Mason was the only adult who ever took that bit of trouble to make a phone call in the three yearly Easter Periods of our travels together – Bill's and Mine. I remember feeling quite indignant at the time but, as I have grown older, I do recognise that Bill and I were being permitted a level of freedom that has certainly dwindled and disappeared over the years and decades for youngsters of that young age. Camping happens of course and is both very beneficial and enjoyable for children. The camping though is usually organised in a more formal, planned, fashion for youngsters such as we were. Hitch hiking moreover is a very different kettle of fish altogether. When I look back, I can hardly believe that my parents agreed to it. That they did is a matter of history, and I am eternally grateful to them for having done so. I must recognise also that both the times and circumstances have changed over the years. If I were ever questioned on the matter myself now; I would have to admit that I am heartily grateful that none of my children ever put me to that question!

Well; to return to the story and to cut the story short we did stay overnight. In fact, we stayed for two full days and nights with the Masons. We camped in what they referred to as their 'home' field. We pitched in the lee of some thick bushes used to border the field and to keep dogs out and sheep and cows in! Fortunately, we went to bed quite literally able to count ourselves to sleep with the noises made by our nocturnal companions. Nonetheless and despite the weather reports, then and now, it was a bloody cold night! It was cold, wet, and windy. I must tell you now and with an accumulation of a great deal of camping experience in Britain that 'mild' is but a relative term. A field in Dorset at night-time in April is not a warm place to be. The sheep however seemed contented enough; and one actually learns to enjoy the crack!

We both slept like proverbial tops despite the abiding lack of temperature. It was during that night that I learned how to keep my sleeping bag warm by directing my outward breathing into the bag instead of uselessly into the cold atmosphere of the tent. Luckily, I am a nose breather and so I was quickly able to adapt to a breathing regime that required breathing in with my nose outside the bag and breathing out through my mouth which I kept religiously inside the bag. A couple of minutes practice and I was in business. The method simply required one holding the edge of the bag as tight as possible against the gap between my nose and my mouth. It was just one more example of that old adage "necessity is the mother of invention" rearing its venerable head once again. The aim was to not waste one iota of the warm breath that has been created inside the body. Try it and see!

In spite of my brilliant bag heating invention at bedtime we awoke to the need to venture out from our nice cosy cocoons, and it was frosty man! The sheep seemed happy enough, moving slowly though, mooching around, and chewing contentedly on the already early spring grass. A few lambs there were not so contented and trying to snuggle into Mum's deep woolly coat. It was a coat though that kept moving around and so it was tricky trying to get a decent snuggle going! That night was so cold that we awoke to find that a bottle of milk that we had purchased en route had acquired a two-inch spout of solid frozen milk while we were asleep.

We, being teenage boys, had thought first of our stomachs and how to get breakfast on the go. We had been sent away with some parental provisioning in the way of breakfast cereals; corn flakes and shredded wheat were the two options. Milk was now required!

"Well!" I looked at Bill; we surely do know where there is milk. I heard Mr. M. herding the cows in for milking a while ago. I'm sure he'd sell us some milk."

And so, we got dressed, washing never featured that strongly in our programs during our camping sessions. Our rules, after discussion, came into the; 'as and when possible' category and we had decided that that would suit us. 'Wrong!' It did not suit Mrs. M.

We arrived at the milking parlour and found Mr. M. hard at work. It was close to 7am and he had nearly finished the morning milking. When we explained that we wanted to purchase some milk from him to use for breakfast in our tent that good man had the first of several surprises that came our way during that morning. He grinned when he heard our request.

"Well, no actually. Mrs. M. says that she's not having you scrabble for your food in that little tent while you're on this farm. It's both too low for comfort as well as too cold for comfort; two good reasons for you to have breakfast with us."

"But…" He held up a big right hand to quell our joint automatic response. "You can argue with Mrs. M. if you think you stand a chance but first…have a taste of this!" He handed each of us what looked like a half-pint beer glass and tipped into each one a beautiful thick creamy fluid.

"It's still warm from the cooler." He explained. Just drink up and I bet you it's the best you've ever tasted…milk that is."

And it was. That milk was the best I have ever tasted. It was like drinking warm cream and has spoiled me for life against anything but full cream milk. I do drink skimmed and semi-skimmed milk on cereals etc. these days but that is only through firm guidance from my wife who claims, nay insists, that the lower quality milks are better for me.

"Right then." Mr. M. seemed to want to say something but changed his mind…" We'll go inside now; the Misses. is preparing breakfast but before that you're going to have a bath the pair of you. When did you last wash all over?"

He held up a huge flat hand to ward off the objections that he could see building up in our young frames.

"My misses has spoken! You can argue with her if you think you're up to it."

That was the second time in just a few minutes that that good man had used his wife to ward off any objections. She wasn't so terrifying as all that, but she did have a firm kindly manner that broached no argument for fear of giving offence.

Mrs. M. was stood in the frame of the back door which also served as the back door of the farmhouse. She moved back and sideways to allow us to enter. She handed each of us a huge towel and pointed up a set of stairs.

"Bathroom's up there first right at the top there's a shower over the bath. You can use that it'll save both time and water. Mr. M's got something to say to you later, during breakfast."

That set our minds to work sure enough. What could he have to say? We hadn't done anything wrong that we could think of. They were giving us use of their bathroom and offering breakfast after all. I was in two minds on top of that puzzle moreover. I wanted to hurry on the one hand to hear what Mr. M. had to say. On the other hand, I had never been in a bathroom that had a shower. In fact, I had never been in an actual bathroom before; just a tin bath in the kitchen on a Friday night. It would be some months before I was to rebel against that regime and transfer my business to a weekly visit to the Town Hall foot baths. At that moment in that farmhouse, I just wanted to luxuriate for as long as possible.

Mrs. M was waiting for us at the bottom of the stairs. That good woman actually gave us a quick inspection before she allowed us to take our places at the breakfast table in the kitchen. I hadn't suffered that particular indignity since my Aunt Joan used to seize me and inspect behind my ears. She though wouldn't simply inspect; she wasn't beyond grabbing a scrubbing brush and finishing the job to her satisfaction. As I write I think of her now, she is still with us and living in her own home fairly independently and has a good old chuckle when I remind her of the indignities, she inflicted on me in those days after the war. Aunt Joan is just thirteen years older than me. I have only recently, in the last two years or so, reverted to using the prefix 'Aunt' when speaking to her or of her. This lies at the feet of her two brothers Bert and Bill who both, when I reached twenty-one, asked me to call them by their first names. I did so with alacrity at the time and included, solely by assumption I might add, that I could include all my Mum's siblings into that request. Once into the habit I continued to take the liberty for many years until I began to regret it. Both my Uncles Bert and Bill had passed away before I began to realise that it had been a liberty too far. I realise that I still had my Aunt Joan but found it strange to break the established habit and revert to using her familial title. I did so just about three years ago and feel more comfortable for that.

For me now, I see any trend to dispense with the politeness of such titles as Aunt and Uncle as unfortunate. For me the titles hold and affection and a recognition of family ties that I am sorry that I dispensed with for all that time. I might have known several 'Teds' over the years but there will only ever be one 'Uncle' Ted for me. That principle applied for me to all my Aunts and Uncles. My Dad' siblings were never reduced to first names, and I am glad of that.

We sat down at the table; a table that seemed to groan under the weight of food that had been placed there. Bill and I were well used to the post-war restrictions on food. By this time most food items were off ration but there were still supply-side shortages, not at this farmer's table though. There were fried eggs, bacon, toast made from fresh home-made Farmhouse loaf. There was a bread saw regarding which I took the precaution of asking if I could cut my own slices after my experience at Bill's Dad's place.

 "Yes, me dear. You go ahead don't stint yourselves. The old man's got a proposition for you two. You may well need your energy before you get too much older."

What a grin appeared on her face at this remark! Mr. M appeared just at the end of that small delivery. He possessed a similar, plotter's smile.

"Tuck in boys. I got an idea you might like but start eating. I can talk while I eat. "

At this point another fellow entered the room and sat down. Now he was the hugest, smilingest man I'd ever seen up to that time.

"I'm Sam." Was all he said, as he began piling great quantities of breakfast onto his plate.

"Right." Said Mr. M as he finished his first mouthful of breakfast. "How do you two feel about a couple of days' work-experience on this farm?" A pause here as he took another great mouthful.

"You won't be paid in money, but you will get two days of the best food in the universe, and you will get to know the ins and outs of the loveliest horses in the world."

Sam nearly choked with laughter at this point. What did he mean….horses? Bill got in first.

"How come we'll get to know horses so well?"

I wanted to know that; I have always been nervous of horses but that has been about sitting on them – the buggers will move about, and they've got no brakes, and, after all we were moving on after breakfast.

"Well then." Mr. M paused only slightly as he took another huge portion of his breakfast onto his fork and swiftly, yet with finesse generated by practice…he continued.

"Well then…" he began once more. "We happen to own four of the loveliest Shire Horses in Britain. We are in the middle of ploughing and sowing the fields. We don't use horses for those jobs nowadays of course but they do still need to be exercised and groomed on a regular basis. You could ease the burden on us for two days or so." Again, a long pause... "And they do enjoy company. That's where you could come in if you wish. They are big chaps but as gentle as maybe. Believe me the next two days or so could be more interesting than whatever else you might have planned."

And that's how it came about. We spent the next two days around four of the biggest, best natured, and awesome animals that I have ever been close to in my life. Mr. and Mrs. M. were the nicest of couples to boot. When we finally left that farm, we realised that we had been as happy as pigs in Sh...!

After breakfast Sam took us in hand but began by introducing himself properly "My full name is Samuel Mason. Yes…he paused at our sudden looks of interest; yes, I'm their son. I also have an older sister who you won't meet. Dorothy er Dot is six years older than me. She's working on a vineyard in southern France. She travelled over there in the early summer of 1947 hoping to find grape picking jobs with all the students seeking the same summer work in those days."

"Surely there was work here?" I interrupted. As we talked, we had been walking across the yard.

"Yes of course but my big sister wanted a change from wheat and spuds." Sam grinned at me.

"The other thing is that her working farm experience and her general get-up-and-go gave her a big edge on mere students seeking picking-money. No; the girl dun good. Dot is now the vineyard's Harvest Manager. She only comes home nowadays for a few weeks over Christmas and New-Year."

Sam sighed at this, but we didn't catch his saddened mood too well because we had entered a long barn of a place equipped with several stables on either side of a central aisle. At the far end several stables had been knocked together to form one larger stable area. In that enclosure were four of the biggest animals I had ever seen; and so close! As we approached four heads appeared one by one over the extended side of the stable.

It is held in horsy circles that Shire horses make an impression. It is after all the draft horse from England, its sheer size – both in height and mass – really is something to behold.

They are the largest horse breed. They can surpass all other draft-horse breeds in both size and weight. The largest horse of the four 'Thunder' was a true shire and stood nearly 21 hands tall, towering hugely over an average horse that stands only 15 hands tall. Sam himself stood a bit taller as he imparted this information.

"I supposed he's called Thunder because of the noise he makes with his hooves when he walks?" Bill asked the question innocently enough.

"Not exactly…" Sam grinned "Just get behind him when he farts; you'll realise then why he's been called Thunder!"

All but one of the huge animals, including the gelding Thunder had white faces and white flowing ankle hair that needed careful grooming as well as careful approach work until we all got used to each other. The contrasting black of their bodies added to their size led to an altogether intimidating appearance. But that proved not to be the case, not by a long chalk.

The fourth horse, one of the mares had almost the opposite colouring to the other three. She had a dark face and ankle hair with a contrasting grey body. She was the largest of the three females. Her name was 'Reckless'. The other two names I forget exactly but were perhaps Bela and, also Sylvie because she was bought from a farm near the New Forest.

Even though the Shire horse is so large, they are known for being gentle giants. These animals are laid-back, calm, and docile. Shire horses are reputed to be popular because they aim to please. They do not mind being around other animals, such as dogs, and even as it turned out, wayward passing young hitchhikers.

Overall, this breed has a mellow personality and state of mind that is typically attributed to the fact that it was originally created to work as a war horse. That occupation required the animals to stay calm and even-tempered during the most chaotic and dangerous situations, and those traits have been passed down through the generations to modern Shire horses.

A gelding is a castrated male horse or other equine, such as a pony, donkey, or a mule. Castration, as well as the elimination of hormonally driven behaviour associated with a stallion, allows a male horse to be calmer and better-behaved, making the animal quieter, gentler and potentially more suitable as an everyday working animal.

Sam explained, at speed because he had other work to do, that the shire Horse had a long history from the early "Great Horse of England" which was bred as a heavy war horse from the hardened horses of Central Europe to carry Knights into battle and one would have to wonder which was the braver, the horse or the man. As a distinction one has to agree that the horse knew no better so it was the man who was the more stupid. That at least was Sam's opinion.

In the short time available to him Sam instructed us in the art of grooming the horses. "Do it right…" he added "and you'll have absolutely no trouble…they love it, and you'll make four very large and co-operative friends between you."

"Start from the top and work down is my advice." He shouted over his shoulder as he finally left the stable as well as us to our own devices. Just for a moment however his head made a brief re-appearance round the door.

"One more thing..." The head began. "In the end stable you'll see a huge black bull. His name is Terence; don't ask me why; I haven't got time. What I've got to say is not advice it's a direct instruction. You do not go into the stable with Terence. That is not because he's vicious, he's a daft old bugger and very friendly but he weighs a ton and loves scratching himself against the stall. If you are unfortunate to get yourself between him and his scratching post when he needs to scratch an itch, you'll die! This is serious, he's so heavy he won't notice poor little old you he'll simply lean against you, and you'll die.

Believe me you won't be able to shift him, and we'll have to phone your Mum because you'll be dead. Clear?" He waited until we'd each made it clear that we understood.

Well, it did almost happen. We did inspect Terence in his stall and were even for one moment determined to test out Sam's direct instruction and enter the stall with him. He did seem to be so amiable, and that characterisation was quite justified, he did moreover love his back to be scratched because I leaned over the wooden fence to his stall to give him a back-rub at which point he turned his head towards me and almost purred at me in approval. I then leaned over a bit further to try to shove him into a slightly different position, but it was like trying to move a house by pushing one of its walls. Terence did not move one iota. I then imagined trying to move that amiable giant if I were on the other side of the stable barrier and he were moving towards the barrier to get a better scratch. I decided at that point that any closer encounters with Terence would be with someone who knew him well and in an open field. His demeanour gave me no reason to fear his moods, but his immovability was frightening. I thanked Sam mentally for his warming. We might otherwise have been tempted….

The Shires on the other hand were an absolute dream to be with. It is no wonder that their ancestors were regarded as the Great Horse of England. That horse was a heavy war horse used to carry knights into battle as far back as the 11th century. The wheel of time turned and the need for war horses declined, and the new requirement was for heavy horses to pull great loads with some ease. From this need came the powerful carthorse. Some will then point to evidence that black Flemish horses with leg feathering such as the Shire horse possesses came into England in the early part of the 13th century and that these horses also had some part in the development of what we now know as the Shire horse. It is believed that East Anglia is the first region where Shire-Horse breeding took place. In the middle of the 1800s these beautiful horses began to be exported to the U.S.A.

All horses need and deserve proper care whatever their role in life work or play. They are 'giving' animals and can become very firm friends. In those couple of days, we were fortunate enough to be in full-time contact with those big beauties. They have the well-deserved reputation of being gentle giants and 'our' four seemed to be in their element during the exercise and grooming sessions that we spent with them. They truly seemed to want to please!

Shortly after Sam left with his final instruction re Terence and just after my attempt to move the immovable Mr. T. Mrs. M appeared round the door and gave us a half hour of her time in order to put us through the very basics of horse care. She began with some sound words of advice.

"Look here you two it's really kind of you to give up some of your free time to care for this big boy and his girls, it really helps us, but I think, and I really mean this, you will get much more out of this time than you could believe at this moment. These are the biggest animal you will ever meet in your whole life that will be as kind to you as they are. They are so laid back. They are kind, they are good with loud noises like dogs barking cars and even children. If you get on with them the way I think you will, I will be able to allow you a special privilege tomorrow that you will keep to your hearts for the rest of your lives; believe me you'll see. Remember always, they aim to please"

Mrs. M would say no more about that but took us through some very basic information regarding the care of all horses and her four Shires in particular, she showed us basic techniques of grooming, of exercise and feeding as well as the need to feel their joints for excessive heat which can indicate disease in those areas. This can be an area where horses and humans have some distinct similarities as I have discovered personally in my later years.

She was right though, Mrs. M. Her four Shires were a delight and as much as we enjoyed being with them, they seemed to reciprocate: with interest- compound! That first day passed so quickly what with us grooming and walking them around the yard. Mrs. M brought us out some lunch in the form of cheese and pickles encased in newly baked homemade crusty rolls. You were never going to die of starvation on that farm, believe you me! The afternoon passed as quick as a flash and the evening meal came and went, slowly. Every member of the family took a turn at quizzing us about our experiences with their horses and laughed at the innocent pleasure we expressed at the enjoyment we had felt simply from being with them.

From that day I have never been as comfortable with horses as I found myself to be during those two days. The Shire is so big in comparison with any other animal that most of us will ever meet that he/she is quite comfortable in himself or herself. They are not skittish and want to make friends at the drop of a hat. After an evening spent with the family we returned to our tent in the field and slept soundly in the land of the Gods.

In the morning, after breakfast Mrs. W. took us to the stables and asked us to make a special job of seeing to her Shires that morning because she had something in mind for after lunch that she thought we might enjoy.

"I know that you two boys must set off for home tomorrow, but you might as well go with a lasting memory of the friends you've made here and you're just about to muck-out four of them. Have a great time!" She left with a huge smile on her face.

We did enjoy our work with the four Shires. I cannot state it too often; these animals are laid-back and very docile. Some would say that these characteristics derive directly from the fact that they were originally created for the task of being War Horses and the need to remain calm through 'shot and shell as it were. Moreover, they really do seem to aim to please. They do also both need and deserve the very best of care.

Those big animals really did seem to enjoy the attention of being groomed and, furthermore, were very well-aware if you departed from their usual routine. Mrs. M had made us aware of this and had given us a detailed list of instructions including the order of duties and the hierarchy of turns. Thunder, of course, expected to go first and was absolutely able and willing to insist on that; with very firm good nature of course. Cleaning coat, removing dirt and dust, as well as twigs and the like were all a part of the routine. There would not be many men tall enough to groom Thunder and access to all areas easily without a 'lift-up'. For us we had the use of both a stepladder and a couple of stools to be accessed as needed.

I swear that Thunder was the only animal I have ever met that could give a damned good impression of grinning at you as well as playing small, good-natured tricks that clearly gave him huge satisfaction thereby came the grinning! For Bill and me this trick came in the form of small movements away from us when we were grooming him from the dizzy heights of one of the stools provided. With that movement away the head would turn, and the teeth would be bared in Thunder's version of a grin. This often came accompanied by a soft neighing; as if to say, gotcher! Yet again. We tried to fool him by grooming him in unison together with a stool place on either side of the cheeky bugger, but he soon understood this to be just another version of the game, he moved forward and farted when we were in range of his rear end. Yes, working with Thunder was a bunch of fun. It might have been different if we'd had to do it day in and day out, but we didn't and we enjoyed the crack as much as he clearly did. On that second morning I decided to show my determination to get the job done so I got down from my stool and moved round to his head and in mock anger I raised my fist right up to his nose. "Listen you old devil we've got to get this job done and you're not helping see! You muck about one more time and you'll get some of this, do you understand me?" Thunder demonstrated his abject fear of me and my warning by licking my clenched fist with his huge, hot and sticky tongue. He flicked his head back in common with a quiet neighing laugh. That was a truly stage-hot horse. Then came lunch. After some quiet chat Mr. M made moved to get back to work. On his way out he threw a few words over his shoulder towards us.

"By the way Mrs. M. has something for you to do before you get back to the stables." We got up, somewhat reluctantly, from what had turned out to be a very welcome rest together with a really enjoyable lunch. But needs must when the devil flies…

We gasped in awe and in unison. Thunder looked magnificent in his full show regalia and rigged up to that beautiful four wheeled [red-rimmed] cart. "We bought that lovely little buggy from a firm of wedding transport providers. We just use it for 'posh' trips to the village and to friends nearby."

Mrs. M. had disappeared half-way through lunch, and this explained what she had been doing. She had been preparing Thunder for a trip out and we were going to be invited it seemed. The big old boy looked great. His tail had been tied into a decorative knot and his mane had been separated into a row of tufts from the crown of his head and over down the back of his neck. The rig was black leather but with red separators. I have no idea if that is anywhere near the correct terminology. I was too in-awe and too excited to ask technical questions at the time.

"Well boys we're going into town and in style! Who wants to drive first?" Neither of us could believe our ears, had she really used the words…" Who wants to drive first?"

"Where on earth are the gears?" Bill joked and my own question had been of similar lines although mine was a question about brakes.

"You don't have to worry about anything like that at all…The public will think you're driving that cart, you may even think that you're driving the cart but just have one guess as to who will be driving the cart in reality." At this she gave a knowing glance towards the magnificent equine standing between the traces of that lovely cart.

"Yes, she smiled. We are all about to be taken for a ride by my lovely horse Thunder. He knows where he's going and you'd have a near impossible task if you tried take him anywhere else, believe you me, I tell you no lie."

With that she got into the cart and sat herself down on the double seat behind the double that was the front seat.

"Com-on-up." She laughed as we dreamingly clambered into the buggy…

"We're just going into the village for a spot of grocery shopping. Thunder looked so good this morning when you were grooming the Shires that it seemed a pity to waste his good looks. He loves showing off anyway. You may have noticed?" There was a short pause during which she explained the simple basics of driving the rig, turning, and stopping being the main actions. We soon learned that Thunder needed no incentive to get moving and that he knew where he was going and just how he was going to get there. For public and social reasons Bill first and then I held the reins and pretended that we were in charge. Even when we came to the T junction at the end of the farm-track that came up to the main road Thunder demonstrated that he knew full well what he was doing. He actually stopped, looked each way, and only then crossed the road and turned right towards the village. Bill and I joked afterwards that when we were 'driving' we felt quite safe in Thunder's hands, or should it have been hooves?

In giving us that short experience in Thunder's care Mrs. M. did us a real kindness. There was a real sadness like a cloud hovering between us as we made our way down the road and back through the village and onwards towards London and the way home. We were two London boys going home to the 'smoke' but there was little joy for us on that occasion. We had made friends and not just equine friends!! No! joking-aside, both humans and horses had made their impact on us two who had hardly ever spent much free time out of the city. A few breaks with parents yes but on our own and actually working for two days with the biggest, the best, and the most intelligent animals in the world! That had been a real experience to cherish. Heads up Thunder!

In fact, we had a further day to spare before we needed to return home. Not wishing to waist even one day of our allotted liberty we hitched a lift into the forest and spent a night full of interesting scuffling animal noises before we made a reluctant return home.

<u>Holiday No Two with Bill F.</u>

I am now including a simple outline here of the second and third trips that we made, always over the Easter Holiday. The trips and the places we visited were important of course but the simple fact that we were able to make them was the prime importance for me. They rounded off the long history for me of being allowed to explore either alone as at Ramsgate by my Nan, in the two summer holidays after the War or with friends: swimming and fishing in the river Lee. Mud-larking unofficially on the 'beach' or should I say the mud-bank just above Tower Bridge was another but less frequent activity. We never discovered anything worthwhile but the 'crack' of being there in the mud next to the Tower of London and that Great Bridge was worth a fortune to us. All that, not to mention the frequent journeys under the culverted sections of Salmons Brook from Bury Street right through to Montagu Road. Life in those days was a series of freedoms only spoiled, but radically so, by the seriously sour relationship between Mum and Dad.

By the beginning of 1953 we were ready for a second go. Good Friday was on April 3rd. The first half of that April was changeable, although amounts of rain were generally small and never enough to spoil our enthusiasm for the trip. It was windy at times and temperatures were mostly below average. On the 6th, the Monday, the maximum temperature was only about 8^0 C which would have been about 46^0 F. Even for us these temperatures felt quite low when camping in fields, which we always asked permission to do when the land was private land. As with all three of our trips we spent four nights away; the Friday to the Monday nights thus for me there was the disappointment for my parents that I spent the whole of the Easter weekend away and so would not be available for family trips. Now that I am older and have had children, I can understand that this would have been hard on them but, with the callowness of youth I did not think of that at the time. We got as far as Gloucester by the Friday night; we were always quite lucky and pleased with our speed of travel. As an adult now I am convinced that we had the scarcity factor of two young boys travelling alone in that fashion to our advantage.

We got as far as Gloucester by the early evening of the Friday. Bill had arranged that we would sleep on the floor of the flat of one of his cousins and her friend. These were two young women in their early 20s and were Welsh Speaking as it turned out. I sat there listening to the two women with quiet fascination. It was the first time that I had heard that beautiful language being spoken. I was at that time in the second year of my studies of French and what with the unconscious assistance of the previous summer term batch of French students together with a friendly rivalry between myself and Mario Dubsky my studies were going pretty well. I was also still on an unsteady path with Geoffrey Thorpe and Latin. I was not so happy with this but willing to soldier on because Geoffrey was such an amiable chap. As I listened to the two women though I made a mental decision to begin one day to study Welsh. I am now 82 years old and must confess that that decision has not as yet come to fruition. Maybe…?

In fact, we stayed two nights at Bill's cousin's place. We slept in our sleeping bags on the floor and passed the intervening day in the lovely city of Gloucester. That was the only time that I have ever visited the place. Cathedrals and the like are not my first interest as a visitor, but Bill wanted to visit the Cathedral. I must admit that despite my lack of enthusiasm at the time it is a magnificent building. I have to admit however that in recent years my lack of interest in such structures has deepened. For this my apologies must go to all the souls to whom they are wonderful and sacred places. I mean no harm, but I cannot set aside the thought that the building of such as those must have crippled the local economy for decades and more during and possibly long after their construction.

The two days following our sojourn at the flat of Bill's cousin we moved on to pitch up for couple of nights on the bank of the nearby River Severn. We passed most of the intervening day simply watching the world go by. The traffic and the wildlife on and by the river were wonders to behold. I have always loved rivers and the Severn was no exception. As a remedy for all your ills there is nothing better that to watch a river flow by. I believe that that is why my favourite book of all time is The Wind in The Willows. I must have read that book many times over the years and always get something different from it depending on my age at the time. I had taken my swimming trunks with me and so was also able to indulge my liking for river swimming at a point where I saw a group of locals engaged in the like. The Severn is a big and powerful river that was and unknown quantity to me. I would have been unlikely to have simply taken a dip in it just anywhere on my own. It's always more fun anyway to have company.

<u>Holiday No Three with Bill F.</u>

 By the time it came to our third Easter together in 1954 we felt like old hands at the game of hitch hiking. We were also much older, by two whole years in fact. It was Good Friday, April 16, 1954, and the day was quite chilly. The beginning of April had been unsettled and even cold at times. In the first few days of the month, it had rained heavily, and the temperature had not even reached 50^0 F that is it was barely at 9^0 C. We had already decided that we would head in a southerly direction to visit the holiday home of Sue's Mum. Sue from Burgess Hill that is. She had a Holiday Home at a small seaside resort called Elmer Sands near Bognor Regis.

Sue and I had surprisingly become boyfriend- girlfriend since the 'Shabbos Goy' argument with that teacher John in the English lesson. We were not firmly in that relationship it was a bit of an on off situation and it was the 'off' bit that Sue's Mum preferred. She did not like me and made that quite clear. She was of a wealthy family. Her cousin was a famous English sportsman whose name I will not mention here. At her daughter's request she had allowed Bill and me to visit on the understanding that we could only enter the bungalow in order to go to the loo. We were permitted to camp in the garden which had direct access to the sea nearby. That was handy because I was quite happy to go for an early morning dip in the sea in those days even at that time of year.

I liked Sue a lot, but she was clearly bullied by her Mum. They were a Jewish family, not orthodox as the Jewish element of my family is. I had had just the one visit to their home: a very impressive house in Wimbledon. I was never invited back. Mrs. W clearly knew of my 'mixed' Jewish status and made the mistake of trying to lecture me about the correct way to use her kosher kitchen. I pointed out some issues to her, perhaps not very diplomatically; that her kitchen was somewhat lacking in one important element to be truly kosher. I was after all, but a brash know-it-all teenager and I had studied more than was good for me about Jewish Law and practice; not because I was or ever have been religious, rather just because it made it much easier and satisfying when mixing with Jewish friends and family.

She had pointed out to me, somewhat pompously, that there were two separate zones in her kitchen, those set aside purely and solely for milchig and fleishig foods and meals. The first of these refers to foods containing milk and anything dairy the second refers to anything containing meat, meat of any kind or any meat product. She continued her mini lecture by telling me that she had crockery and cutlery that was dedicated to these zones and so I would not be allowed to use the kitchen unattended for fear of making a mistake and thereby upsetting the balance and order of her kitchen. In all honesty this information was of the utmost unimportance to me, but her delivery was so pompous that I could not refrain from bursting her bubble just a bit.

"Oh yes, thank you Mrs. W. but where's the pareve section? You surely have a section for pareve foods?" Pareve foods are those that fit into neither camp, such as fruit, vegetables, eggs, fish, water, even alcohol if it is otherwise kosher. These foods can be served together with foods that are either milchig or fleishig but should be kept separately from both in a strictly kosher kitchen. For that reason, a truly kosher kitchen will have a third separate section for storing and preparing pareve on the basis that 'the twain should never meet' that is meaning that a pear that has been in either of the aforesaid zones is no longer pareve and cannot be used with foods of the other category. Please do not try to scold me for making this too complex I didn't make up the rules and I could go on to make this section really confusing if I wanted to do so. The guys that did make up the rules had centuries to work on them and refine them. They did a thorough job. One of my female cousins, orthodox, once had the honesty to state that in her opinion "the rules of kosher were designed by men for the confinement of women." I have studied those rules and my vote would elect my cousin, by a mile!

Whatever the case of this, my intervention with Mrs. M did nothing to elect me to a position of popularity in her book. I was not actually banned from her newly labelled 'semi-kosher' kitchen; I was simply never to be invited back to her home. Sue was instructed to inform me of my newly 'segregated' status on the next occasion that we met at school.

I remained friends with Sue on and off for a couple of years; until I left Burgess Hill in fact. I was though very surprised when, after overhearing the third Easter Trip planning session between Bill and me, Sue came back the next day with an invite for us to spend a couple of nights in the garden of their bungalow in Elmer Sands. This came with the proviso that we could only enter the actual premises in order to use the toilet. I'm not at all sure how she thought we might otherwise perform that function but, nonetheless she had made the concession that we could camp in her garden and a concession is a concession after all. "You're to go nowhere near the kitchen." Sue managed a sweet smile together with this piece of information.

That then is the tale of one of the nicer elements of my childhood, my series of Easter camping trips with my school friend Bill. We did not keep in touch after I left that school which is something I do regret. I have tried to make contact on Facebook but to no avail.

I am Definitely NOT Flavour of the month

At the age of sixteen I took and failed my first ever set of exams. That is I almost completely failed. I did pass in French but for my poor old Dad this was merely rubbing salt into the wound because I failed English.

"How in God's name did you manage that?" He demanded, throwing the results letter at me. "Right." He continued. "We're taking you away from that school."

That school was the private school BHS that my parents had been paying for me to attend for the past four years. Despite my protestations, I loved the school, Burgess Hill School in Hampstead. True to his word Dad sought a meeting with the headmaster of the Latymer School in Edmonton Mr. Victor Davis and somehow secured a place for me there in the fifth form there for the following September.

That was in the summer of 1955. I was just about to undertake the BHS school summer holiday to Yugoslavia which was due to happen in a week's time and was to be my first foreign holiday. I cannot describe the heights of anticipation with which I had waited for that holiday.

<u>Chapter Twelve</u>

<u>A Border Incident 1955 Belgium/Germany.</u>

At the age of sixteen I had taken and failed my first ever set of exams. That is almost completely failed... I did pass in French but for my poor old Dad this was merely rubbing salt into the wound because I failed English. Nonetheless my parents had already paid for my holiday in Yugoslavia with BHS, and they were not mean enough to prevent me from going away with the school and so, as a final gesture in my direction I was allowed to go.

By July 1955 I had been attending the private school, Burgess Hill School, in Hampstead for four years; very happy years. Burgess Hill School in Hampstead was an unusual school. It was designed on what its founders formulated as 'progressive' lines. The only forms of compulsion came from the school council of students which sat every Monday. It is true that attendance in lessons was voluntary but, other than that the school bore very little resemblance to that portrayed in a later editorial by the Daily Mail which depicted it as a school from hell. As I say attendance at lessons was left as a matter of personal responsibility and in that the regime was perhaps somewhat naïve. The main ethos was, however, civilised and I have many happy memories of my four years there.

It was Saturday morning, and we were about to embark on a two-week holiday to Yugoslavia crossing Europe by train and I was so excited because this was to be my first holiday abroad. It was, or it seemed to me, incredible that this was just about to happen. The school fees were not expensive as far as those things went but for my parents it was a difficult task for them to afford to keep me in the school let alone pay for the holiday on which I was about to embark. They had even gathered together enough money for me to have some spending money whilst on holiday. Dad had bought me an ex-U.S. Army two-person tent, a sleeping bag and groundsheet some three years previously when I had started camping each Easter with my school friend Bill F. What with that and the hitchhiking around the southern counties I was both very well equipped for this coming holiday as well as being also quite experienced as a camper.

We all met at Victoria station and gathered together to catch the train which apparently was going to take us all the way to Rijeka which would be the end of our train ride in Yugoslavia but not quite the end of the journey for us. From Rijeka we needed to make a short boat trip across the bay to a village called Lovran not far from Opatija on the Croatia Instrian coast. We were a really excited bunch of kids many of whom were going to leave the UK for the first time. Many of my friends, four years beforehand in my previous school had never even seen the sea and here was I about to cross Europe, four countries away to spend two weeks in the final one.

The trains in those days were not constructed in open carriages as they are today. Each carriage had a corridor with sliding internal doors which opened into four separate compartments made up of two opposing bench seats for four people. Groups of eight of us were therefore piled into several compartments together in one carriage. We were a happy, noisy group of youngsters as we settled ourselves down into our compartment. We had enough reserved seats to almost fill up the whole carriage. I had already spotted that if we arranged ourselves properly a couple of us might be able to sleep in the luggage racks two on the floor and the others arranging themselves on the seats, we could use our luggage as pillows. That though was a problem for later; we were all too excited to think too much about that at that time.

We were about to cross a Europe which was still suffering the aftermath of a terrible war. Although it was 1955 many cities in Great Britain still bore the scars of bombing campaigns carried out by the Luftwaffe. I had spent much of my childhood and early youth playing on bomb sites in London. The transport systems across Europe were not as they are now. We had been told to expect a train journey of some 36 hours before we reached the Yugoslav Adriatic port of Rijeka from where still that short boat journey had before, we would reach our campsite further down on the shore of what was then the province of Croatia. I was surprised when I was told that we would stay in the same train way throughout the journey even across the channel in the ferry.

The journey started out well enough; we were too excited to worry about the length of the journey. We arrived at Dover from where we crossed by ferry to the Belgian port of Ostend where border guards boarded the train to inspect our passports. They were dressed very smartly, very officiously and were to my shock and horror armed. I had lived through the war and the aftermath of war and was used to seeing soldiers carrying rifles and I had never seen or expected to see a border guard or a police officer carrying a side arm. This was though something I got used to seeing during the next two weeks in Europe.

The train puffed its way across Belgium towards the border with Germany. Now for me going to Germany, even crossing the country was something that I had sworn I would never do because of what happened to my family and to the whole Jewish people during the war and perpetrated by the then government of that country. For this trip I had bargained with myself that I would go on this holiday to Yugoslavia because although we were going to cross Germany we were going by train, and I would not need to set foot on German soil. That was the compromise that I had made with myself in order to allow myself on this one exciting trip.

I do have to admit that nonetheless I felt a degree of tension as I realised that we were getting ever closer to the German border. This tension though was tempered by the general excitement in the compartment and the high-level chattering going on among friends. I had also spent much of the time with my nose glued to the window as I enjoyed watching out at the unfamiliar landscape and townscape passing by. Finally, we reached the German border at Aachen, and this is where a few moments of anxiety, fear and anger regurgitated all thoughts of the personal bargain I had made with myself.

In those days when you crossed the border between two countries in Europe there were two sets of controls that had to be satisfied before you were allowed to continue your journey. The Belgian border control came on board the train and with the very little fuss and bother they came and went. It was then the turn of German border control which was altogether a different kettle of fish. I do remember that they were dressed in a much more military style and had a very much more military briskness in the way they set about their business. The whole affair as conducted by them was much noisier and unfriendly than the Belgian border control had been.

We could hear the sound and noise of their approach as they came down the carriage compartment by compartment well before they reached us. They came through the sliding door from the corridor; a man and woman and the woman seemed to be in charge. They demanded to see our passports in a quite unfriendly manner. One does not expect to make friends with officials but it's not too much to expect a friendly and helpful manner when they are conducting their business. I produced my passport it was examined briefly and handed back to me, not a remark being made, not even a smile, not a please nor a thank you.

In our compartment there happened to be a young lad who was born in India, the son of an Indian diplomat now serving in London. His name was Bashir Ahmet, otherwise called Bushy for short. He was a young lad of about 14 and very slightly built; he was also very nervous about travelling without his parents. Up until the time that they got to Bushy I had taken very little interest in their progress or their work. They had checked my passport and handed it back with only a bit of grunting and sighing here and there. I began to take an interest though at the time they were taking looking at Bushy's passport. They seemed to be taking an inordinately long time to peruse the document and I could see that Bushy himself was becoming very nervous.

"This passport is not good." This sharp utterance came from the woman who had been scrutinising poor old Bushy's passport. "Needs visa!" She stated by way of short explanation. Her English was actually quite good. "Passport Indian!" the sharp explanation continued. Bushy is in tears by this time. My stomach is churning because; it was selfish I know, because I was beginning to sense the possibility of this, my first holiday abroad, and going down the pan.

"May I look at the passport?" I had decided to take an interest, both for Bushy and myself, another lad in the group, a good friend at that time by the name of Mario, Mario Dubsky, also began to take an interest, "Yes let's see the passport please."

The officer held the passport towards us but obviously had no intention of relinquishing the document. She held it very firmly whilst making the reluctant gesture to allow us to look at it at the page where she had spotted the place of issue. It had been issued in Bombay, as the city was then called.

"But it is not an Indian passport." I exclaimed. "It is a British passport issued in Bombay." "Issued in India it's Indian." She retorted, totally ignoring our pleas for her to consider the wording on the face of Bushy's perfectly legal passport. She then instructed our, by now terrified little friend to get to his feet and, with her partner officer, proceeded to march him out of the compartment as if he were a criminal and along the corridor towards the exit in like manner. Before I realise what was happening, I found myself, together with Mario, following the threesome out of the train and towards a door into an office in the station building.

Bushy was well past terrified by this time. I had forgotten my own feelings about a lost holiday. For me the War had returned. I could not shake the sense that this was all about Bushy's colour. Mario and I followed the three through the door and into a gloomy room. There was a radio on a table by the left-hand side wall that looked remarkably similar to one that Dad had 'liberated' from a German railway station at the end of the War.

A few yards inside the room there was a desk behind which the two officers stood with our friend standing between then. The situation had all the hallmarks of becoming a 'Mexican Standoff.' I suddenly realised that they could hardly allow the train to leave whilst they had three British boys in custody, in effect. I felt that the female officer had overplayed her hand. If we had been grown men, the situation may have been different. Nonetheless the argument continued for several minutes with Mario and I both insisting vigorously that the passport was a valid British passport, and that Germany was legally required to honour it. We explained, not that she needed any explanation, that British Passport Offices all over the world had the power to issue valid passports. She would have none of this and so the stalemate looked set to continue for a while at least.

At this point I would make observation that there are two situations in life that have the power to greatly improve one's ability in a foreign language. The one that was present in that room during those moments was 'anger'. I had become so angry at the sight of our little friend shedding totally unnecessary tears that my poor German became a veritable weapon. I had never sought to study the language up to that point but had absorbed some from German speaking students at the school. The second of these miraculous aids to language I intend to elaborate in a later story when a friend and I decide to walk across Liechtenstein. We had been bantering angrily for some time.

Suddenly a new face appeared around the door. It was Ken, one of the teachers accompanying us on the camping trip. "What's going on?" He demanded. "The kids in your compartment ran to tell me that you'd all been marched off the train."

The atmosphere in the room changed tangibly at the appearance of an adult who was demonstrably on our side. The two officials turned respectfully towards Ken as their mood changed. My mood had not changed; however, "They're all still bloody Nazis here Ken." I heard myself saying. "Bushy's skin colour is the problem here 'cos there's nothing wrong with his passport." I hurried to finish what I wanted to say to Ken as I saw the woman beginning to voice something by way of interjection. "It's a perfectly valid British passport that happens to have been issued in Bombay and not in London."

Ken began to walk towards us as the first signs of anger appeared in his expression. As he came forward though, another figure previously unnoticed by any of us in the gloom of the rear of the office, moved towards the female officer. "Ich glaube, ich habe genug davon gehört."

My German lacked a great deal at that time, but I quickly realised that he had heard enough and that he was bringing the incident to an end. The man clearly had final authority in that room for he quietly relieved the woman of the passport of disputed validity and handed it to Bushy, with a soft word of apology. Thus, we were able to board the train that had been gently puffing away beside the platform whilst the incident resolved itself. It had all taken approaching twenty minutes or so from beginning to end. Our friends on the train in other compartments had become quite anxious at the break in normal service. It was, moreover, an incident that I am sure that Bushy will never forget. I certainly will not for it forced me to break my lifetime resolution never to set foot on the soil of Germany. The passage of years however has led to greater maturity. I have changed my view on this matter. I am over 80 years old at the time of writing this piece and I have visited Germany very happily on a few occasions since the end of the 1980s.

Chapter Thirteen

Four Incidents in Yugoslavia. Circa 1955

My one chess win in Rijeka station.

The train finally puffed satisfyingly away from Aachen, the town where the Belgian/German border was met, we began to breathe properly again. For those of us in our compartment the passport incident had been a shock. This was particularly the case due to the racial undertone of the event. We were all very well aware that such prejudice was not at all foreign to Britain, but we were naïve enough to believe that that level of demonstration by a public official; in public, moreover, would have been very unlikely back home. Furthermore, it was difficult to imagine how far the border officials in question could have hoped to maintain their stance. We were a group of schoolchildren venturing on a school holiday in our school summer holiday period.

Bushy was the son of an Indian diplomat. He was only 14 years old; to have taken him or any of us or indeed all of us from that train would have provoked an international incident for which the German Government would not have thanked its border force. The Third Reich was a thing of the past, German officials needed to be seen to be more flexible than in those times of recent history. That was the opinion that I came to at the time. We have all unfortunately seen such intolerances enacted even in our own Dear Old Blighty through the years.

It took me a little while to shake off my negative thoughts as the train steamed away from the scene. With the passing of time however I did begin to be aware of the passing scenery. I became intrigued by something that I had never considered; that Germany was a beautiful country with a very varied range of vistas. Not only was the countryside somehow different from that back home the architecture was also a pleasure as well as a very interesting experience for a young boy on his first holiday abroad.

It was high summer; the weather monsters were behaving themselves. Crops were either ready and being brought in or were coming to the point of readiness. The year was 1955 and European farming was not yet as mechanised as it is today. There were many more workers in the fields than 15-year-old youngsters will see today. As the train passed through towns and villages full of people, I had my nose almost glued to the window in a need to absorb the scene. I became very defensive of the seat that gave me access to this exciting new world. I just could not get enough of this newfound, albeit temporary, freedom from the stringencies that were still in place back home.

If asked I would have acknowledged that the people, I could see from the distance of the train had also suffered and were still suffering the shortages that we had come to know so well. In the ivory tower of the train though, that all seemed so very far away from my world. At that distance people appeared to be dressed well in summer-appropriate and colourful clothing. I could see no signs of the poverty that would have been no doubt in evidence at closer inspection. My train and my excitement rumbled on through German towns, villages, and countryside.

The train was delayed frequently as we crossed the country. This would have been largely due to the aftermath of the destruction that most European countries had suffered during the Second World War. Germany's infrastructure had been a prime target during that terrible time for the whole of the continent. Germany was moreover a divided country both literally and figuratively.

After the war, Germany was left defeated; Britain and France moreover were both left drained and exhausted. The United States and the Soviet Union each held considerable power, and both soon rose to superpower status. The two became rivals through their conflicting ideologies and mutual distrust. They constantly competed for power. In March 1946 Winston Churchill had already delivered his famous speech that *"From Stettin in the Baltic to Trieste in the Adriatic, an iron curtain has descended across the continent."* This speech was later considered to be one of the opening volleys announcing the beginning of the Cold War.

Germany became divided by war time allies and the powerful political aftershocks of World War Two were what shaped Cold War Germany. The post-war state of the country was grim: about 1/4 of all housing had been destroyed, the economic infrastructure had largely collapsed, inflation was rampant, there was a shortage of food, and millions of homeless Germans from the east were returning. After its unconditional surrender, Germany was divided into four zones of Allied military occupation: American, French, British, and Soviet. The old capital of Berlin was also divided into four zones, but Berlin itself remained inside of the Soviet zone. In 1949, the French, British, and American zones merged and formed the Federal Republic of Germany with its capital city Bonn. This was more commonly known as 'West Germany'. Also, in 1949, the Soviet zone became the German Democratic Republic with the Soviet sector of Berlin as the capital. This slice of Germany was known, unsurprisingly, as East Germany. Our train travelled exclusively through 'West Germany'. For decades after the war West Germany had to concentrate on a huge rebuilding programme in order to restore its infrastructure as did all the erstwhile combatants.

We finally reached the German-Austrian border at Salzburg. The journey had been slow by modern standards. This took nothing away from my enjoyment of it all. I had had no similar experiences with which to compare and so it could not become devalued by any, "comparison that is the death of Joy" (Mark Twain). It was night-time by the time we reached the Austrian border. There was no repetition of the unpleasantness of the earlier border between Belgium and Germany. Salzburg impressed me hugely by the beauty of its architecture, glistening and dancing an evening-time wonder at me by the paler light of the moon. I made myself a promise to revisit the place as we passed through. This promise was extended to a second vow, to tour wider Austria someday, for repeated vistas of that country's beautiful moon-lit scenery began to flow, as if in a soft kaleidoscope of subdued colour by the train window against which my nose was permanently pressed. Mountains topped with white, valleys deep in the mystery of darker greens; villages and rivers there were. For me, a largely untraveled boy from North London, it was a magic lantern show. To this day, though, I must admit that I have not yet kept either of my Austrian-made promises to myself. I have kept myself too busy with other travels, other journeys.

We entered the, then, Yugoslavia near the Austrian border town of Villach. The Austrian border guards were very calm, even laid back, with all the passengers as far as I could see. This may well have been because they knew of the different experience to which the forthcoming Yugoslav guards might subject us when we crossed into Yugoslavia to the check point at Lesce-Bled. True enough; it was different. Firstly, they bounded noisily onto the train brandishing rifles and demanding loudly to see our documents. We were not slow to spot, though, that it was all *'Lärm und Wind',* 'noise and wind' and largely good natured once you saw beneath the skin-surface of a group of young men and women, mostly doing compulsory military service, who were seemingly putting on a 'show' for their superiors.

Morning had broken a while ago by the time we left our well- armed but youthfully friendly Yugoslav border guards. Slovenia is an independent country in its own right these days but at the time of which I am writing it was one of the states in the Federation of Yugoslavia. The journey across Slovenia and into Croatia took longer than it would by rail these days. This was, just as it was across the whole of Europe in those days; countries were intent on rebuilding their infrastructure and civilian traffic did not have the level of priority that it holds in Europe these days. There was, in any case, much more by the way of 'goods' traffic on rail services then than we see nowadays. We had, moreover, a longer stay in Ljubljana than we had expected.

The result of this fairly slow journey across the region was that it was approaching night-time by the time that we pulled into Rijeka railway station. The town of Rijeka is on the Croatian Adriatic coast and was the end of our rail journey across Europe. It was not, however, quite the end of our journey; that was to take place on the next day. We still had a short journey to undertake the next morning by boat across an 'elbow' in the coastline to the village of Lovran. We did not have accommodation booked in Rijeka, firstly, because we had not anticipated arriving so late in Rijeka and had hoped to make the short sea crossing that same afternoon. Secondly the holiday was to be a camping holiday in order to keep the costs manageable for everybody. We looked around to settle ourselves down as best we could in the large waiting area in the station. There were a good number of benches in the large hall but already many of them had been taken by other passengers. I was too excited, in any case, to attempt to settle down to sleep.

I left my rucksack with a group of friends and began to walk about the station. I had no local money, there was no obvious place open at which to cash some of my precious pounds, and so I only had whatever food was left over from the journey. Some local people were settling down to rest or to sleep but many were playing board games. One seemingly popular game was one that I now know to be backgammon but one that I did not recognise at the time. One very popular game being played was one that I did recognise, however. I had played it with my Dad since he began to teach me at about the age of eight. It was chess and people were playing everywhere. I have to admit that I thought of myself as a pretty fair player. My Dad had not beaten me since I was about thirteen or fourteen. I had obtained books on chess from the library in Edmonton. I had replayed some of the famous chess games in order to analyse them and to understand the depths of the game. I knew some of the best plays by heart; the Ruy Lopez opening, invented by Lopez circa 1400,the Sicilian defence which came into being in 1604 or thereabouts, the Queen's gambit that came into being at least as far back as 1490, and so on. I still have some of the books that I purchased and studied when a teenager. I must admit that I have studied the game very little since those days.

I moved from game to game, and no-one seemed to mind the audience. I had known that chess was a very popular national game in Yugoslavia, but the fact had gone out of my mind with the excitement of the journey. Some minutes into my wanderings I noticed a group of young people, about my age, perhaps a year or two older. The group was intent on watching the proceedings as two of their number played each other. The group watched respectfully, in a deathly silence. The two had just begun their game and as I watched them, I realised that I recognised the opening moves that one of the two players had used. He was playing a fast tempo game and using the King's Indian Attack. Despite the respectful atmosphere I could not help honouring my own perspicacity in recognising a pattern that I had only read about. I uttered a single sharp hiss and the word '*yes*' to myself. At least I thought that I had kept it to myself, until I was made very quickly aware of my error by sharper hisses directed back at me from the group.

I continued to watch the game, in silence now, until one of the young chaps in the audience moved over to me and quietly asked if I was English. I readily replied in the affirmative. "You want to play?" he asked me in reasonable English. "You bet". I responded. He may not have recognised my colloquial language, but he clearly got the gist from my huge grin. Suddenly a space was made on a nearby bench, a board and pieces appeared, we had chosen colours and I was white. I opened in a standard fashion with the Queen's pawn. Within a couple of minutes, just a few moves later in fact, and I had won the games using, unbelievably, a simple fool's mate play. I got up to leave, thanking him. His name was Antun, the Croatian equivalent of Anthony, my own given name. I was very pleased with myself and perhaps wanted to quit while I was ahead. Antun was now finding himself the centre of attention from his own crowd and had no intention of letting me get away easily. He was the subject of some ridicule. He grabbed my arm in a vice like grip and pulled me back into a sitting position. He was still grinning in a very friendly way. I could not understand the language but, in a mixture of broken English and fluent Croatian, he let me know that it would be very unfriendly of him to let me go, having given me only one very short game. I had clearly made a huge mistake in beating him in such a humiliating manner. He was determined to try to restore the international balance as far as the chess world was concerned.

I tried very hard to keep my end up but Anton had clearly had enough of the ridicule to which his friends had subjected him. It was all very friendly, but I did not win another game all night. In fact, the more he won the friendlier the atmosphere became. I tried all the famous plays that I had read about, but Anton had clearly mastered more of the game than me. He finally let me go at about one o'clock in the morning. I made my way back to where my friends had long settled down. I spent a half hour or so reflecting on the merits or otherwise of so easily beating a man at his national game, on his own patch, in front of his friends.

<u>Shark Attack</u>

The next morning gave promise to a beautiful day. We arrived, hot and bothered and lacking sleep, down at the dock, where we were due to board the boat for our transfer to the village of Lovran, a town in Istria, Croatia. It is situated on the western coast of the Kvaerner Bay. It is best described as a large village or a small town. As I remember it the population was not very large. Apparently public transport around the bay was not too reliable in those times; we were, therefore, booked to take a boat trip across the corner of the bay to our final destination, a camp site near the beach at Lovran itself. This was a pleasant prospect for most of us.

The boat, naturally, was not there waiting for us. The boat owner had given up hope of us arriving the previous afternoon and had decided to take on another job for early that morning. We were assured, by people at the dock, that he would not be long as he was only on a short trip. The various assurances were all given in a high decibel mixture of languages, but with comparatively good humour.

It was hot, we were sticky and tired, and our luggage was duly stacked neatly on the dockside. One look into the dock revealed a very inviting and crystal-clear expanse of water that was simply waiting for swimmers to take advantage of it. Within seconds, and in spirited abandon, five or six of us had stripped and changed into swimming trunks and were racing each other to be the first to jump into the water. There was, in fact, a set of stone steps down to the water for the convenience of boat crews but jumping was much quicker and met with the collective enthusiasm off the moment.

Hitting that water was one of the most delightful memories of my young life. It was so refreshing after the night playing chess followed by hours of trying to sleep on an uncomfortable bench seat in the station building which became stiflingly hotter as the night progressed. We were able to make really good use of the stone steps up to the jetty because the best fun was to jump as far as we could into the water from the end of the jetty using it as a running launch pad. From there it left us with a 30 yard, or so, swim back to the steps on the side of the projection. I for one felt the cloak of fatigue washing away with each leap into that deliciously cool water.

We had been enjoying the fun for about 15 minutes when we began to hear some shouting from somewhere along the harbour wall. We took no notice of this at first. It could be nothing to do with us after all. It was also in Croatian which removed it even further from being any of our business. Gradually, though, as we jumped into and then climbed out of the water, we noticed that the clamour was approaching us and appeared to be directed at us. It was being generated by an older man. When you are 15 or so anyone over 20 is an older man. He seemed to be seriously agitated however and we began to wonder amongst us what on earth he could have against us enjoying ourselves in the water. "Ignore him, we're doing no harm". We voiced between ourselves however we could not help but try to hear what the man was shouting at us, however. "He seems to be shouting something about fish", thought someone. "Don't be daft", was the reply, "we're not harming any fish," "It's something about high fish. What does he mean high fish?" "Get out of there quick you damned fools." This came from one of our friends on the jetty. "The man's trying to save your lives. He's speaking in German and saying there are sharks in the water, Haifishe that is."

Well, we broke all local swimming records getting out of that water. When we were all safely out, up the stone steps and back with our friends we began to receive a series of animated explanations from a committee of locals. This committee was led by the man who had run round the harbour shouting helpful warnings in German. The series went something like this; there are sharks in the Adriatic, and they are dangerous to humans, leisure beaches have the protection of anti-shark nets as a safety measure for swimmers, the harbour, for obvious reasons, was not enclosed by a safety net. Swimming in the harbour, clean and crystal clear as it was, was a very stupid thing to do. We thanked our 'saviour' profusely and very sincerely in the best German that we could summon up between us. He, as well as most of the explanation committee, spoke very good German.

By way of understanding why there was a general ability in the local population to speak German, it is helpful to remember the very recent history of Yugoslavia at that time. The year of our holiday there was 1955 a mere 10 years after the end of the Second World War. The invasion of Yugoslavia, also known as the April War or Operation 25, was a German-led attack on the Kingdom of Yugoslavia by the Axis powers which began on 6 April 1941 during World War II. The German occupation of the country ended in 1945 when the Germans were finally defeated. During that period of occupation, the Yugoslav people suffered many privations and indignities at the hands of their captors. Much of the land of Croatia and Slovenia was cleared of indigenous population to make room for 'Lebens Raum', living space for Germans. The story of Axis occupation of the country is extremely complex. It does help though to understand the high level of understanding of the German language in the population at the time of our holiday in that beautiful country.

Olive Oil and Spinach

the time that the brouhaha over our 'illegal' swimming escapade had died down we began to receive the welcome news that our transfer boat had been spotted approaching the harbour. This meant that the eagerly awaited final leg across the bay could be happening quite soon.

It was very fortunate that there was a direct boat or ferry service from Rijeka to Lovran even in those days for there were very suitable docking facilities there. That transfer was a welcome rest from all the activity in Rijeka and a very welcome cool, breeze-generated respite from the heat of the sun from which there had been little shade on the dockside from which we had now departed.

The boat owner was taking us across the bay direct to Lovran in a private capacity. He explained, in a beautiful mixture of broken English, German, some Croatian aided by a huge variety of hand gestures, all of which were applied by the trowel of genuine good humour, that he himself lived in the lovely town of Opatija. He explained as well as he could in the above-mentioned complicated melange of languages etc. that he would be staying dockside at Lovran for just over an hour. He would then be returning to Opatija and would ferry anyone back there who would be prepared to pay him a small fare for his trouble. He advised that it would be very easy to get a local bus back to Lovran; the two towns were, apparently, a mere 5km apart along the coast. The man added, very helpfully, that such a short distance would also be an easy walk for us at our ages, a simple stroll, he smiled a knowing smile. As it turned out a small group of us did manage to pitch our tents and organise the rest of our travel paraphernalia in time to get back to the dock within the proposed time for departure back to Opatija. Once back at the dock though it became clear that our enthusiastic ferryman had badly misjudged the time of his departure. His boat was still there, just as we had left it; the man himself on the other hand was not.

One searching glance around the dock quickly located the miscreant, however. He was sitting with a group of pals having a chat, a comradely smoke and sharing with them a bottle, or two, of a drink, alcoholic of course. The bottles containing this beverage were striking. They were round with colourful labels and held captive a beautiful golden liquid. We later discovered that this drink, Slivovitz, was a very important Slav drink. It is a Plum Brandy, and very potent. This we discovered once we found out that we would offend no local customs or laws by giving it a try! Slivovitz comes in a variety of colours from crystal clear to quite dark. According to locals there is a range of qualities from excellent to pthxxx! There is also a widely understood table of strengths which rises from very potent to bloody overpowering!

We finally convinced our now reluctant guide that the time had come to depart for his hometown. We overcame his initial unwillingness to move by showing him some money. A comparatively short while later we were docking at the small harbour of Opatija. This led to my first encounter with two further staple elements of 'Mediterranean' diet, spinach, and olive oil.

About eight of us had decided to make the trip back with our newfound sailor friend. Four of those of us decided to have a bit of a wander round away from the quite attractive harbour area. We did not plan to go far but just enough to stretch our legs. The others decided that they would prefer to hang around near the harbour to see if they could find a café and have a snack.

Opatija is a very prepossessing town. Yugoslavia was a communist country in 1955.It did manifest some of the privations that had become the fuel of much of the media criticism of such regimes in the western press. Those were, however, tempered by the fact that the whole of Europe was still suffering shortages on a grand scale due to the ravages of six years of war. Britain, for example, had only just, in the year of our visit to Yugoslavia, been able finally to shed the regime of managed rationing of most goods; coal remained rationed until 1958. I stress the word 'managed' here because many things, both foods and manufactured goods, were still rationed by both availability and affordability. We, as teenagers, did not realise that we were deprived, though; for the situation was normality to us. Everywhere we looked in Opatija seemed to be very pleasant in our eyes. People were friendly. Police carried guns but broke into decent enough smiles when greeted with a polite "Dobar dan, kako ste?" "Good day, how are you?" Which was the sum total of our competence in the language at that time. As I say, people were friendly, so much so that, when we had walked only about a hundred yards or so from our friends and the harbour, a man and his wife called to us from the tiny garden of their house. They had some English, enough to ask us if we were hungry. As far as we were concerned that was the correct question at that moment. We were both hungry and thirsty.

In a totally friendly and open way this lovely couple sat down with us around a large, rectangular, wooden table. It was a truly beautiful experience, in the sunshine, with absolute strangers, and in a foreign country. These lovely people shared food with us when, it appeared, they had little enough for themselves. I say this because what they put before us was a huge, deepened plate of spinach in olive oil together with a large plate of coarse bread. It was a banquet and we lapped it up in that company.

The spinach was steeped in olive oil to which my stomach was unused at that time. I did suffer some revenge-taking from my mid-region later, but it was worth it. I have adored olive oil since that day. Halfway through the meal the man produced a huge Tate and Lyle tin that did not contain syrup, no, not at all. It contained a couple of gallons or so of homemade scrumpy. Needless to say, we four, in the spirit of not wanting to offend our hosts of course, each took a good quaff of that delightful brew. With some regret we took our leave of that lovely couple, with firm assurances that we would return to visit them again. Unfortunately, these promises were not kept. We had so many things to do, to explore and to enjoy on our holiday that we forgot all about our very generous newfound friends. Such is the fickle face of youth! Those Tate and Lyle tins are mentioned in similar vein later in these pages.

We returned to the group, now waiting at the bus stop, to discover that they had found out that a bus would probably be along in another ten minutes or so. This was not a figure set in stone, it was information extracted from a passer-by, via the rapidly developing mixture of English, German and wild hand gestures. The group were becoming anxious that we would put in an appearance before the bus arrived as they were quite reluctant to catch it without us. They were, however, very interested, even envious, to hear our story of the spinach and olive oil mini break that we had experienced although they themselves had found a café that offered bread, cheese, and coffee to quench their appetites. The bus arrived and we all climbed aboard still engaged in an excited discussion of how we met the generous couple, how we communicated with them and whether we were going to visit them again during the holiday.

We arrived in Lovran very quickly as the distance between the two towns was not great. Lovran was not a big town, and we already knew of course the location of the campsite as being just the other side of the coastal road from the beach. In fact, as it happened, the bus stopped just a few yards from the camping ground. The others were glad to see us. They had already settled in and had taken the best places, naturally, but happy to help us finish making camp and stow our things. I had my own tent. I had had the same tent since the age of 13 when I began my camping career. Together with my friend Bill from school I had begun my lifetime in joyful experience of the art of travelling by hitch hiking around the southern counties of England at Easter time during the school holidays. We would set up impromptu camps wherever the notion took us and whenever permission was obtained. My friend Bill and I had discovered early on that farmers were always very obliging, as well as frequently generous with such items as milk and eggs, when permission to camp was requested.

My tent was an ex-US army two-man ridge tent and was my pride and joy for many years, decades even. I was an experienced camper. I had learned to make myself as snug and as comfortable as a small tent can achieve. I then set out to walk around the site and survey the place.

I am not writing this as an agent of tourism for Lovran but, if I were, I would have to say that Lovran was a welcoming, quiet town and resort on the eastern coast of the Istrian peninsula. Like Opatija, Lovran has a mild climate as it is protected by the Ucka Mountains. It also has a rich architectural heritage. In addition to several Baroque houses on the town square and a medieval tower, the 14th-century church of St George has a spectacular series of wall paintings.

Although slightly less famous than Opatija, Lovran was equally lush with flowering gardens and plenty of greenery. I have never returned there since the age of 16 but I have always intended to do so. There are just so many lovely and interesting places to visit in this beautiful world. I do, still, intend to return. I have often 'googled' the place which has fully whetted my appetite for Lovran and the idea of retracing my steps. I am definitely not intending, though, to spend any time, in that hopefully soon to be future, in a small two-man tent!

It is not to be a feature in this short story but, in the spirit of widening our enjoyment of this holiday in Yugoslavia, the school had arranged a bus trip to Postojna to see the wonderful caves there. It is a truly captivating experience for all ages. The bus takes a little over the hour from Opatija to Postojna. The tour around the caves can take longer and is very well worth the time spent. We did not have the power of the internet in those days, but you do. I urge you to do a search and you will see...

The first thing to do, of course, once I had set up my tent was to take a look around the site and to take in the views. It was a reasonably well-equipped site for those days. There was a block of very clean toilets, showers etc. The shower was not always hot but. I have to say, it was much better than the facilities I had at home in those days. A stream ran down from the Ucka mountains. The water in the stream was quite cool even in the summer it seemed. We later found a very handy use for the cool of the stream. We could use it to keep things cool, for we had no other form of refrigeration. Watermelons were delicious and very refreshing after they had spent some time in that water. We were not sure about the water from the stream itself for drinking. It looked clean, crystal clear in fact but some of us had left home with deeply felt parental warnings along the lines of "mind the water, it's not safe" and that applied to the tap water. Water from a natural stream was, therefore, off the menu. There is after all always the thought that a herd of cows just upstream might be peeing in it just at that moment.

The cool water from the stream ran through the site, beneath the coast road, and emerged from under the pebbly beach, directly into the sea's edge, thus making the first few metres of sea water surprisingly cool. There was, though, a way around this for those who were too 'sensitive' to brazen the cooler water. The beach was shaped into a small bay. At the southern end of this bay was a collection of large rocks. They formed slabs that swimmers used for sunbathing. The rocks also protruded into the sea just beyond the cool ribbon of water bubbling up from the beach. One was, therefore, faced with a choice. You either had to brace yourself for the walk into the sea through the refrigeration strip or dive directly into the briny from the rocks. It was not really a harsh choice either way although some made a real meal of it. On a reflective note, the bay was protected by an anti-shark net.

We spent much of the first few days lazing by the sea. Many of our group had never had the luxury of spending a holiday in such a wonderful spot. Then there came the very successful trip to the caves of Postojna. Whilst on this trip a group of five or six of us had got together and decided that we wanted to explore the countryside and hills behind the campsite. The whole area was one of natural beauty. We had a long discussion with the teachers who were managing and agreed that we arranged that our group could go off into the hills and, if we did not get too fed up or bored, we could sleep out for one night. Thus, we set off with food, water and sleeping bags for our previously unexpected adventure. I was quite comfortable with the idea of wandering off like that as I had after all been camping and hitch hiking, in southern England since the grand old age of 13.

War Games

We set off after breakfast, in good spirits, on the designated morning. As is the nature of youthful optimism we were carrying ruck sacks that contained only the bare-essentials, food, and a sleeping bag. Food and water were the first essentials, by far ahead of the sleeping bag when our short list of necessaries was organised. The nights so far had proven to be quite warm and so I had been in favour of leaving even my sleeping bag behind. It had been pointed out, however, that we were about to set out to climb a path up into the lower hills of a mountain range. It was not going to be a mountain climb but, nonetheless, it might well have been cooler up there than on the campsite. I was looking forward to spending the night up in the hills, particularly because I had never slept out under the stars, even though I was a quite experience camper. The fact was that all of my previous camping had been in southern England at Easter time. Call me 'softie' if you like, but that part of the year in England had never presented itself to me as an ideal time for sleeping out under the stars. I was camping with a friend at Easter one time when we bought a bottle of very fresh milk from a friendly farmer. We went to bed that night with the said bottle safely inside the tent. We woke up in the morning to discover that the milk had frozen solid. The bottle top had been lifted, an inch or so, by a cylindrical shaft of frozen milk. No! Sleeping under stars in southern Britain at Easter had never seemed to me an attractive proposition but now, in southern Europe in the summer it was a great idea.

The walk began as a quite easy saunter up a gentle slope beside the stream. We continued to be in very high spirits, chatting happily and joking as we made our way to what appeared to be an easy destination. This was a particularly attractive hilltop that could just about be seen from camp. That factor, I believe, made the whole escapade more palatable and agreeable to the staff members of the group.

As we proceeded, however, the terrain became more and more challenging. There were rocks, large and small, that occasionally made progress quite slow. As the morning drew on the heat of the sun became more and more draining. On more than one occasion a small cliff face forced a detour away from our predicted line of passage. When I say 'cliff face' it would be closer to the truth to consent to the fact that the path had become too steep for us, the sadly untrained! There came an untimely, but popular, call for a rest and an early lunch. We had been on the move for little over two hours by that time. We had all taken repeated looks at our target hilltop. As much as we looked at it, though, it did not seem to come any closer.

We agreed to stop for a while to refresh, to eat and drink some, and to relax some before the next stage required a further discharge of effort. I was quite surprised at how tough the amble was becoming for me. I had been under the impression that I was pretty damned fit. At home I had been used to cycling to and fro from school. That is Edmonton to

Hampstead, return, daily for much of the previous four years. I had to admit that this ramble was becoming more of a trudge up the hill. It wasn't going to beat me, I decided grimly, but it is doing its best! We soldiered on, after a while even the moaning and groaning faded away. We were all feeling the heat as well as the effort when suddenly we reached the crest of a small rise, and our destination hilltop came into view again. It had been out of our line of sight for quite a while during which time we had been making progress towards it, so much so that it appeared before us, across a shallow valley to be sure, but manifestly now well within reach. Furthermore, we could now see that there was the skeleton of an old and dilapidated church just beyond the crown of that hilltop. We were both elated and enervated by the realisation that, within the hour, we would achieve our objective.

We puffed up the final incline in the approach to the hilltop and flopped gratefully on the grass in front of the ruins of the former church. Why had it gone into decay and neglect? Was it simply, now surplus to requirements? It seemed logical to me that the changing attitudes of both the Nazi regime and the Communist one to follow to religion and churches generally had probably played havoc with the upkeep of out of the way country churches. It may well have been that the 'Lebens Raum' removals of Yugoslav citizens from that beautiful area into concentration camps in Germany and Eastern Europe, had initially so reduced the population that it could no longer support the church. That, followed, as I say, by an unsympathetic communist ideology could have led to the decline and eventual fall into drastic disuse and dilapidation of a once beautiful building.

I had no facts to support any of these thoughts as I lay there in the sun. I was young, somewhat brash, and opinionated and I did not need facts on which to build theories. Besides which the warm sun was so relaxing that the mind- building of theories was such an easy game to play. Finally, however the others were becoming rejuvenated after the effort of gaining our objective. I became aware that they were making noises about being hungry and thirsty. We looked around for the makings of a fire. There was plenty of such fuel about and around the old church. We were also able to gather some slabs of stone together to make a very passable and safe fire base. We had been able to carry sufficient drinking water for the walk. The nearby stream though seemed to us to be clear and clean enough for us to use its water for cups of coffee and tea and so preserve our drinking water.

One or two of the group were not wildly happy about using stream water but those of us who were keen managed to persuade them that it would be quite ok because after all the water would have to be boiled first. At that point I remembered the story of tea, in Britain, when it first became adopted as our national drink. As tea became more and more popular in the British Isles so the rate of infectious diseases began to decline significantly. This was solely because the water to make the tea had to be boiled. And so, it was agreed, and we began to settle down for the evening.

I have to say that, as far as my camping experiences are concerned that night was the first that I had slept out under the stars. I have had the pleasure of repeating the experience quite a few times since then, but that first time became a magical encounter, for me, with the sheer wonder of the universe in which we live. Firstly, the sounds of the night are so much closer, more immediate to you and they change subtly during the night as different insects and animals have their impact. Even the soft wind felt different, friendlier somehow, as it rustled the longer grass a few feet away from my sleeping bag. More wonderful, though, even than the sounds of the night was that bowl of wonder which is the night sky in all its glory.

From the moment that I got into my sleeping bag I began to lose contact with my companions. I could hear them chatting away of course but my actual awareness of them faded as I drank in that first real visual encounter with the Milky way which, I discovered a few days later, has the name *Mliječna Staza* in Croatian which, in its turn, is a translation from Latin. Traditionally it was named *Kumova slama* (Godfather's straw). I also discovered that the galaxy in which we live has a different name in Slovenian where it is called *The Rimska Cesta,* The Road to Rome. In my youthful English arrogance, I had assumed that all languages would have simply translated the English name into their language. Another important lesson learned!

I really do not think I got much sleep that night. I lay there in my warm sleeping bag simply gazing up at that inverted arena of dreams, drifting in and out of sleep. I had never noticed it before, but it really is true; the darkest hour of the night is that hour before dawn. Then just as I began to feel that the sun was about to appear –BANG! A series of bangs, some louder than others, had disturbed the quiet peace of that night of dreams. I jerked myself out of my reverie but, before I had managed to escape from a sleeping bag that seemed to be doing its best to keep me prisoner and to fight my irritated efforts to escape; I began to see those white mushroom puffs of marshmallow drifting down from the now lightening sky. A barrage of light bangs snapped rat-tat-tatting from the dark objects now to be seen dangling from below the mushrooms. My God, I thought, the war's started all over again. We're right in the middle of it! I turned as if to wake the others but there was no need. They were all well back from their night's sleep. By the time that we had gathered our thoughts well enough to think of hiding in the old church the dark objects had begun landing, all around us. They, of course, had also noticed us.

We came to our senses enough to stand up, somewhat nervously, as several of the dark objects strode determinedly towards us. They were not happy! One of them, not much older than us, seemed to be in charge. The rest of the mushrooms had landed by now and were making their way towards us. That seemed to irritate the 'in-charge' one even more. He waived his arm angrily at them as if to motion them away. Then he turned back to us, barking at us in a language that was way beyond my local knowledge which only went as far as 'Dobar dan, kaku ste?' I tried that, but for a moment I thought he was going to hit me with his rifle yet then, quite impossibly, he burst out laughing. "You're English" he spluttered. I tried to simulate his accent in script, but it looked so patronising that I decided to give that attempt the miss and leave the accent to my reader. Sufficient to say was that he had a strong Eastern European accent. As I had already exhausted my total knowledge of Croatian, I reckon that he was well ahead of me in any language duel.

"Did you not see the signs?" "Why did you come up here?" "Are you watching us?" The laughing had stopped. He was back to business now and appeared to want answers. I looked around at my friends as if to ask them to help-out with some of the clearly needed answers to his questions. Between us we explained where we had come from. Yes, yes, he knew about the campsite. We explained that we had seen some signs by a small bridge over the stream but, as we could not understand them, we ignored them. That admission did not please him. Mario went on to explain that the Ucka Mountains were so beautiful that we just wanted to camp here for one night. It was an opportunity of a lifetime for us to sleep out under the stars when, coming from London, with its smog, we could not see the stars shining so bright as here. There was, in fact, some reality in that response by Mario even though he was trying as hard as he could to 'butter' his man. The atmosphere began to change again. The young soldier was not yet fully pacified, but he could clearly see that he was not dealing with a group of War Games saboteurs. He, together with another young soldier whose English was even better than his own, went on to explain.

They explained that they had had to halt a training day for young Yugoslav men who were undertaking their National Service. He was initially very angry with us because notices had been posted to keep civilians away from the area for the day. This was in order to prevent accidents. The senior officer, a young captain, went on to explain that some of the rounds they would use that day were live rounds. These would only be used at certain times and that the rules of usage were well understood by his soldiers, but the accidental involvement of civilians could make the situation quite dangerous. He graciously accepted our explanation that we did not understand the nature of any posters we might have seen as well as our apology for interrupting his training day.

After apologies had been offered and accepted the tone of the conversation became much friendlier. The captain even offered us breakfast while he and his colleagues took time to re-arrange the day's training for the young national servicemen. We all felt strongly that they wanted a half hour or so with us so as to practice their English, which was generally very good. We began the walk back to camp after a short breakfast of bread, cheese, tomatoes, and hot coffee.

Walking downhill can sometimes be just as tiring as the struggle uphill. There can be a greater downhill strain on the knees and ankles as one works to prevent slips and out-of-control descent. On that day, however, we were in such high spirits that we hardly noticed the effort of the journey down to camp. I must admit that we did not manifest any guilt at having put their plans out of joint for the day. The opposite, in fact, was the case. We saw our escapade as having been a fun and very interesting ending to our visit to the Ucka National Park. We 'dined out' on it for the rest of the holiday.

It was during that holiday that I made friends with a girl from Slovenia called Marian. She spoke excellent English which in fact quite a lot of the young people in her group did; others spoke good German and another large group favoured Russian. On our last day of our holiday, I handed Marian a slip of paper with my home address on it. I did not really think that she might respond but she did to my surprise at that. She and I became penfriends and corresponded for the next two/three years during which I became very interested in trying a summer holiday hitch-hiking trip across Europe to Slovenia I just needed to convince one friend to accompany me. I had already had plenty of hitch-hiking experience in England. To visit Marian and Yugoslavia, the country that had repeatedly defied both Hitler and later, Stalin, would be a good reason to cross Europe.

Before I leave my memories of Burgess Hill School, I realise that my affection for the place and its occupants has not diminished over the years. They were happy days, never to be forgotten. I met and became friends with people whose influence on me has been ongoing. Mario for one; he and I had planned a trip to France, just hitch-hiking for a few weeks here and there, no particular plan, just to enjoy the place for a while. My parents had agreed to the idea, and I thought that Mario had gained the agreement of his parents. When I think about it, I am still surprised that my Mum and Dad were so ok about my hitch-hiking adventures. I am so very impressed that they were though. The Mario trip never came about however because his Dad put a stop to it. Mario told me about the ban quite at the final moment of planning and after my parental agreement. I think that he had assumed permission but had approached his parents late in the day and the result was disappointment for both of us. I felt doubly aggrieved and fell out with Mario big-time for a while. I pleaded with my parents to allow me to undertake the trip alone but that was a step too far even for them. I was still only fifteen at the time of the discussions but would have been sixteen by the time of the holiday. I do think though that that disappointment was one of the factors that induced them to support me to go on the BH trip to Yugoslavia where Mario and I made up our differences during the fracas re our young companion 'Bushy' and his passport.

Mario and I were good friends who had had a disagreement and had made it up. We drifted apart once I left BH, but I followed his career for a while. He became quite a well-known and respected artist. I finally learned that he had sadly passed away in the early 1980s due to an AIDS related illness. That news made me feel both sad and guilty; sad for the loss of a childhood friend and guilty that I had so reprehensibly lost touch with him. Farewell Mario! Alev-Ha- Shalom!

Chapter Fourteen

Latymer School Edmonton

After two years of more intensive study at Latymer's than I had ever undertaken previously I took another set of exams and passed in nine GCE 'O level subjects including both English Language and English Literature as well as an A/S level pure maths which is the highest level I was ever to achieve in Pure Maths. That was in the summer of 1957. I was therefore two years older than others by the time I was ready to enter the sixth form.

As an aside I would like to add here that during the school summer holidays of 1957 I had taken a summer job as a 'washer up' in a holiday camp in Norfolk. It is not a vain boast to add at this point that I have been, ever since that time, the best hand 'washer up' that my family has ever known.

It was during the after-lunch washing-up session that one of the supervisors 'flustered' towards me just as I was about to tackle my last huge pile of dishes. We used two sinks for the task both contained very hot water, one for washing the second for rinsing. The dishes were then stacked to dry thus obviating the need for hand drying. The water was usually too hot for bare hands, so we used rubber gloves, often extra heat protection was achieved by running some cold water into the rubber gloves. I gazed with some astonishment at the supervisor as she hurried towards me. As she neared me, I gathered that she was trying to stutter something about my parents. This caused me some immediate concern which was not quickly alleviated because she was clearly trying to hurry too fast with her message for her mouth and brain to deal with it.

Finally, I got the gist which seemed to be that my Mum and Dad and even my sister were parked outside the front reception office and were asking to speak to me. It was such an unusual event for family members to visit workers at the camp that I immediately absorbed her apparent concern as to the reasons for the visit. I scampered the couple of hundred yards towards the front office, but the boom was lowered on my very sincere sense of doom and gloom when I got my first look at the huge grin on Dad's face. He was waving an envelope at me long before I got close to him. In my work I had forgotten all about my exams and that I would be getting the results at about that time. Nine O'levels including one A/S level maths! Superb! Just for once I was in everybody's good books. I basked in that glory for a further very short three weeks.

I do not want to spend much more time on this venture into the holiday job world, but I do intend to pass just a few words of warming onto anyone bathing in a seemingly passive sea. On my second week of that venture, I sadly saw my first dead body. I was only seventeen or so at the time and the circumstances surrounding the death of the young man were wholly avoidable. It appeared that that fit young man, on holiday with two friends at the holiday camp had died in comparatively shallow water whilst playing ball with his friends.

At that very section of the beach a sandbar ran parallel to the beach and about twenty feet from the beach at high tide when the bar was hidden. It seems that the three young men were playing in the section between the beach and the bar at high tide when the tide turned. The ebbing tide caused a strong sideways current around the sandbar that took that young man off his feet. He disappeared under the water and being dragged sideways it was too late before his friends realised the seriousness of the situation; they were still in 'play' mode. It has been a lasting memory; that of seeing that young man being carried up from the water's edge, so young and because of such seemingly innocuous circumstances. I have often thought of the reaction of that boy's poor mother hearing of the death of her young son whilst on a holiday with his friends. Back now though to my own situation…

There was the beginning of a clash about to arise in my life moreover despite my very recent exam success. For years Mum and Dad had had the dream that their son would become a medical doctor. I had gone along with this dream until I began to realise at Burgess Hill that I was more interested in Modern Languages, including English as it happens. But even though I had achieved one significant success for them they would not consider a sideways move for me to study languages in the Sixth Form and then on to Uni. No, that apparently was not a suitable route from which a son of theirs could earn a Living. We had many bitter arguments in subsequent years, but I was entered into the sixth form to study solely maths and science subjects. It did not work for me. It was not until autumn of 2014 at the age of 75 that I finally achieved my initial wish to gain a degree in the study of Modern Languages.

I did so when undertaking my final year of that degree which began with the O.U. in 2008 but unfortunately required me to spend time in hospital in 2011 with an operation to mend my left ankle the calcaneus of which had split vertically. This required me to spend about six months in all of re-hab. and light work. It did not stop my studies but did hinder them.

In 2013 I had a further operation this time for prostate cancer and ended with nearly seven weeks of radio therapy in July/August of 2014. By the time I got to the point where I received my degree result together with an offer, by way of email, to attend a degree ceremony in Versailles I was totally knackered.

I made my way downstairs from my computer to inform my wife and two of our granddaughters, who were spending a few days with us that I was too weary to think about going to France for my degree. To my everlasting gratitude those three persuaded me in very powerful terms that I would regret it ever after if I didn't take that opportunity. They pointed out to me that although I felt quite tired at that point, I had only just finished the R.T. and that I had three/four weeks to recover before the trip to Versailles needed to be undertaken. Joyce and I did make the trip to France and spent a very happy long weekend in the lovely City of Versailles. Many thanks then to Joyce, to Lizzie and to Jenny for 'bullying' me into one of the most enriching holiday weekends of my life.

Back now to the 1950s! I had done as well as I felt possible in the 5th form having passed a decent group, of nine o'level G.C.E subjects, in those two years including both English

Language and English Literature. At Burgess Hill School my sum total, after four years of 'study', had been one pass in French and fail English; that was the final insult for my Dad; that I had passed French but failed English. Even at that time, I could see his point.

Almost immediately following those dismal exam results and following some discussion between my parents as to how they could redeem their errant son my Dad had arranged an appointment for him and me to meet with the Head of Latymer in order to petition for yours truly to join that school. I, naturally, was very fond of Burgess Hill and did not want to move. Burgess Hill, however, was costing my parents more money than they could afford to throw away on an apparently lazy so-and-so. The decision was made on the joint grounds of my previous lack of effort allied to the cost to my parents of that lack of effort.

As I have already outlined I did quite well in the 5th form. The day that the exam results came through my parents and my younger sister drove up to Caister-on-Sea in Norfolk, where I was doing summer work at a Holiday Camp, to bring my results to me was one of great relief and celebration for me. They were absolutely delighted that my exams had been so successful. It was not just that I had achieved 9 subjects but that the actual marks were also very good, even in Maths, Applied Maths and all the science subjects. Unfortunately, though, those results put my parents into an overconfident frame of mind as to what could be achieved at the higher, Advanced Level.

I really pleaded with my parents to change direction and to go into the 6th form to study languages. They would not hear of it. They could see no career future in my studying languages. They actually wanted me to study medicine but that was never to be. As it turned out my first year in the 6th form did nothing to change my view that the science and maths subjects were not for me. The results of my mock exams were not a total debacle, but they did come close! Chemistry and Applied Maths seemed as if they were going to be manageable and Pure Maths did get off to a good start when it came to the Binomial Theorem. I got that straight away as it is to do with numbers, albeit complicated numbers in complicated systems. I could understand that because it had to do with things that I could visualise. When it came to the Calculus, however, I was totally lost. Calculus never meant a thing to me because I could not visualise what was happening nor, more importantly, why.

And that was it. Both Pure Maths and Physics involved absolute acres of Calculus; fields of the stuff, as far as the eye could see. I knew before the end of the 1st year in the 6th form that my final year at Latymer was not going to be the great success that my parents were hoping for. I had been forming a different plan for some time. It was that I was not going to raise my level of expectation as regards any success probabilities for my A' Levels but, just thinking about it in that way gave me some mental relief. I elected on all possible occasions to remind my paters that the outcome of my final exams was not going to be anywhere near as distinguished as my O'level exams had been. They seemed, tragically mistakenly, to put my protestations down to natural modesty whereas that is a commodity with which I am not particularly well endowed!

Chapter Fifteen

Sammy and I go to Europe

In that summer between the two, 6th form years I planned a hitch-hiking trip across Europe with a school friend of mine Sammy S.

Part 1. The first Day – We're under way.

To summarise then; it was the summer holidays of 1958. I was 19 years old and just finished the first year of my two years in the 6th form of Latymer School Edmonton in north London. I had undergone a belated entry into that form due to my late entry into the school altogether. I had transferred from Burgess Hill School in Hampstead at the grand old age of 16 but had spent two years in the 5th form so as to catch up with my general education before being acceptable for the 6th form.

Three years earlier I had travelled to Yugoslavia by train and had had some quite exciting adventures both on the way and while there. I had made some friends one of whom was a girl, Marian. My plan was to hitch-hike to that country, stay there for a few days and return home by the same means of transport. I needed to recruit one friend to accompany me for I knew from past-experience that my parents would be more likely to agree to the proposal, and thereby fund me, if I had a companion.

The sticking point was the notion of hitch-hiking. Some friends were keen on the idea of the trip per-se but hitching was a notion too far. I, on the other hand, had been hitching rides in order to travel and camp around this country since I was 13 years old. Getting into other people's cars was not a strange concept to me. I liked to meet people and to see more of the country, as I did when I hitched. I also spoke good French as well as by now some German, and so language was neither a barrier nor a problem for me. In the end one brave sole, Sam, agreed to come on the trip with me. He was a keen motorcyclist and did try to sell the idea of a faster journey to me. I made it clear though that it was not an option for me as I really did want to meet people and see places rather than see them all whiz by in a flash. It would be fair to say that Sam and I did not see completely eye to eye throughout the whole holiday, but we got on pretty well for the most part and for most of the time. You can't really say fairer than that we didn't do bad for a scratch made crew!

The first day of the school holiday was taken up with last minute preparations; collecting holiday money, packing etc. Then, early the next morning, we met up at Lower Edmonton railway station for the trip to Dover and the ferry to Calais. Once we were in Calais, I knew that my longed-for trip across Europe had truly begun.

Even now I can remember the sense of freedom and relief as I stood on the deck of that ferry and caught sight of the coast of France slowly drifting towards me through the morning mist. It was Monday July 28th. 1958, and the world was still upside down and inside out from the six years of war. Britain and France had seemingly been in non-stop colonial conflict since the 2nd world war; France, first in Indo China and then in North Africa and as for Britain, well, all over the world really. Yet here was I, leaving England under my own steam for the first time in my life.

I had only been abroad that once, three years previously, with my former school. That was exhilarating and proved to be quite exciting. This though was different, the sense that for the next, however many weeks, there would be no-one on my back telling me what to do, or when to do it or why! It was also different because we were beginning this trip in France. I was then, and I always have been, more excited about being in France than any other foreign country except, perhaps, many years later, Argentina. I have realised gradually that I am one of those strange creatures that enjoys cities. I love Buenos Aires!

The ferry pulled slowly into the dock in Calais and suddenly everything came to life again. Sam and I were, of course, foot passengers; and as such, once the ferry was secure at the dockside we were told to disembark. We gathered up our belongings which consisted of little more than our rucksacks, but they were full to the brim, if a rucksack can be said to have a brim. Mine was a Bergan framed job, second hand but one that had served me well for the Yugoslavia holiday those years before.

Our tent was my trusty old ex-US army two-man ridge-tent. You know by now that it could be divided into two halves by unfastening a double row of heavy-duty press studs that ran from end to end over the ridge of the tent. That tent had already served me well during camping holidays since I was thirteen years old. It had been second hand then and was quite heavy by today's standards but was my pride and joy. At that point in our holiday Sam and I were carrying half each, poles and pegs having been divided neatly into two equal bundles and wrapped with the tent halves.

We arrived at last onto French soil and our first concern; how to get through and out of Calais onto the road for the Swiss border, was answered almost at once. Towards the end of the dock, I spied what looked like an argument between a man trying to unload his van, a Citroen 2cv van, and some type of official that was unknown to me at the time.

As we approached the argument, an animated mix of arms and hands with enthusiastic verbal accompaniment, I gathered rather than understood that the van owner had a delivery of goods that he needed to unload. He apparently needed to leave the van where it was while he went off to find the recipient of the goods, but the official was having none of that. The van could not be left where it was, unaccompanied. By the time we arrived at the spot I believed that I was quite apprised of the situation. It also appeared that both men were quite tired of the argument.

Opportunism being the name of the game I approached the van owner and announced Sam and I as the two English students who had come to help him to unload the van. 'Were we in time'? I asked the question in my best French and as innocently as I could muster. The official's face gave the clue that he didn't believe a word of it but on the other hand it gave him a way out of the hole that he and the van owner had dug for themselves. The van owner held out his hand to shake mine and smiled at me as if he had known me for years. The official walked off having given me a last evil look that conveyed the message that he had well and truly 'marked my card'.

It was not love at first sight but that 2cv was an answer to our initial problem of how to move away from the dock and onto the road away from Calais. The van owner turned out to be a farmer from a small village near Arras. He was delivering food produce to a cafeteria serving dock workers. We helped him to unload his goods. It took no time at all between the three of us and the man was very agreeable to giving us a lift to Arras afterwards. The only drawback to this arrangement being that poor old Sam had to makeshift in the back of the van. I took the front seat as the only practical arrangement, for Sam had learned to use very little of his 'school' French.

The farmer was a man of about 40 years of age and, as far as I can remember it his name was Jean Luc. It was a sudden upwards learning curve in the French language chatting with Jean Luc in his battered old cv2 van. The vehicle was a decrepit and ancient grey affair. The ancient aspect of the van was the least of my worries though, compared with effort I was having to put in to keep up with the man's chattering conversation in the strange, to me, version of French that was the local dialect. We were entering "Le pays des Ch'tis!" My difficulties were not helped by the persistent enquiries from my colleague Sam in the back, demanding a word for word translation of the conversation. I had not taken the difference in dialect on board when we first met at the dockside. Firstly, I had done most of the talking and the official had also thrown in his two-penny worth.

Now, it seemed that Jean Luc could understand me well enough. It was I who was having all the problems. Jean Luc's pronunciation was quite different to what I had been used to up to that time. After a while I realised that it was also about rhythm, and I began to tune in to that. In due course I was relieved that I was beginning, just, to understand our friendly farmer well enough to keep the conversation going. He asked me where we were heading for, and I explained that it was our aim to hitch hike to Yugoslavia. When I told him this Jean Luc whistled quietly, he was apparently, a communist as many French men were then and are nowadays. He admired our plans to travel across Europe and to end up behind the Iron Curtain for, as he put it, there you will see social justice really working.

I was having enough problems with his accent, thank you very much; to be much bothered with social justice in Yugoslavia just at that moment. By the time that we parted though, in Arras, I felt quite pleased with myself that I was beginning to, just about, get the hang of it. Jean Luc lived and worked his farm, in a small village about ten kilometres outside of the city of Arras. He was kind enough to say that he had enjoyed meeting us and pointed out some of the attractions. He explained that Arras was an ancient town with an interesting history. Jean Luc also felt that it would be a good place for us to get something to eat at a reasonable price before continuing on our way. He advised us to head for Reins and Troyes at which point we would pick up the flow of traffic from Paris to the Swiss border. We said our goodbyes as Jean Luc left us in the main square of Arras. Before we finally parted company, he indicated the direction in which we should head to continue our way towards Reins.

During our journey thus far, I had explained to our new-found friend that I did not want to set foot in Germany and preferred to travel the longer route to Yugoslavia via Switzerland. As a Frenchman and a communist Jean Luc fully understood my attitude. That was, indeed, my attitude for many years but has changed little by little over the decades since. One cannot live a full life if one lives it chained to the past!

Arras is the capital (chef-lieu/préfecture) of the Pas-de-Calais department, which forms part of the region of Hauts-de-France; at the time of which I am writing it was located in Nord-Pas-de-Calais. The historic centre of the Artois region, with a Baroque town square, Arras is situated in Northern France at the confluence of the Scarpe River and the Crichoh River

The Arras plain lies on a large chalk plateau bordered on the north by the Marqueffles fault, on the southwest by the Artois and Ternois hills, and on the south by the slopes of Beaufort-Blavincourt. On the east it is connected to the Scarpe valley.

Established during the Iron Age by the Gauls, the town of Arras was first known as Nemetocenna, which is believed to have originated from the Celtic word nemeton, meaning 'sacred' space.

That battered old cv2 van was the first lift I had ever had in a foreign country and Jean Luc was a very kind and thoughtful host. Ever since that time I have fostered a real soft spot for the cv2.

Arras town square was a sight to behold for two young men abroad on their own for the first time. These days much of it is taken up with parking. In 1958, though, it was almost empty except for shoppers and visitors. There were shops, there were restaurants and there were cafes. As we walked slowly across the square Sam reminded me that we both had a sandwich lunch prepared for us by our Mums earlier that morning before we left home. In the excitement of arriving in France and meeting Jean Luc we had forgotten these now very welcome provisions.

We sought out a café, with outside seating, at the edge of the square. In this way we could order drinks and eat our sandwiches surreptitiously whilst enjoying both our drinks and a tranquil half hour or so. In fact, we passed a tranquil hour plus at that café. Since that time, I have always argued that one of the best ways to begin to enjoy a foreign language is to sit and listen to it going on all around you in an open-air café. There is the hustle and bustle of passers-by, all chatting as they do so. There are the smells, the scents that will bring back memories in the future. As Marcel Proust reminds us in his « A la recherche du temps perdues. » Past scents often return us to past-memories. It is one of the ways in which we learn our own language. We absorb it. That was a simple meal but one of the most memorable of my life. One of these days I plan to return to Arras for a longer visit.

We left Arras sometime between 2pm and 2.30pm. We were hoping to make it to Troyes before time came to settle down for the night. There remained, however the rather large town of Reims between Arras and Troyes. The walk, through Arras gave us an opportunity to stretch our legs. It did not take too long to get to the spot that Jean Luc had described as a reasonable place to begin to hitch towards Reims.

A number of cars vans and Lorries came our way; some passed us by, and some stopped but were not going our way. Finally, there was one lorry driver who stopped and who was able to offer a lift to us. Again, he was connected to the farming industry but was carrying farm equipment to several farms in the region between Reims and Troyes. This was handy for us in that he was able to take us past the city of Reims. The drawback from our point of view was that he would not be able to take us as far as Troyes. The best that he could do was to leave us at a spot on the road to Troyes but still some sixty kilometres from the town and in a country district. We accepted the offer gladly on the basis of never looking a gift horse in the mouth.

In fact, the place where we were dropped was a quite isolated lay-by on a very quiet section of road. The driver gave us a cheery waive as he pulled away and then turned off to the right about a hundred yards from where we were now standing alone; with just the birds for company it seemed. Sam looked at me with a glare that was a mixture of concern and anger. I was waiting for him to blame me for something. I'm not sure what but, whatever it was it was clearly my fault. Perhaps it was because we were both hungry but had no food left after we had eaten all our sandwiches at lunchtime. I waited for his bubble to burst because I had noticed something that he clearly had not. The bubble seethed away for several minutes but finally he managed to get control enough to grin at me. "What now". He asked quietly. "Well then, as you ask, let's go get some food". "Bloody where?" was all he could muster. "Follow me". I grinned and walked away.

I led Sam back the way we had come for about three hundred yards and, in a lay-by just like the one where we had been dropped off was an older woman who was just about to pack up her wares for the night. Our saviour was just about to go home but a few seconds of quick conversation changed her mind. She was the proud proprietor of a lay-by fruit and fresh food outlet. It was not absolutely ideal, but it was a lot better than we could have hoped for, there, way out in the sticks, as it were. The woman seemed very old to us but, at the age of 18 or 19 years everyone over the age of 25 seems old. Looking back, I guess she must have been about 50 years old. She wore a long black dress with a flowing skirt.

We were able to buy some apples and plums. Also available were two French bread sticks; not at their best at that time of day but, nonetheless, were also in the 'better than we had a few minutes ago' category. She also had butter, some eggs, cheese and two bottles of cider. This was all very welcome and just enough to provide for both supper and breakfast. Before we parted company the lady pointed to a clearing behind the roadside hedge. "Camp there"! "You'll be OK there for the night. That piece of land belongs to my husband and me".

The clearing was not large but was quite clean from our point of view. It also had a stand tap for fresh water. Despite all the warnings that I had had from my Dad about 'drinking the water' it tasted fine and; no-one died! The only other occupants of the clearing were the inhabitants of a long chicken run, from where, no doubt, came the eggs we had just bought. I set about hard-boiling those at once on our small camping gaz single burner stove. We decided that that was safer than trying to carry fresh eggs around with us in our rucksacks. In any case we had bread; we could make quite a good tea/supper with a couple of hard-boiled eggs bread and some cheese. The cider went down well too.

It was a warm evening, and so we settled down to sleep in just our sleeping bags. We didn't use the tent. There were many nights on that trip when we wouldn't bother with the tent. Sleeping out under the stars can truly be a magical experience. The chickens didn't make for good bedtime neighbours; however, they seem to be squabbling and cackling on and off throughout the night. They also have truly scant respect for the mornings. The cockerel makes sure that everyone knows he's awake and in charge. By my count he began his own reveille at about 4am and was still going at it when we finally gave up the idea of sleeping anymore and stowed our sleeping gear away.

<u>Part 2 A Smuggler Emerges</u>.

We then had a wash using the cold-water standpipe, after which we made a breakfast from the hard-boiled eggs, some of the now well past its best 'bread', some of the very tasty butter and a slab of cheese each. It was not sumptuous but good enough for two growing lads in a hurry to get moving. The cider had been consumed the night before, but the bottles came in handy as refills from the cold-water tap. We kept the remainder of the fruit as a reserve snack for later in the day. Toiletry arrangements were concluded 'au nature' as they say, and I do not intend to illuminate any further on that subject.

We then set out for the nearby road hoping to get under way quickly along the next section of our journey to the beautiful town of Troyes.

Troyes is a town in the Grand Est region of north-eastern France. Its medieval old town features narrow, cobbled streets lined with colourful half-timbered houses, mostly dating from the 16th century. If one likes sight-seeing of ancient buildings, then Troyes is a town that has a fine selection. The town is home to several Gothic churches with striking stained-glass windows. These include the Troyes Cathedral, the Église Sainte-Madeleine and the Basilique Saint-Urbain.

Troyes is the capital of the department of Aube in north-central France. It is located on the River Seine and is about 150 km (93 mi) southeast of Paris. This area is known as the Champagne region of Northern France. Many half-timbered houses (mainly 16th century) survive in the old town. Troyes has been in existence since the Roman era, as Augustobona Tricassium, which stood at the hub of numerous highways, primarily the Via Agrippa. There is the junction of the main highway the A26 which we were on and the A5 which is a main highway connecting Paris and the Swiss border via a direct connection to the N19. We were aiming for the A5.

We walked back the short distance to the stall where we had bought the very welcome provisions the night before. We had it in mind to but some fresh bread as well as something to go in it. As we approached the stall, we noticed that the old woman was indeed there and that she appeared to have already set up her stall. We were, therefore, ever more hopeful that we would depart with something for the journey.

As we came closer the woman seemed to be crouching close to the as-yet empty road. We began to get a sense of running water as if a nearby tap had not been fully turned off. The woman took no notice of us but, as we came alongside the stall, the sound of flowing water ceased, and the woman stood up. The sound stopped sure enough but her motion of standing up revealed her reason for crouching in the first place.

A very large puddle of liquid in the gutter gave notice that the woman in black had been doing a long pee, al-fresco so to speak. She turned towards us as if nothing had transpired and made to ask us if she could help us. Sam looked at me and a silent message passed between us. I advised our friend from the night before that we needed nothing but had merely come back to thank her once more for allowing us to sleep in her field. She smiled and held out her hand as if to shake hands. As there had been no apparent attempt to wash that hand since her open-air ablution I pretended not to notice the appendage. I stooped and gave her a kiss on both cheeks instead. I then walked briskly away with my friend in the knowledge that we had each just received a small but interesting addition to our collective worldly wisdom!

It was a very pleasant morning and that being so we decided to walk the short distance to the A5 where we hoped to pick up a lift towards Switzerland or even into it would be better. We had walked about a half mile when I slipped in the grass by the side of the road. I did not actually fall but, what with the heavy rucksack on my back I had stumbled forward for several paces before I regained control. At the final stumble I twisted my ankle. It hurt only slightly but as soon as I tried to walk my ankle began to click at every step. The ankle caused me no pain and absolutely no inconvenience except for the click every time I put one foot before the other. It became so persistent that Sam often chose to walk a few paces behind me so as to escape the disconcerting click. That was inconvenient at times as well as embarrassing. That 'clicky' ankle remained a persistent reminder of that nearly-fall for the whole of the holiday, almost six weeks as it eventually became.

We reached the A5-A26 junction after about 45 minutes. My nearly-fall and the discovery of the persistently sonorous reminder had delayed us by several minutes. Sam had, by now, made his choice to trail behind, out of earshot of the offending ankle. My experience of hitching rides in Britain told me that motorists prefer not to stop near busy junctions to give lifts. I turned eastwards towards Switzerland, walked a few hundred yards, and stopped; both for a breather and to allow Sam to catch up. Sam was still about 50 yards away though when the most unexpected and amazing car hove into view along the road behind Sam partly hidden, initially, behind his shoulder. The car was a huge, light blue American convertible. I signalled it, more in hope than expectation, in the time-honoured manner as befits a hitchhiker.

To my total astonishment the car came to a halt just a few yards past me and about 30 or so yards past Sam. By the time that he caught up, puffing, and blowing what with running under the weight of his rucksack, I had replied to the driver's enquiry that we were on the way to Yugoslavia, ever hopeful me, via Switzerland. He grinned at the mention of Yugoslavia but said that he was going to a place just across the Swiss border. After all the years that have passed, I cannot remember the name of the man's destination in Switzerland.

Our New driver, I discovered, was a Russian Jew who had managed to make an escape from the Russian Army in the confusion that existed everywhere in Europe in the months after WW2. His name was Mendel Abramsky, but I never got past 'Monsieur Abramsky' in the few hours I knew the man. His first name though was the same as my Dad's first name when written in Yiddish in the form Mendel ben Shimon. Mr. Abramsky was originally from a town called Grodno in Western Belarus. I did not discover until much later that his action in stopping for us was not predicated solely on kindness. He had an ulterior motive but needed some time with us to check us out first.

Our new friend introduced himself at once. I recognised his name as being Jewish and was not surprised when I heard that he came originally from Russia. Once I had informed Mr. Abramsky of my own Jewish connections he seemed to become more interested in Sam and me. Where were we going? Why? Why were we hitch-hiking? Stuff like that. He also opened up with some information about himself. As I say he was a Russian Jew who had been conscripted to Stalin's wartime army. He had no serious objection to that in itself. Russia had to be defended from the Nazis and in that he was very willing, like any good Russian, to do his bit. What he did object to though was the constant anti-Semitism that pervaded in Russia generally and in her armed forces in particular. The moment that the opportunity presented itself in the confusion after the Russian invasion of Berlin he took his chance to simply move to the West. He finally settled in Paris where he founded his business as a Jeweller in the Jewish Quarter of that great city. He seems to have used funds acquired as the Russian Army made its way across Asia, Europe and finally into Germany. I did not wish to or in fact attempt to enquire into the details of the acquisition of those funds.

I listened to the man's story in a mixture of genuine interest bolstered by natural politeness to a man who was, after all, doing us something of a favour. Not, though a totally unconditional favour, as I was soon to find out. What really interested me at that point, however, was his car. I have always loved cars and his really was something special! I had realised that it was a Cadillac even before we got into it. Some careful questioning revealed the further information that it was a 1954 Cadillac Eldorado convertible. Abramsky had used money and influence to import the car from new; following a business trip to New York where he had fallen in love with the vehicle in a cars-sales showroom. I could not blame him for any of that. It was a real beauty! The car was an example of total comfort allied to fulsome power. A real gas guzzler as they say! Abramsky apparently did not care about any of that, he just loved his car. I had been in the car for a total of perhaps fifteen minutes by that time and I loved his car too. Sam must have appreciated the car also, because he fell asleep in the back just after his whistle of delight as he fell onto the very sumptuous rear passenger seats. It was becoming a very hot day, but the open aspect of the car provided a very cooling breeze as we moved gracefully along the straight-as-a-die French road.

Then came a few preliminary questions; "What do you think of the exchange control regulations?" Now, I was a teenager. I was not used to discussing such things at that time of my life. I understood the French but not the reason for the question. I was not really affected by exchange control. The limit for me as an ordinary traveller was £25 and that was a great deal of money to me at that time. Dad had provided me with £25 in travellers' cheques as well as a ten-pound note and a few pounds in French francs which he told me to keep in a separate pocket. "If anyone notices plead youthful ignorance." Were his only instructions on the matter. When Abramsky asked his question; I replied by telling him what I had and added that it seemed OK to me. He spluttered and nearly choked in his vain attempt not to roar with laughter. "Well, it sure as hell isn't enough for me." He then noticed a sign for an upcoming service area. "Let's have some lunch; I need to get petrol anyway." The car pulled gracefully off the road and into the service area.

French service areas have always been superior to those of Britain. This one had not developed to the exquisite standard of variety that one experiences these days but the selection of food in the cafeteria was very good. It was, then, a very welcome as well as very surprising when our car host offered to pay for our food. I managed to whisper to Sam that it was a bit fishy. Sam grinned back something about looking gift horses in their mouths. "Besides," he added. "What can he do to us? There are two of us and he's just an old geezer. He's not out to steal our rucksacks that's for sure." Sam's assessment was sound enough even if it was based on the judgement that, at our age, anyone over the age of about 35 was well on the way to meeting his maker.

We enjoyed our lunch even though I could not shake off the feeling that all was not quite kosher. That thought however was quite cast aside when, after the meal, I went to the loo and had my first encounter with the ferocious French loo that was standard in those days. This comprised a hole in the porcelain on either side of which were a pair of slightly raised China footprints on which you were required to squat in order to do your business. It was anything but a comfortable operation. The danger to personal comfort was by no means over though even when you thought that the affair was over and when you had cleaned yourself up and had pulled your trousers up etc. The most dangerous moment was still to come, so beware! As a mere unsuspecting Englishman, one pulled the chain totally unaware that a spiteful wave of water would rush at you, intent, it seemed, on soaking your feet and the bottoms of your legs and your trousers if you were not wearing shorts.

French loos of that epoch were one of life's great learning experiences. I returned to the car with both my feet and new walking boots in a sad and soggy state! I tried to hide the feet as I returned to the car but Abramsky simply grinned and suggested that I might like to remove my boots and socks until they were dry.

The three of us continued for about a half hour with Sam trying to enter the conversation where he could or where he could persuade me to keep up a running translation. I was not too keen on this chore however because it tested my French at a level of speed at which I was at the very edge of my capabilities. At about the half-hour mark though he got bored and fell asleep again in the comfort of the rear seating and with the warmth of the sun adding to his dive back into siesta mode. Then came a question that I had been half suspecting although the route that it took was something of a surprise.

"Would you be willing to do me a favour?" He smiled conspiratorially as he asked the question. "If I can." Was all I could think of by way of reply. "It's like this. The French government only allows me a small amount of exchange control money if I leave the country. I have a house in Switzerland and my daughter lives there and goes to school there. It costs a lot of money. You're not a French citizen so you're not bound by French exchange control regulations. We'll be at the border soon. I would like you simply to carry some money across the border for me. It won't be too heavy!" He added with a mischievous grin.

It only took me a couple of seconds to think it over before agreeing to the man's request. After all, he had been pretty good to us and, well, it would be a bit of a lark. If he was telling me the truth about us not being affected by French law on the matter, then we would be fire-proof anyway. He dug into the inside pocket of his light jacket and pulled out a really thick roll of currency, all French francs, and handed it over to me. Sam had been asleep up to that point but began to rally as the money was handed over. I don't think that he realised straight away just what was being handed over, but he was suspicious enough to demand exactly what was going on. I quickly brought him up to speed and a series of questions followed as in a torrent, the torrent of someone who feels that he has been left out of something important and now wants to make his presence felt.

Sam's questions left no doubt as to how he felt once he knew about the money. The two most important were, "How come there's no danger for us?" and secondly, "What's in it for us?" On the first I let him know Mr. Abramsky's explanation of the lack of danger for us. On the second point he was more insistent, which I found both less understandable as well as quite unreasonable considering that we had had a very good ride in great comfort. What we had been asked to do did not involve any hard work, after all. My friend's attitude was beginning to irritate me. I must admit to being rather pumped up at the thought of smuggling money across an international border. Sam, moreover, was in no way mollified when I suggested that if anything went wrong, I would be carrying the money. He himself could claim total ignorance of the deed. That seemed to aggravate him all the more. Nonetheless, as we passed a particularly lovely stretch of country and through a very pretty village our Russian driver announced that we were only a couple of minutes from the French border with her neighbour Switzerland.

On a point of European history, it needs to be said that international borders within Europe were quite different that you would experience these days i.e. across the Schengen zone. We arrived at the French side where there was a customs house. I cannot remember exactly the name of the place where we crossed the border, but we had driven past the French town of Mulhouse and very quickly were at the point of crossing from France into Switzerland and into the Swiss City of Basel. At the post resided certain officers who, between them, incorporated the several offices of customs, border control and security.

Once the car had pulled to a halt outside the customs house and the officers had established who we were, that is Sam and me. They waived us out of the car and pointed us in the direction of the Swiss side. There was a strip of territory between the two sets of officials known universally as 'no man's land'. We crossed that strip in a few strides as the French border control guys set about taking Abramsky's car apart with the obvious intent of searching it thoroughly. We both looked back towards our erstwhile Russian driver and friend. His face was ashen as he stood helplessly, totally helplessly, watching as his money was apparently disappearing from his control, in the pocket of a young stranger, one who he had only met a few hours ago and one who he had trusted to protect it for him. How quickly can life reverse one's fortunes!

There was nothing we could do about the situation. The French authorities wanted to search the car, and nothing would prevent them from doing so. The Swiss border guards had observed the interesting events that had begun to play out on the French side of the tracks and were not at all interested in two scruffy hitchhikers. They waived us on and so we had free and uninterrupted passage into the land of the toblerone.

We walked in silence for perhaps two hundred yards and until we were quite out of sight of the border. Sam suddenly stopped and turned around to face me. "Let's have a look at what all the fuss is about." I took the roll of banknotes from my pocket and passed it over to him. He bounced it in his hand as if trying to weigh it. "Bloody hell." He almost whispered the two words. "There's a bit of a bundle here Tone. What are we going to do now?" We looked hard at each other. The same thoughts were being considered by each of us. We looked hard at the bundle that had fallen into our hands as if by providence. We looked at each other then, as if by telepathy, we both shook our heads at the same instant. He said the words. "I can't do it to the man Tone. Scrumping yes but we're not thieves." "Yup, me neither, let's find a place to wait. He's got to come this way." We walked a short distance further and actually found a wooden bench on which to wait, hoping that the French customs would not find anything in the car and thereby would actually release our man.

It must have been at least an hour and a half later when this blue bullet came racing down the road like the proverbial bat-out-of- hell. We had been at the point of thinking that the

French had found some further miseries with which to delay, or even arrest, our man. The look on his face though was well worth waiting for as he screeched the blue bullet to a halt

"I knew I could trust you." He lied. We accepted his lie gracefully however and handed his money back to him. He did do us the courtesy of putting the wad back into his pocket without examining it.

"I will not offend you by offering you money as a reward."

He had reverted to speaking to me, now totally in French although we had just discovered that he did have some passable English. I can remember thinking that I would not have been in the least offended but what came next was actually quite acceptable even more so when considering our circumstances.

"You waiting for me not only saved my money but also cost you some time. I cannot spare the time to take you the whole way across Switzerland, but I can take you as far as Zurich. I have a friend who has a small family hotel on the outskirts of the town. We can have a meal together and I'll pay for you to have a room for the night. That way you can have a good wash and brush up and take away the dust and dirt of the road. In the morning you should be well placed to get on your way. There is a direct road to Liechtenstein."

Sam was delighted when I explained to him what was in Abramsky's mind.

"I told you so. Honesty always pays." He chirped.

And that's just how it happened; Mr. Abramsky drove us to and through Zurich where he pulled up in the driveway of a beautiful small hotel. It took him a while to find his friend and to explain what had happened that day and to arrange for our room. We took our rucksacks into the hotel and left them in the charge of the staff in the reception while we took some time to stretch our legs with a short stroll around the gardens of the hotel'

"Well Tone, this is a bit of all right. We've done OK here. Wash and brush up; nice meal, comfy bed, shower and whatever else you might want to do in comfort followed by breakfast and on our way, all freshened up!" Sam paused for breath. He had done more sleeping than talking that day.

"You know what Tone; I might even begin to like this Hitch-Hiking lark!"

I grinned and walked back to the hotel smiling all the way. I had heard Mr Abramsky calling us. I was really happy though that Sam had begun to enjoy the trip. Motor biking was his real forte and preferred option for travelling about whereas this trip had been my proposition and that included hitching because it's a dammed good way to meet people.

We had our meal with Mr Abramsky, but it became a somewhat rushed affair because he was clearly anxious to move on to meet up with his daughter at their home in Luzern. Otherwise, the meal was quite genial because he brought Sam into the discussion by bringing out and dusting his English.

We said our goodbyes immediately after the meal. It was a slightly sad affair, that parting, because we both felt that we had made a friend, albeit a transient one. We had also hoist up the flag for honesty in travelling. That in itself was a good feeling.

We did not rise too early the next morning. The luxury of the en-suite room and comfy beds was hard to leave. Remember that at home I still lived in a house with an outside loo and a tin bath; although, as I have previously explained, I had not used the tin bath myself since the age of 12/13 years of age. We took ourselves down to breakfast at about 9.30. That was just a half hour before the hour when breakfast was due to end.

We were able to partake of a very substantial meal nonetheless as we were able to choose from a range of options that enabled us to select from both continental and British options. Being healthy young Brits engaged in a holiday choice that implied, ostensibly at least, a decent amount of exercise in the form of walking we expanded our selection by choosing from both of those alternatives. By mutual agreement we felt that it would be churlish and ungrateful to avoid anything that was on offer. We had a dammed good breakfast that morning; we also managed to procure, surreptitiously, enough items of food to last us the rest of the day.

Justas we were finishing our feast the head waiter came to our table, he grinned hugely at the devastation we had wreaked on his food supplies. He spoke to us in absolutely perfect English.

"I see that you have broken your fast very enthusiastically." He turned his head to look in the direction of a table about fifteen feet from where we sat. He turned back to speak directly to me.

"I understand that you speak French." "Yes" I replied." But your English is very good."

The smile was resurrected. "No, it's not that, it's about the two people on the table over there. They are a father and daughter. They would like to speak to you. But they speak only French and German".

Nothing ventured nothing gained we looked at each other and immediately nodded our agreement. We heaved ourselves up from a table that had erstwhile groaned with the weight of food.

« Bonjour Monsieur/Dame, Le maître d'hôtel nous dit que vous souhaitez nous parler. »

I spoke quietly looking at each of them in turn indicating that we had been given the message that they wanted to speak to us. The young woman turned her head to speak to me in French. "Our friend Mendel left a message with the waiter that you are heading towards Yugoslavia".

I nodded my head and acknowledged the truth of this in very urgent agreement. It seemed that the good Mr Abramsky had left us with one more gift of gratitude. She noticed my excitement at her early comments.

"Well, we're not going to Yugoslavia, but we can give you a lift to very close to the border between Switzerland and Liechtenstein if that's any good to you."

The lady smiled as I tugged my left elbow away from Sam's urgent grip. He just could not come to terms with the fact that although my French was pretty good, and I say it myself but that it just did not want to be pushed into the role of instant translation whilst it was girding its loins in preparation for the next bit of dialogue. I held my hand up by way of apology and explained to her that my friend was anxious to know what was going on. A huge grin indicated that she understood the reasons for Sam's impatience.

Sam was as pleased as punch, just as I was, at the news that we were getting a lift to the border. Surprisingly we had discussed, only the previous evening, that if we reached Liechtenstein in reasonable time the next day that we would endeavour to walk across the country and into Austria; just to be able to take into the future the true tale that we had walked across a whole county as part of our journey to Tito's Land! I am shortly about to bring that true tale into the future from the past whence it comes.

We thanked our new 'friends' enthusiastically and returned to our room to collect our things. Back down in the foyer very sincerely and where we thanked both the Owner of the hotel and the head Waiter. We had no money to spare for tips to the latter, but our thanks were truly sincere.

We sank into the luxury of yet one more car ride for which we had not had to wait ages by the side of the road and in the heat of the sun. Our baggage neatly stowed into the boot, and we were off, having waived to a small group of three waiting to see us off at the entrance to the hotel. It was with a mixture of sadness and relief that we pulled away from that hotel.

Jeanette broke the spell; she spoke to me in French but asked me to apologise to Sam on her behalf for not having any English. Sam asked me to tell her that he wasn't bothered at all. I did so but with more diplomacy than Sam had indicated.

"We are going to a place called Buchs, very close to the border. We can drop you off though, very near the border close to a town called Vaduz which is inside Liechtenstein. You won't have much trouble at the border here; it's very relaxed across this section. You might not even see a border guard."

."Wir fahren entlang der Nordseite des Zürichsees. Es ist wirklich schön." This came from the father; telling us that we were about to drive along the North bank of a huge lake called the Lake of Zurich which he added is very beautiful.

I am ashamed to admit that I saw little of the lake as we drove along its northern shore. I was too interested in the structure of the conversation between the father and daughter to spare much thought for what was a beautiful journey. I did read somewhere that Lake Zürich is formed by the Linth River, and that this rises in the glaciers of the Glarus Alps and was diverted by the Escher canal, which was completed in 1811, then into Lake Walen from where its waters are carried to the east end of Lake Zürich by means of the Linth canal which in its turn was completed in 1816. The waters of the Lake of Zürich flow out of the lake at its north-west end and pass through the city of Zürich. At this point the outflow is then called the Limmat. See that? History and travel guide all in one!

I do remember that the valley of the lake seemed to be both beautiful and peaceful; particularly as most parts of Europe were still edging themselves out of the 'pit of war' and had not yet entered into the bright sunshine of more hopeful days yet to come.

I also remember that I was quite captured by the style of conversation between father and daughter. It was fascinating. She spoke wholly in French to her father, and he kept his side up entirely in German or, actually, Schweizerdeutsch. I could understand her part of the conversation and, obviously they could fully understand each other yet each was speaking an entirely different language.

I have thought long and hard about this phenomenon over the years and have now come to explain it from my greater familiarity with Yiddish and its counterpart –Yinglish as well as from my studies in Spanish and its alter ego Spanglish. I have grown to believe that what I heard in that small car travelling along the north shore of the Zurich See on the summer's day in 1957 was an extreme version of what happens when people at different levels speak to each other in either Spanglish or Yinglish. Let me explain!

My paternal grandparents emigrated from what is now Poland in 1906. The family language was Yiddish. This is a language that developed from Old High German but with strong additional influences from Polish and Russian as well as Hebrew which is of course the language of the religion for Jewish people. Yiddish does have dialects, but they are mutually comprehensible with some difficulty. Hebrew is now of course the daily spoken language of Israel.

 My Bubbah, my paternal grandmother had ten children. They were five boys and five girls. All grew to become adults although two of the girls sadly passed away due to disease in their early twenties. From discussions that I had with my uncles Harry and Rueben the language of the home was ostensibly Yiddish but that it changed in character as more children came along. The older three or four children were exposed entirely to Yiddish in the home but as more children came along, they were exposed to more and more English. Children started to go to school and to mix with other children many of whom were Jewish but that the language that they spoke between them became mixed with more and more English and so took on the mantle of Yinglish. Bubbah still spoke Yiddish of course because she had very little exposure to English. All her friends spoke Yiddish and she shopped solely in shops where that language was spoken.

Thus, it came to pass that the children developed from Yiddish speaking to speaking Yinglish to a time where the young people were entirely more comfortable with English. As this development took place my Bubbah learned to understand what her children were saying but continued to speak in her preferred language. Yiddish by the way is called, in Yiddish, Mame Loshen; literally 'Mother Tongue'.

I am not absolutely convinced that those children were entirely conscious that these dramatic changes were occurring. I remember that my Dad always maintained that the language of the home was Yiddish. I do however have a short story related to me by Dad's older brother, my uncle Harry who had several episodes of passing time in Israel both before and after the declaration of independence. On one occasion he arranged to stay for a month or so with an orthodox and Yiddish speaking family in Safed. Although he was by no means orthodox in his own religious views Harry felt that he would be comfortable with the language. To his huge surprise he quickly realised that linguistically he was way out of his depth. He hadn't realised just how much his knowledge of the language had been eroded over the years.

As I relate in Chapter 18 of my first Book, I did not truly meet the main element of my Jewish family until I was in my early twenties. I did then notice that it was my oldest aunt, Pearl, who conducted the major part of the discussions with her mother and in Yiddish. They were not in-depth discussions, however. I took the trouble to learn all the Mame Loshen that I needed, and I would refer to it as 'pass me the salt' Yiddish. They were not a family for deep discussions over world issues!

…………………………………………..

I did not take in much of the beauty of the journey along the north bank of that lovely and huge lake. I had been too interested in listening to the quaint twin language discussion and remembering the evolution of language in my own Jewish family. In recent years I have begun a study of modern language with the Open University. Part of that degree course involved an introduction to World Spanish which led to a window on Spanglish as spoken in parts of the USA. There is a multitude of individual family stories of course but I remember that there were many situations that were clearly developing along very similar lines to that of my family.

My mental wanderings then had taken my mind away from most of the journey when I suddenly came back to the world and realised that the daughter was talking to me to say that we had arrived at the chosen drop-off point. Sam insists that earlier in the journey that kind young woman had told me of their plans to take us a bit closer to an appropriate road into Liechtenstein and that I had briefly discussed it with her and thanked both her and her Dad but, for the life of me, I remembered not a word of that discussion; chalk that one also to my concentration on the 'loom of language' bloom that had occupied my head for most of the trip! I tried to make up for my lapse in concentration by apologising to them and thanking them profusely for their kindness. They had the good grace to smile and wish us very good heartedly a happy onward journey to Yugoslavia. I believe that they put my apparent lack of memory down to a 'sleepy head'.

Hitch Hiking Across Europe into Yugoslavia

Liechtenstein

We began our short walk into Liechtenstein in very good spirits. We actually turned down a couple of kind offers to give us lifts during which I used up much of my precious German vocabulary with:-

 "Danke Sehr mein Herr, aber wir wollen heute spazieren gehen und die schöne Landschaft sehen."

As these conversations were not destined to be long by their very nature my mere thanks in this way may well have given a couple of German speaking drivers the mistaken illusion that here was at least one wandering Englishman who spoke passable to good German. I just hope that they drove away determined to spread the WORD! - Just doing my bit!

As was predicted we walked across the border unnoticed and unchallenged. Border control appeared to be out for the day! We continued to walk into the country towards Vaduz which is the capitol of the small state of Liechtenstein; officially the Principality of Liechtenstein and is a German-speaking microstate situated in the Alps between Austria and Switzerland in Central Europe.

It was a lovely day and just like a couple of carefree British twits we began our walk towards Vaduz singing tunes from old sea chanties. Quite out of sync with the countryside around us but we didn't care. To say that it is German speaking is a slight misnomer; the dialect there was strong; more of that in just a few moments.

Vaduz is the capital of Liechtenstein and also the seat of the national parliament. The city is located along the Rhine River and had just over 5,000 residents. We could see the most prominent landmark of Vaduz long before we reached the city. Vaduz Castle is perched at the summit of a steep hill in the middle of the city. We had been told that it was home to the reigning prince of Liechtenstein and the Liechtenstein princely family. There was more distinctive architecture such as the Cathedral of St. Florin, Government House, the City Hall, and the National Art Gallery, as well as the National Museum, although we did not intend to stay long enough to do any sight-seeing in the city. We did express the hope that we might be able to return some day to do the place justice. Vaduz is the best-known town in the principality internationally, it is not the largest. In the short time that we were there it gave the vibes of a city that would be well worth a longer visit

Vaduz is only few miles or so from the Swiss border. We knew that it would not take long although my ankle was still playing its timpani chorus as we walked. We arrived in Vaduz in time to sit at an open-air café to grab a bite and a mug of coffee; no arty tiny coffee cups for us. We did not want much as we'd had the breakfast of a lifetime at the hotel not all that long ago. We had also taken part in the disposal during the day of the elements 'stolen' from the overladen breakfast table.

We hiked out of town after eating drinking and performing other ablutionary functions whilst we had nice facilities to do so. Again, we refused one more offer of a lift as we left the place which gave me the opportunity once more to offer up my own short selection of decent German; one more messenger to deliver into Europe the good news that some Englishmen make the effort!

The road along which we were walking seemed to be set into a wide and not very deep valley. There was the suggestion of mountains in the distance, but fields of various crops lay on either side of the straightish road. [Word says that I've just made up a word there. Don't care!] Suddenly we were hailed by a guy working about fifty feet away in the huge field to our right. He saw that we had noticed him, and he began to walk towards us. He stopped, turned slightly, and waived at us to follow him.

I must admit that both Sam and I were just a bit cautious at this sudden and unexpected summons from a complete stranger in a country in which we had only been walking for a very short time. We began to catch him up but the caution, the concern mounted when he disappeared into a somewhat scruffy but sizeable shed in the middle of that large field.

"There's two of us. What can he do to us?" Sam whispered into my ear as the man poked his head back out and waived at us to follow him. We entered the shed, and the man made no effort to close the door.

"So far so good!" Sam again, this time in the other ear. The man pointed into a far corner at a second man.

"Mein Bruder Markus. Ich heiße Leon".

So, we were into introductions. It all seemed a bit sudden from just now walking along the road. He looked at us as if expecting a reply. So, in for a penny…I pointed at Sam.

"Mein guter Freund Sam. Ich heiße Tony". Well then! My poor old German had held up sofar. Mind you we were not on to world affairs yet! Another test however from the basic German primer!

"Sind Sie durstig, hungrig?" I looked at Sam to translate but he was well ahead of the game.

"Not hungry, thirsty a little thanks." I turned to Leon, but he had not understood Sam's reply.

I obliged. "Nicht hungrig, durstig ein wenig danke." Leon grinned a wicked grin and chuckled something at his brother who reached behind a cupboard next to his rickety old wicker work chair and pulled out an object the like of which I recognised instantly from a previous holiday. It was a very heavy, two gallon, Tate and Lyle syrup tin but I realised at once that it no longer would have contained syrup! Leon produced four plastic beakers and set them down on an up-turned tea chest that served as a table. I quickly explained to Sam what we were about to be offered.

"How can you know that?" Looking back towards the tin that had been opened ready for pouring I explained.

"I've been down this way before!" I beamed at him. "Well," he replied, "The door's still open."

We each accepted a beaker of dark and tasty home-made scrumpy. Leon fished around in the darker depths at the rear of the shed and came up with a couple of fold up chairs for Sam and me; we settled down to drink with our newfound and somewhat strangely found friends. Leon had a chair that was an exact copy of his older brother's rickety cane chair.

Leon sat back and raised his beaker to a toast to the then current Prince of Liechtenstein Franz Joseph 2nd who was apparently their monarch at the time. Not to be out-done Sam immediately raised his glass to the Queen.

"Not letting him get away with that one!" Was Sam's response to my quizzical look.

I am not going to claim here that the level of conversation included anything more deep than short episodes into football and including a tsunami of questions; where did we come from? Is Glasgow far from Edmonton? They had a cousin living in Glasgow. Is Edmonton far from the sea? What does the sea look like? Could we swim in the sea? It was, though, very cheerful and I am very clear in my memory that my German improved dramatically the more I drank. When writing these words, I would remind my reader that many pages ago, in Aachen, I stated that there are two mental states that improve one's proficiency in speaking a foreign language; the first of these if you remember was 'anger' the second of course is a decent intake of alcohol! These might be a useful clue for all students of modern languages, or indeed, in principle, for students of any kind in any subject?

Well then, we passed a very pleasant and much unexpected couple of hours with those two brothers. We had to leave eventually however in the way that all good things must come to an end. We said our goodbyes and shook hands with those two very kind young men. We were not too steady, I must confess, on our feet, as we left and made our way back to the road.

"Well!" Said Sam, as we began to walk. "That went well, better than I thought when they first invited us in. I must say that I wondered a bit what was going on; what they might be up to…"

"Me too", I admitted. "Still, what could have happened, there are two of us when all's said and done."

"By the way." Sam turned to stare at me. "What on earth did you mean; I've been down this way before?"

I smiled and referred him to the contents of Chapter thirteen 'Olive Oil and Spinach'. "I had been in almost exactly the same situation three years ago, in Slovenia." "It's a small and predictable world" I added.

As we continued walking, I noticed that my ankle had stopped clicking for a while. "Must have been the scrumpy" I muttered to myself, grinning.

We walked out of Liechtenstein that evening whilst it was still light. We got to the outskirts of Bludenz and got ourselves into some sort of argument on matters that I can no longer remember. Sam and I argued very rarely during the six weeks that we had together that summer but on that occasion, he became so exasperated with me that he actually walked off as if he was intending to leave me and go ahead alone.

The road we were on was still a comparatively quiet country road even though we were not far from Bludenz. It was getting darker, and we had had a long day during which we had achieved our first foreign 'binge' and had walked across a whole country. I decided that that would be a good place to bed down; a grassy bank wide enough to choose a spot far enough from the road for comfort. Sam was still well within earshot.

"I'm going to bed-down just here Sam. It's a nice warm night, the stars are coming out and they will make a beautiful eiderdown under which to sleep."

I really meant that. I have had many opportunities to sleep under the stars and it is an experience that just cannot be over-rated. I certainly recommend it, but I shouted to Sam just to give him some bearings as to where I was if he wanted to get back to me. We had had an argument, but he was my friend, and I was just arrogant enough to realise that, under the circumstances in which we were travelling, he would have been better off with me than not.

Happily, for both of us Sam made his way back to where I was trying to conjure up some tea with a simple meth stove that we had brought with us; somewhat messy and odorous but those were days in which the luxury of 'camping gaz' had not introduced itself to me. We sat for a while chatting about the pros and cons of the holiday that far. I was pleasantly surprised that, on the whole, Sam gave the trip the thumbs up. He did miss his beloved motorbike but admitted that we had met some really interesting people on our journey that far. We enjoyed our cuppa and spoke nothing of our earlier disagreement. It was all in the past, which is just as it should be.

It was a beautiful night during which I lay awake for an hour or so just drinking in the beauty and majesty of it all. There was very little light pollution and so the sky was clear, and the stars were clear and bright. I actually saw a couple of shooting stars which my Dad, albeit a non-believer would tell me stories about these being regarded by some people as messages from the Gods, they are indeed for they add to the beauty and interest of the sky for anyone who might take the time to simply lay down and look skywards. Are they omens of bad luck, good luck, bad weather, good weather and are they are not stars at all? Whatever the case may be, just layback one cloudless night, look up at the sky ask yourself if you've ever seen a sight more beautiful! Whatever they are I say to the heavens; please don't turn them off; and I am just like my Dad, an absolute non-believer.

We did get some sleep that night. I cannot speak for Sammy, but I lay awake for an hour or more simply drinking in the night and its wonderful canopy. We were woken with a real shock though at about 6am with the racket and rumble of a train passing by not more than ten feet from below OUR feet. We had parked ourselves for the night on a grassy embankment just above a train line. It could well have been a route from Vaduz to Bludenz for all I know but it was a real close and early alarm call that's for sure. We tried to lay there for a while longer, but it didn't work.

"C'mon!" Sammy groaned in my direction. Let's go and find a café where we can have a bit of a wash and a bite to eat before trying to get ourselves into Yugoslavia." He paused, looking at me and grinning.

"That is still the object of this exercise is it not?" "You bet! I shouted - Ljubljana by tomorrow morning!"

Bludenz to Graz to Ljubljana to Novo Mesto

 The walk into Bludenz did not take long but there was little traffic on the roads, and we were not actually looking for a lift, but our luck ran true to form. We had hardly got our rucksacks onto our backs when a man driving a small green van stopped and waived at us. He wound the window down and shouted; "Bludenz?" I gave him the international thumbs-up sign and there it was, our ride into Bludenz. We had decided that we would probably walk in, but the distance was more than I had anticipated. It was a good ten miles and so would have taken a couple of hours or so out of our day.

The driver who had so kindly given that unsort lift was an elderly man with a very strong local accent which turned my struggle into the complexities of German language into a real battle with reality. We did achieve the management of the linguistic struggle between my weak knowledge and his apparent lack of hearing with some good humour. I was able to convey the understanding that we were intending to continue hitching to Graz after we'd had some breakfast. I did manage to answer some of his questions about us and where we were going and so on. He did moreover express some surprise that our destination was Yugoslavia, but we didn't have time to go into any details about that. It may have been that he was surprised that we were leaving Austria. I would not blame him if that were so.

I have been through Austria and part of Austria twice in my life but have never stayed there. I just cannot explain why not. It is just such an eye wateringly beautiful place. The trouble is that there are too many corners of this world that are either too lovely or too interesting to miss or where there are friends of family that you simply cannot visit them all and spend a normal life with the normal amount of money that may come to you during it.

Our unintended friend dropped us off in Bludenz but about three quarters of the way through. As far as I could gather, he was intending to visit his daughter who lived nearby. We thanked him and he wished us well during which exchanges I was thereby back fully into familiar Teutonic territory.

A short walk brought us to a café, and we sat down and began to interpret the breakfast menu. I seem to remember that Sam was for coffee, and I preferred tea and that was the simple part. I did not want a cooked breakfast as we had had an enormous meal the previous day which had left me somewhat bloated.

I then chose what is called a 'Mehlspeise' which I discovered is simply the German for 'sweet' breakfast. With my tea I chose some home baked rolls called Kaisersemmel with butter. I added a croissant for luck together with both strawberry jam and honey. I had given in to Sam's insistence that I was not allowed to take with me a pot of either marmite or Bovril.

Sam vexed me by insisting that he felt like a cooked breakfast thus highlighting my language deficiencies in that part of Europe once again. These were days after all when not everyone in Europe spoke English. It is one of my greater sorrows that so many of them do these days. Nonetheless we had a pleasant breakfast which cost much less than I had anticipated. This was welcome because we did not have a fortune with us although I was keeping secret for the time being the 20 mark note that Mr Abramsky had given me just before he left. I was keeping that for emergencies and necessary purchases that might occur towards the end of our holiday. I stuck it away in a pocket in my rucksack where it became a forgotten item at first and then an embarrassing one later in the holiday.

During the meal we took turns to go to the toilet for a bit of a wash and brush up; as well as what else might be necessary of course. The toilet arrangement were more than adequate I have to say; very much better than one might have expected in a similar establishment in England in those days.

We then set about the task of hitching across Austria to Graz where we needed to catch a train to Ljubljana in Slovenia, and which is both the capital and largest city of Slovenia. It has been the cultural, educational, economic, political, and administrative centre of what was then a simple province of Yugoslavia under Marshal Tito.

I remember little of the journey across Austria other than the place is so beautiful that I made a hundred self-promises on the way that one day I would spend some time there for its own sake. Already discussed as a promise as yet unfulfilled…

We arrived in Graz just in time to catch the last train to cross that border that night but one that went direct to Ljubljana. Our final car owner, one of four or five to take us the whole way across the length of Austria that day dropped us off right by the railway station. She did so because she felt that the departure of the last train was not far off. She was good enough to save us the best part of a day by getting us to the station on time for that last train of the day. She was, by the way, the sole lady driver to give us a lift in the whole of our travels across Europe. That was quite an ask, in reality in those days moreover; for a woman to give two scruffy male hitchhikers a lift.

It took only a few minutes to buy our tickets, the cheapest possible of course and returns so that we would not have the embarrassment of not having the fare back across the border. I still hadn't mentioned the twenty mark note to Sam.

The journey time from Graz to Ljubljana is just over three hours these days a few minutes more if a change is needed. Yugoslavia was still a communist country at the time of which I am writing even though much less indoctrinated than the others because of Tito's independent spirit. It still meant that the border inspection was by both an Austrian team followed a few minutes later by an inspection force of young soldiers, mostly conscripts. These inspections did not take up much time as it goes and were also very good natured to us on both sides as the young hikers that we were. Our main gripe was that they woke us up during what had promised to be a near three-and-a-half-hour train ride. Not too happy about that but very happy to say we'd made it into Jugoslavia. Notice that I have changed the spelling now that we're in the country!

We arrived in Ljubljana at about 3 am. It was dark of course. One of the station staff somehow recognised us as English; damned annoying that, even in the dark. He was useful though…

"Youth hostel down that way." My eyes followed his finger towards a large dark building about fifty yards across the road from the station entrance.

"Reception open all night." Useful info again…

That had been our immediate worry, where to get a bit more kip somewhere organised, in a city.

The entrance to the hostel did seem somewhat drab and forbidding when we first saw it through quite dim public lighting in the street outside. Sam rang the bell; and I mean he rang it; it was an actual bell with a short rope to swing so as to strike the clanger onto the bell sides. It made a bit of a racket in that public street. No matter though; it did the trick for shortly afterwards a young chap, about our age answered the door and smiled a wan smile through his early morning tiredness.

"English?" He asked at once. Even more aggravating that; instantaneous recognition even at that ungodly time of the morning and about 1000 miles from Blighty.

"Yes." I answered wearily. "How on earth did you know?"

"Well actually I didn't know. That why I asked." His English wasn't perfect, but it was pretty good and of course he was quite right. He had asked. It had been too long a night to argue the toss, however. I showed him my passport.

"Beds for two please."

"No beds for two." He grinned hugely. "Bed for twelve only. Come, I show."

And again, he was quite right. The 'bedroom' was on the ground floor but that was its only advantage. It was a long room about twenty feet or so long and fifteen or so feet wide. Along each of the long side of the room was a bed, a long bed, a very long bed.

"There," He smiled. A very smiley man this one! "Beds for twelve." Luckily the spaces were not all taken so the space on each of these communal beds was not as cramped as it could have been. I sighed, there was no good arguing, it was what it was, and it was far too late to go looking elsewhere. I threw my rucksack at the 'pillow' end of the bed close to the wall and took my place as about the sixth person in a twelve-person bed. Sam became number seven very soon after me. We slept well until the noise of the hostel morning woke us up.

Sam did not look his best when we began to gather ourselves together in the morning amidst all the clanging, clattering and loud talking.

"I hope I don't look as rough as you." I said to Sam. "Piss off!" was my reward for that.

"I don't suppose there's any breakfast." Opined my friend. Indeed, though there was. We followed our noses and the crowd into what was a quite respectable dining room and managed a very decent breakfast. There were washrooms but there was also a very inviting open air swimming pool with showers sited so that you could shower before and after your swim. It was a lovely morning, so we decided to have a shower and then a morning swim and then another shower. All in all, it was a good end to what had been a tiring and uncomfortable night. The best part came when we went to pay because albeit that the beds were not up to much the whole deal had cost us not much more than frumpence! That's not a bad price in any language.

The guy at the desk gave us the necessary Griff regarding buses to Novo Mesto. It was a journey of precisely 45 minutes during which we had some quiet minutes to gather our thoughts and realise that we had finally arrived at our destination. Suddenly Sam made as if to punch me.

"Well, you bugger, I know why you've come here but why the hell am I here?" He chuckled as if he had only just thought of a funny joke.

"Sam this is a new country. Not many Brits have been here yet. Marian is just a pen friend and I think that she has an interesting family. It's new stuff, so enjoy!" And thus, we arrived in Novo Mesto. It was close to midday by that time.

I had no idea where Marian's house was, but I did have the address of course. I picked on a woman who had just got of the same bus as we had. I was about to excuse myself by saying good morning in Slovenian. But wasn't too sure of the pronunciation after three years. I remembered that most adults spoke German because of the war. So once more I dug some of my first-year German course out of the bottom drawer.

"Gute Morgen gnädige Frau. Kennen Sie diese Adresse?"

"Good morning, madam. Do you know this address?"

"Guten Morgen junger Mann. Bist du Deutscher?"

"Good morning young man. Are you German?"

"Nein, Ma'am, Englisch."

"No, Ma'am, English".

She smiled and asked me in perfect English.

" Why didn't you ask me in English?"

I grunted an apology along the lines that I hadn't expected such good English just off the bus.

"Well now you know!" She took my piece of paper and squinted a bit clearly trying to decipher my 'beautiful' handwriting.

"Ah yes, I think I've got it now - Just go down there to the corner, yes that's it opposite the bend in the river. You'll see a path going up the hill to a cottage next to a quite large and elderly barn. That's it, about five minute's walking."

"You're English yourself, aren't you?" My truly agile brain had kicked in at last.

"Yes, I've lived here since right after the war. There's not many of us here in this town although it's a nice place. Are you staying long?"

"Not sure really. Here to meet friends . Four weeks tops!"

"May see you again? By the way, Tito's visiting in a couple of weeks, big parade, and all that. Be there!"

She smiled again and waived over her shoulder as she walked away in the opposite direction to that that she had directed us. "Bit of luck that." I grinned to Sam. "One of the few English people in the town, off of the same bus! How about that?"

Chapter Sixteen.

Novo Mesto

The name of the place, Novo Mesto, translates easily into both English as a language and English as a culture. Purely and simply, it means New Place. At the time that Sam and I arrived there many New Towns were being constructed or envisaged in England; Harlow New Town for one. We meet Marian and her family. Her Dad greeted us half-way up the path to the house from the road. He was not a big man but one whose stature rose the more you knew about him and of him.

The family and Background

We discovered that his was a both an amazing as well as a truly interesting family and, in its cohesion, and history a remarkable example of family unity to remember for me. Its formation, structure and cohesion were direct results from the onerous and despicable Nazi application of the arrogant and cruel policy of 'Lebensraum' during the recent war.

In Nazi ideology, Lebensraum meant the expansion of Germany to the east in search of a unity between the German Volk and the land (the Nazi concept of Blood and Soil). The Nazi-modified theory of Lebensraum became Germany's foreign policy during the Third Reich. It was a cruel policy presumptuous of self-importance above the needs of others.

At the beginning of the war Lia the mother together with her baby Marian was deported from the beauty of her native Slovenia to a concentration camp somewhere in Poland or Hungary, along with many others of the region for the sole reason that it was a beautiful place and that the Germans wanted it for themselves. Marian's natural father was deported into slave labour in one of the Nazi 'work' camps in Eastern Europe. He was never seen again nor did any records indicate his final fate.

Marian was therefore deported as a baby, together with her mother, into the extreme world of Nazi ideology and suffered many traumas accordingly. It was one of life's inexplicable eventualities that Lia survived the war with both Marian still alive as well as Sofia, Marian's younger sister who was born in the camp as a result of the frequent rapes that Lia suffered, and which ended in that one pregnancy. One can only suspect that she experienced just the one pregnancy because her health had deteriorated so much during her incarceration. Again, the fact that all three survived was one of those few but welcome wartime mysteries that one encounters from time to time.

It is probable that Lia engineered the survival of herself and two children by using the fact that she was a handsome woman whose company was sought by German officers and through which she also obtained some necessary additional food to the very meagre rations that she was allowed. She apparently received some extras in consideration of the facts that she was not a political prisoner or someone who had been accused of activities against the Reich. She was merely one of the 'sub-humans' who had been re-located in the pursuit of 'Lebensraum'.

I found these conundrums interesting at the time but was only nineteen and a young man as well as a stranger to boot. I did not feel confident enough to delve any further into the details at that time although I do regret that failure now. You see, I feel that a remarkable story is there to be written about this one family and its experiences during that evil period in the history of Europe.

The girls had both suffered traumas because of the vicissitudes of their early lives; neither Marian nor Sofia could sit comfortably on grass. When they were first liberated, they were terrified of the stuff. The reason for this was that there was no grass in the camp; anything green that manage to grow was quickly picked and eaten.

Dogs of any size or breed were objects of absolute terror for both girls even at the time that Sam and I came to meet them. Dogs, in the camp, were not pets in the way that they usually are in our comfortable lives these days. They were tools of terror used by the camp guards to control the poor defenceless inmates. They had both witnessed as children the terrifying scenes of an inmate being 'chastised' for very minor offenses by guards who, often for the pleasure it gave them, would set their dogs on the poor devil.

Finally, I remember that they were not comfortable around small animals either. This seemed to be a continuance of the 'dog' trauma; rats, mice even cats and rabbits all came firmly into this general category.

The father, Lando, was not a Slav at all. He was an Italian who had rebelled against the regime of IL Duce [The Leader] in other words; Benito Mussolini; who had allied himself to Adolf Hitler during World War II, relying on the German dictator to prop up his leadership. Mussolini was executed by firing squad shortly after the German surrender in Italy in 1945.

Lando was no fascist and had made his way to Jugoslavia where he allied himself to Marshall Tito for the period of the war. For those activities he was something of a local hero and even used that status to his own advantage from time to time. More of that in a while!

After the cessation of war there came a long period of very uncomfortable peace. Millions of people were on the move in and around in Europe. Most of them were trying to get back to the life and the homeland they remembered. Others were trying to move to places they preferred to be in and hoped for better things to come. Our aforementioned Mr. Abramsky was a very successful one of those.

Many of the Jewish population, much reduced by mass murder at the hands of the German Nazis and their sympathisers, were desperately trying to find some still living relative to offer them home or help; others were trying to get out of Europe to the USA or to Palestine which, in 1948 declared independence as the New State of Israel after a majority vote in the U.N.

On his way back to Italy Lando making his way home from the northern part of Slovenia came upon little boy of about five years of age. The boy was in a bad way, hungry and dirty and grieving for his lost family. He was now abandoned and homeless. Lando adopted the boy at that moment. There was no court involved, no judges or other officials of any sort. He just took the boy under his wing. The world was totally unconscious of that adoption just as it was unconscious of each of those individuals moving en-mass around the continent at that time. Chaos reigned!

The boy spoke Slovenian and so Lando, who had fought underTito for some four years, was able to communicate with him. As far as he could understand and reconstruct the sad tale the child's family had all been killed by a direct rogue bomb hit on their home. He had been playing outside the home with friends because there had been no warning of a bombing raid in the area. Lando searched for a while for some family member who might be able to take the boy in but to no avail. They were times of chaos everywhere there seemed no option but to keep Jurij with him, which he did right willingly.

Lando and Jurij continued on foot through Slovenia. They stopped for a few nights rest in a town called Novo Mesto [New Place] Lando liked the sound of the name although many years later he discovered through his then children now at school that the New Place was in fact, founded somewhere around 1365.

Lando and Jurij crossed paths whilst in Novo Mesto with a woman and two young children. These three were Lia, Sofia, and Marian. He was attracted to Lia, and she responded to a kindness from this man that she had not experienced for years. They met together and stayed together in Novo Mesto and eventually acquired the house on the hill with the barn next door, which is the home where Sam and I came to see them. Vita was the young daughter of about three years of age and who was a result of their union. Thus, Lando was the father of just one of the four children but very clearly the Dad of all of them.

Lando's full Italian name had been Lando de Luca, but he felt that that suited only him out of the whole family group He consulted with Lia, and they decided that their family name would be Praha [the h pronounced like the (ch) in Loch]. Praha is the Slovene name for Prague the capitol of what is now the Czech Republic. Czechoslovakia had been the first friendly country that Lia had encountered after being released from the camp.

I realise that what I have written here is but a bare glimpse into the history of this remarkable family. The information here is a result of simple conversations that I had with those members of the family who spoke English. They were not statements taken under oath nor were they dedicated research. The two principals, Lando and Lia, spoke no English. Jurij spoke very little English when we first met him, but he was a decidedly remarkable fellow. He was like the amiable uncle that we all had in those days where every family had a piano. He was that guy who could walk into the room and sit down at the piano and play any tune that he had ever heard without any music. I had one of those, my uncle Les. He could do just that.

Jurij could not play the piano, but he had an equivalent talent. Language was his piano! He already spoke several languages; Slovenian, Russian and German and by the time we two left to go home he spoke very decent English simply by listening to Sam and I and our conversations with Marian and Sofia. I mentally took my hat off to that young man although he had given me some very pointed stares when we first met. He clearly did not trust the stranger in the midst of his family. Mind you, he had had a whole lifetime of reasons to mistrust, I understood that even as a brash nineteen-year-old.

There was some initial confusion and misunderstanding at our arrival. Marian had only told her family of our intended visit a couple of days earlier and they knew nothing of our intentions. That was in-line in fact, with our own lack of planning as to the time we were likely to be spending in Novo Mesto. The original plan, the one we had discussed with our parents had been for a two-week holiday in Europe with the main element to be spent in Slovenia. We had in fact enjoyed the trip down, much to Sam's surprise, that we had taken five fays to get to Novo Mesto and not really noticed the time. We now had to make decisions both because the Praha family needed to know and so did our own families if we intended to stay longer as seemed likely.

At this point I must remind any reader that this was 1958. There were no mobile phones and very few domestic phones in family homes in England. My Mum and Dad had one but it was a party line shared with our neighbour and they had to wait six months to get that. The Prahas laughed at the idea that they might have a house phone.

The Usual system for making international calls whilst on holiday in those days and not staying in a hotel was to use a public telephone kiosk but not as a payphone system. There would be a range of kiosks, say six or more, all organised by an attendant who would dial up for you and give you a time that you would be able to receive your call; that might be quite quickly, or it could be longer even an hour or so. None of the family knew of such a system operating in Novo Mesto so I took the lazy route and decided to send a series of postcards to let my parents know what was happening. I decided to begin straight away and so took a stroll with Sam and the two older sisters to a local shop about a quarter mile away to buy both cards and stamps. The girls provided the language although it turned out that the lady in the shop had enough English to deal with the transactions. I began as I intended to continue. I wrote out a quick card and posted it there and then. Walking back to the house I was full of myself and the care and attention that I had shown for my parents' feelings. My Mum's reaction to my care and concern for her feelings will be revealed at the end of this chapter.

We returned to the house when it suddenly hit me that we had no idea how to address Marian's parents. We asked the girls who asked their Mum and Dad who in their turn were somewhat embarrassed at the question. I suppose that they had only met us an hour or so previously and the thought had simply not occurred to them. They slowly came up with the idea that we could call them by their first names. Sam and I exchanged looks that said that we were neither of us happy with that arrangement. Then I came up with the idea that we could do as we would often do at home'

"Perhaps we could call them Aunty and Uncle? That is what we call neighbours who are not relations but who we know well?"

The idea was passed on to the Mum and Dad who immediately looked pleased as well as relieved in fact. And so, Aunty and Uncle it was, that they became Slovenian Tetka Lia, and Stric Lando or simply, Tetka and Stric most of the time. That was one sensitive issue put to bed.

Talking of bed, it soon became clear that the discussion had moved on to where we were going to sleep. It was not easy to understand the language of course but the general flow of the conversation was clearly going in that direction, and it became clear that there was a movement towards kicking Jurij out of his bed and for Sam and I to share his bed. Sam and I were well ahead of that one and were not in favour on two very strong accounts. First and foremost, we neither of us fancied sharing a barely single bed and secondly poor old Jurij was already suffering due to the sudden invasion of his home, and we did not want to pick at that wound. We had the joint story all ready and waiting; that we had always wanted to sleep in a barn like the one just a few yards away across the way.

I simply do not believe that anyone gave that story any credibility, but they would not call us liars outright and Jurij actually smiled for the first time since we arrived. I was later convinced that it was something that he had tried and knew what it was like.

We lasted about half of the night! At about 2am I felt and heard Sam moving towards the rickety step ladder that had been our modus for lifting our weary bodies up to the straw on the 'mezzanine' floor! I now know from that one experience that there are all sorts of reasons for not doing what we had briefly attempted. Firstly, straw is bloody uncomfortable when it is left to its own devices, such as not as part of a strong, a very strong canvas mattress. When it is not strictly confined in such a way it works to spear, to scratch and to dig at all the parts that you would much prefer to be left alone, thank you! In a word it is damned uncomfortable. I know that's two words, but I just don't care. Secondly, and completely without one's say so, it harbours visitors! These visitors come in a range of sizes but act as if in unison. They seek to annoy, to wake and to bite lumps of various sizes out of you. You never get to see these creatures, but they are there, and you can hear them and feel them. What you cannot do is to get rid of THEM!

We decided to escape to a much more amenable bed and so to sleep in the most beautiful bed of all, in our sleeping bags and under the stars! The Milky Way scribes a wonderfully milky arc in the sky over Slovenia from the Arctic to Rome such that it becomes the Road to Rome! And so we made the change and enjoyed every night when it didn't rain. Try it for yourself I have done it many times, in England as well as in Europe. Believe me, as I have mentioned previously, it just cannot be overrated!

Outside of the house was a small but adequate courtyard part of which was closed off as a small poultry area. Lia kept a small collection of chickens.

"Not pet chickens you see…" Lia managed a few words in English as our stay grew towards the end of the first week "No not as pets. Eggs and food."

It was when she spoke about food that my feeble teenage brain finally kicked in and reminded me that Sam and I were probably, in my mother's ethereal words.

 "You're eating the woman out of house and home Tony."

Sam and I had both been quite thoughtless about providing ourselves with money for lodgings while we were staying in Novo Mesto. After some thought when I finally got around to thinking I did the one thing that I thought might help a bit towards the extra expense we were causing. I gave her the 20 Mark Note that Mr. Abramsky had thrust in my hand as we parted from hm.

Lia, or 'aunty' as I was still calling her at that time, made pretence at refusing but I could tell by the way she looked at the note that it was going to be a big help towards our board if nothing else. Remember the passing of the years what would be regarded as a mere 20 Mark or Euro note now represented a reasonable amount of money then. In 1958 my Dad, who was thought of as earning good money, was only earning about eight pounds a week and he had just purchased our home in Winchester Road. I have no idea how the rates compared exactly but the post war Mark was growing stronger as Germany moved away from the catastrophe of the war. Wage rates in Slovenia were not high in those days and so I have always been content in my own mind that the note would have represented a reasonable substantial amount of money to 'Aunty Lia'. The one problem over that note came when 'aunty' tried to exchange it in local money.

"Need's passport!" she came back to me near to tears. Marian explained to me that the officials at the local state bank were not happy that a local woman would have been in the position to have such a thing as a foreign banknote. They were, indeed, quite suspicious until 'aunty' explained that she had receive the money from an Englishman as payment for food. Her name and address were taken as well as a direction that the Englishman in question should bring his passport to the bank so that the exchange could be done properly. Lia was quite nervous of the attitude of the bank officials. I am convinced that she would have preferred never to have been given the banknote in the first place. I made my way back to the bank immediately together with 'aunty', still very nervous but less so with me with her. I on the other hand still had the anger of Sam to deal with.

I had only told my friend about the note the day before it was given to Lia. I had stuffed it into my rucksack and had forgotten about the dammed thing until I began to ponder about us scoffing the food of a family that had such a restricted income. He was still furious with me for keeping him in the dark as he saw it. I tried to explain the facts several times to my friend, but he would have none of it! I just had to leave him alone to mellow under his own steam. I certainly had never had the intention of keeping it for myself.

I need to spend a few moments here on the potentially more serious issue that arose on me giving the money to Lia to exchange. Again, it was the thoughtlessness of youth that came once more into play. Even our own experience of the issues for our Russian friend Mendel Abramsky did not give me a warning nudge that Lia might have a problem walking into a bank in a communist country in those days with a hard-currency note.

All communist countries were in dire need of hard currency such as the Dollar or the Pound sterling and, indeed, there were many so-called "Dollar" shops in existence all over the communist world. These were shops where visitors could purchase only in a hard currency. They were though universally suspicious of any local person who might be caught in possession of such. They immediately suspected smuggling or illegal money transfers. I had put the poor woman in danger of arrest or, at least, an interview with the police. In Auntie's case though they had been happy to take her address and demand that I should go with my passport and exchange the money myself. I did so and all was forgiven. That one 20 Mark note yielded quite a welcome wad of dinars for Lia at that time though. That relieved my conscience somewhat.

The days passed and Sam cheered up and forgave me and, all in all, we were in heaven. Beyond the yard and the barn, in which we now did not sleep unless rain was imminent, there was a path that led the short distance to the main road that led through Novo Mesto. A few yards beyond the road on the other side there flowed the beautiful River Krka. In the middle of the river rose a mound of rocks, flat areas on top, suitable for both diving off and sunbathing on. {'Word' keeps muttering to me about 'verb confusion' but I don't care, you know what I mean.}

Sam and I made friends with several of the local young people, both boys and girls; young men and women we would say these days. It is quite astonishing what a huge social difference came about with the lowering of the age of majority from 21 to 18.

The river Krka was not a fast-flowing river but seemed so in comparison to the River Lea which had been my local river bathing experience during my early years. I had, of course, had quite a bit of experience in 'wild swimming'; in ponds such as the Hampstead Ponds on the heath there' in the serpentine in Hyde Park an even in the River Thames up by Richmond. More recently I've done some swimming in the River Medway and in likely rivers wherever I might be camping.

The experience of wild swimming takes some getting used to. Firstly, you have to be very careful of swimming in very deep water such as lakes formed in former quarries. Those waters may look inviting but firstly the waters therein may be of an unpleasant chemical mixture whilst secondly because the water is inordinately deep in comparison to its surface area it may take an unusually long time to warm up in what we in Britain humorously refer to as summer. Many would be wild swimmers have died through swimming in deep lakes in order to take an inviting dip on a hot summer's day. Not a good idea!

Ponds in old quarries due to the former nature and use of the place tend to be in deep pits that are sun-deprived places. The water itself will often be very deep in proportion to its surface area, again due to the nature of the former activity there. Both of these aspects lead to a very slow warming of the water such that they are often very cold and dangerous waters in which to swim. Every summer it seems that people ignore good, common-sense public warnings and die while 'having a quiet dip' an inviting-looking quarry. Don't indulge! There are better, safer places for wild swimming than old quarry sites.

Wild swimming itself can also seem to be uninviting at first, taking the plunge into water where you cannot see the bottom. In fact, it is wise not to 'take the plunge' until you are sure of what it in the water where you are. There can be all sorts of objects dangerous to would-be swimmers; tree roots and other natural objects as well as unnatural objects discarded recklessly by members of the public thoughtless of the damage or danger they may cause. It is therefore simple common sense to avoid 'the plunge' until you are sure of your waters! Take it slowly and safely and you will have fun without having to pay the cost of entrance to a crowded swimming pool.

In the river Krka there were no such concerns for us. The locals had done all the investigations needed during the many years that they had been using their lovely river. As the saying goes I 'would have given an arm' to have had a river such as the Krka 150 yards from our house in Winchester Road, Edmonton. The weather was great, the river was sound, and the company was good. The locals, many of them anyway, just seemed to like having us there; for most of the ones we came to know a bit it was because they wanted to practice their English on us. In the most part their English was of a very decent standard.

As I say, the Krka was not a fast-flowing river as I remember it but it did have a pleasant current which gave you a different experience to that of the good old River Lea which was in reality not a river at all but a canal; where it flowed through Ponders End anyway.

By the time that we began our second week Lando had insisted that we called him by his first name. Lia though seemed very content to be referred to as 'aunty', Tetka of course in Slovenian. They were both hard working people although their work was focussed on their smallholding. I believe that Lando also received something of a pension based on his wartime record in Tito's army and that Lia had been, or was, in receipt of some war compensation from the West German government based on the enforced removal from her home during the war. If I am correct in these two beliefs, I can only say that it could never have been enough, particularly in Lia's case. She had suffered very harshly as well as over a period of some three to four years and all at the hands of an evil and arrogant Nazi regime over which the current German Government was paying some financial compensation for many years. This I know from personal experience of matters within my own family. What I would say about the compensation is quite simple; it helped some people over some practical issues but could never be a vehicle with which to begin to eradicate the everlasting nightmares, self-recrimination and downright grief that befell whole nations because of those dreadful, callously delivered and murderous years.

Lando loved to fish which was something on which we two could both agree and activate. As well, then, as the swimming and sunbathing in the Krka with as many of the local young people who chose to do the same, I now had a new friend, of like mind but no common language other than some basic German which, for my part, included no specifically piscary, or angling vocabulary.

The beauty of fishing however lies in the fact that speaking is quite simply not much needed; it is in fact actively discouraged for the most part. Lando and I got on very well for these very reasons. He taught me how to catch decent sized pike and trout with a short rod and hook and line. This was equipment that would have been scorned on most rivers in the UK at the time; the fish he caught though would not!

I have not ever been pike-fishing since the time that I was in Novo Mesto fishing with Lando and so I have had to try to reflect from a temporal distance on his method and to compare it to what I have just read on Mr Google wherein lies the wisdom of the great. Lando's method was quite different. He had no commercially produced trace wires but some bits of wire from an old rattrap he had salvaged for a better use. Lando used lures for bait but nothing fancy; just strips of fish skin kept from previous catches and kept in pickle for safe keeping then thoroughly washed for use on the day.

Lando's rod was a short and rather beefy tubular rod of wood about 7feet long onto one end of which he had wound some strips of leather to make a workmanlike and comfortable handle. His line was sturdy and rescued from the cast-offs of more affluent anglers. His reel he had adapted from a child's discarded bicycle wheel. The completed contraption had the aura of being a small crane rather than a state-of-the-art fishing rod and line. Hooks and so on he had cadged over the years from angler friends and there was no finesse of a landing net. He pulled his catch as close as he could get it and whacked it with a club. As I say he was more of a crane operator than a fisherman. I was his assistant in reality because he had no reserve set-up to loan to me. Despite the 'Heath Robinson set up I have just described I have to say that Lando was not the worst fisherman 'on the block'. During the time that Sam and I were there I went fishing twice with that amiable man. He caught a good-sized Pike on each occasion. His motto.

"Just what you need"   "Genau das was du brauchst"   That seemed to be a firm principle of his and a good one; one not adhered to evidently by some of his fishing fraternity.

When we got back to the house on the first occasion, I made the mistake of asking Marian how one cooks a pike. I say a mistake because it is a lengthy process and I'd only asked to be polite.

Firstly, one had to gut and clean the fish. The head could not be thrown out for the dog, as was my first thought, because the teeth of the pike, even in death, would have killed the dog. Once cleaned and washed the pike is soaked in brine; I've just looked this on my mobile and this s a process apparently, known as brining, well! Wouldn't you just know? The fish is cut into pieces the size of fish fingers and soaked for 24-48 hours. Lia preferred the longer period as it removed the slightly 'muddy' taste of river fish.

At the end of this process the pieces are dipped in batter and fried. They looked just like fish-fingers and tasted much better. This was in the days before commercial fish-fingers ever entered our house at home. "Bloody good – Chips as well!" Lia had heard that all Londoners just loved chips with their fish, and she wasn't wrong!

 I have just read on yet another search on my ever-reliable mobile phone that the first fish fingers were made by Birds Eye in 1955 at its factory in Great Yarmouth, Norfolk and the official launch took place on 26 September that year. But my Mum didn't believe in them! Fish had to be fish shaped for her and fish and chips came from a good old-fashioned chippy, so there!

By the middle of the second week in Novo Mesto Sam and I had a conference about our prospective plans for the immediate future. We were well aware that we had already begun to exceed our proposed two-week holiday and that leaving, there and then, would take us a week over the previously allotted two weeks.

"Well then." Sam began the conversation. "My view is – in for a penny etc.! We're already in trouble even if we go back now."

Well, I thought, he's dammed right there. I could just imagine the racket that my Mum was making already. But we had sent cards; so, I consoled myself.

"When, then do you think we should leave?"

"If it's ok with Lando and Lia, we could leave it so late that we get back just before school. They won't have so much time to get on at us then."

And that's just how we agreed it. We sent off yet another batch of cards and salved our tattered consciences with that. Our two weeks planned holiday has now become an 'on the fly' decision that has morphed into and become six. Telephone kiosks and holiday cards have both been investigated and cards have proven to be by far the easier option. Judgement day was still four weeks away and we both knew that it would be a long while before circumstances would fall so as to give either of us a six-week window such as the one we were about to steal. I felt that I had got to know Lando fairly well during our fishing trips. They were only two though and our conversations were lacking any depth due to my lack of depth in German.

I came to realise that most Slovenians had fair to very good German because of the failed Nazi attempt to over-run and subdue their country. They over-ran but never subdued. In fact, the German invasion into Jugoslavia was a failure on a profit and loss basis as they did invade but they could never rest on their Laurels. The ever-present activities of Marshal Tito and his partisans meant that they had to keep some eleven full divisions in the country and all that considering that some elements in the country were strong supporters of the German cause. The fact remains that although the linguistic capacity of our fishing trips together was pretty limited, we always returned to the house laughing and seemingly joking just as if we had spent all our time in a continuous joke telling session. Even limited linguistic capacity, it seems, can go a long way; even when you're neither drunk nor angry!

My full realisation of the strength in depth that presented itself in that man of small physical stature came one morning in our third week in Novo Mesto. Lia had asked us to come into the house for a wash-up and breakfast while we were there. ·I must say that the traditional Slovenian breakfast she managed to provide in those hard times was a real pleasure to behold and to enjoy. The platter could consist of a selection from a range of home baked bread, butter, honey, milk and apples, there might also be eggs on offer, even porridge occasionally but always honey. Lia managed a couple of beehives, and both loved and prided her honey. Yes, there was always honey.

Well then to return to that particular morning there was a harsh and aggravated rat-a-tat-tat on the front door just as we were in the middle of breakfast. It seemed to me that Lando was expecting the call because I caught a look of something that I can describe as 'determined awareness' on his face as he rose to answer the door.

As soon as he reached the door the row began. Sam and I were both alarmed because one glimpse in the direction of the row gave the view of two young soldiers armed with rifles as the originators of the racket. Yes, we were alarmed, even scared at first, until I caught the look on Lia's face. She was not at all alarmed, she was grinning hugely. I looked around and everyone was smiling as if at quite an enjoyable cabaret.

A second glance towards the door provided the spectacle of Lando, tiny by comparison to the two young giants before him. He was poking them fiercely in turn, in the chest. Suddenly all became peaceful, and he beckoned his adversaries into the room. After a few moments of this robust entertainment, the depths of which Sam and I had no notion, Lando turned strode back into the room where we were all sitting. He waived the soldiers to follow him. During those few moments of quiet Marian took the opportunity to bring us up to date.

"These soldiers are visiting all houses with teenage children to tell them that they have to do public service on the new road from Ljubljana to Zagreb in Croatia. It's Tito's way of confirming the unity of Jugoslavia."

[We now know well enough how that turned out once the great man himself had passed away.] She continued:-

"They told Dad that we three all must work for a month on the Novo Mesto section of the road during our holidays this summer. They tried to tell Dad that we must report tomorrow for our month's public duty." I believe that the plan was to construct a 'unification' road eventually from Ljubljana to the southern border with Albania.

To sum up it appeared that Lando had told the two young soldiers that they could shove it. He had told them that he had served with Tito for four years, suffering the hardships of a guerrilla war for the benefit of young people just like those two and that he and the great man had become good friends and that he, Lando, would complain direct to Tito when he came to Novo Mesto for his long-awaited parade through the town; due to take place in a few days' time. He was, apparently, somewhat out of breath after that diatribe.

 As a compromise Lando had apparently finally offered his three children for just one day provided that they could be 'chaperoned' by his two guests from Britain. He had then graciously given permission for them to enter the house to meet us and to examine our credentials. I looked at Sam at which he grinned and shrugged in acquiescence.

"Well, it could be fun, and we will always be able to claim that we helped build the road from Ljubljana to Zagreb. And that is just what I am doing at this moment. I am telling the absolute truth when I write that Sam and I did just that. We spent time on our holiday to Jugoslavia helping to build the 'unifying' road from Ljubljana to Zagreb.

One item that had not been made clear at that precise moment however was that when the soldiers had exploded with indignant protest Lando had graciously compromised and had extended our participation to two days. After further bartering of our time Lando had finally agreed to three days, i.e. two nights away. At this point the two soldiers, who would never fight a fiercer opponent than the one who had just ousted them, approached us. No smiles! Just; "passports!" No pleases no thank yous. And there we had it; signed up as the chaperones to Lando's three kids although, as time was about to tell, no chaperone would ever have been needed with Jurij present.

Tito's parade through the town took place and I have to say he was greeted by the population of Novo Mesto with genuine affection. That may not have been replicated in Croatia were he to visit Zagreb? The crowd in Novo Mesto though was clearly happy to greet their leader, their Wartime Hero. Sam and I had a good view of the Great Man as he came past us and within twelve feet of where we stood. I later took great pleasure in telling my Dad, an ardent follower of the communist cause, that Tito not only travelled in an Open Car that the car was a lovely, Tan, Rolls Royce. As a socialist Tito really knew how to travel!

The very next day I happened to arrive back at the house just before lunchtime and was surprised to see Lia sitting on the wooden bench by the door of the house, a large cottage really. Lia was clearly distressed and weeping I didn't, frankly, know what to do. I was a young man, and she hardly knew me plus we had very little mutual language. Without much ado I simply walked over to the bench, sat down beside her, and put my arm around her shoulder; praying at the same tie that she would not take my action amiss. I was never sure if she was crying over times past or whether it was simply something that had happened that morning; we had no common language of course. She made no attempt to shrug my arm away and so we simply sat there for a while as Lia gradually composed herself. After a short while Jurij appeared from around the corner of the barn. He stood for a while, simply watching that strange scene of me with my arm around his mum's shoulder; then as if satisfied that nothing untoward had happened he just smiled at me and walked quietly past us into the house. A few moments later Lia placed her left hand on my right knee and used it to lever herself very slowly into a standing position. As she rose, she turned her head towards me and said "Hvala vam" at my puzzled look she added "Danke schön".by way of explanation and kissed me softly on the cheek.

A few days later we arrived at the site that had been prepared for the young conscript workers. I can remember very little about the work we undertook during the day. There were of course engineers and other experienced people in charge. We were split into gangs of ten or so at which point Jurij insisted that we five stayed together although there was very little problem over that.

Surveyors and 'chain' boys or girls marked out the dimensions and route of the future road but much of this had been done on the section that was allotted to our gang.   The earthworks are the first step that most people would recognize as part of a road construction and maintenance project on sight. The intent of this step is to provide a firm, stable foundation that the road surface will then rest on top of.

This road was being built-in Post-War Slovenia and heavy equipment was scarce and so the lifting, moving, and spreading of the hard-core foundations had to be by hand and we were there to supply the hands and muscle power. The heavy gear was to come along in its turn to make firm the base foundations of the road. It was hard work but was undertaken in a public-spirited way for the most part.

I stipulate above that it was for the most part that the work was tackled in a congenial fashion. There was, however, some real discord between some of the gangs if they came from different regions of the country. This tension existed only here and there but right next to our camp section were some members of a Croatian group who quite clearly were not content to work peacefully next to Slovenian groups. This tension almost erupted into open fighting during the first evening of our stay on the road workforce.

We had eaten what I can only say was an adequate evening meal and had taken to rest our weary bones around a campfire when some of the group began to sing Slovenian folk songs; Sam and I joining in where we could!

As far as I could tell Croatian, and Slovenian were pretty-much dialects of the same language. To me they sounded different, but they could clearly understand each other without too much trouble.

Suddenly something hit the fire causing sparks and small fire debris to scatter among the group and thereby some alarm to those who were sitting closest. One girl, I remember, we later discovered received a small but unpleasant burn on her lower leg.

Someone laughed; the sound came from the gloom beyond the fire and a small group of five or six young men appeared into the firelight. They continued to find our discomfort amusing as they spoke and apparently mocked the 'soft' Slovenians for being scared of a few sparks I got this from Jurij later. At the moment he was too busy with the matter In hand.

Jurij muttered something under his breath as he rose from his comfortable sitting position very slowly. It was a speed of rising that was so determinedly slow that it in itself indicated a considerable inner strength.

For much of his young life Jurij had lived it at its extreme raw edges. He was going to take no crap from anyone. 'Start with me buster and it's going to be really costly!' was his philosophy of life in general. He had the physical build and the mental attitude to back it up.

Sam and I both rose as Jurij responded but in truth we were only there to make up the numbers. Jurij was the main event and, as it turned out; after his one and immediate first and only action no-one wanted to take him on so we all lived to fight another day.

As Jurij rose to his full height and in one movement that completed that action he used his momentum to punch the guy nearest to him full in the face. For some twelve years later in my life I studied karate to a high level, but I have never witnessed such a blow as that ever in my life. With that one blow Jurij smashed the young man's nose and removed most of his front teeth. He was not going to smile again for a long time. He then turned fiercely towards the rest of the small group and stared them a stare that demanded:- "Well then, anyone anything more to say?" They clearly felt that discretion was the better part of valour. They scraped up their fallen comrade and we heard no more of the matter until the morning.

 Just as we were having breakfast the enquiry began but Jurij was having nothing of it. He explained, very forcibly, the event as an attack on our group and had the burn on the young girl's leg to show as evidence of the serious nature of the provocation. At that point the court of enquiry ended and, we heard later, that the offending group were sent home to whence they came.

As the days moved into weeks, we passed the time quietly at the river swimming and sunbathing and generally making friends with the local youth and improving their English. I also took a bit of a shine to little Vita. She was such a sweet kid and clearly the apple of her parents' eyes. I occasionally played with her using her set of wooden bricks or her train set. We also went for short walks along the paths between the trees and bushes above the cottage. The heavens alone know what we used for language, but it didn't seem to matter. We just got along.

One day, as we were all going down to the river to swim Vita demanded to come with us. Her mum was very clear that her answer was no, absolutely not and I could understand that. Vita became so upset that she was being left behind that finally, after the persistent pleading that only a determined three-year-old can inflict, her Mum agreed on the provision that she was in my charge, and would do as she was told because the river was a dangerous place for little girls. [translation of this to me by both of the older sisters in loud unison].

As we walked together down the hill towards the river, I suddenly felt the impact of the responsibility that had been thrust upon me by a mixture of a lack of appropriate linguistic ability and a tiny child's persistent chatter. If only her mother had known about my reputation with tiny girl's and muddy ditches, she would never have agreed to that particular care provision. Poor little Vita! I stuck to that child like a leech all the time we were anywhere near the water. It didn't seem to worry her though and she did enjoy the afternoon despite my petrified state of worry. Actually, I hope that I'm exaggerating because we all had a lovely time. Vita could swim a few strokes and so I allowed her, with me very much by her side and helping her, to make her way out to the rocks. She clearly felt 'made up' with her afternoon with the 'grown-ups'. I, on the other hand, came out in a funk-sweat that night thinking of how things could have gone badly wrong.

We did repeat the exercise once or twice more, but I always felt the weight of responsibility so heavily when I thought about the tragedies that had dogged that family that I could never relax fully. Perhaps that was just how it should have been anyway? Responsibility is not a relaxed place to be!

The time was passing so quickly but Jurij's command of English was coming on in bounds. One day after breakfast he made a proposal.

"Why don't us make trip to Gorjanci, to top?"

Gorianze – a stiff climb – hostel at the summit - those beds again!

In Slovenian Folk law there is a Magic zone in the forest of Gorjanci that became a reality for three heroes: Godfather Janez, Medo and Kroki. One day they decided to go on a trip out of town. On their way among scary forest, they meet giants, golden bird, a very evil lord who wants to rule the village people, they lost in scary desert, unfulfilled love between fairy and brave soldier hit their hearts...{If you're interested in such folk tales from this wonderfully beautiful part of the world, you'll want to pursue them further}I advise strongly a visit to the region. Stay like I did with some good friends, Sam in particular, and sleep like we did in the open air on the top of the Gorjanci Hills! You'll see the stars as you've never seen them before. The 'Road to Rome' the Milky Way as the

Slovenians would have it, hovers like a frozen arc in the sky above you and lulls you to sleep as you try to count the star groups within it. Magic is not the word!

I am no visitor guide for the region, but I could be I'll try to give it a go for the next few moments.

Gorjanci are the best known and visited mountain chain in Dolenjska. They rise above the Krško valley to their peak Trdinov. The Slovene Gorjanci are a part of ecologically integrated area that spreads out far over the Croatian border. The Gorjanci hills are an important reservoir of drinking water for the whole Novo Mesto valley as there are numerous springs on their steep hillsides. Most famous of those are the mythological Gospodična and Minutnik, other clear streams like Kobila, Pendirjevka and Klamfer had carved deep and picturesque vales into northern hillsides.

We began our hike into the Gorjanci hills the very next morning. At Jurij's advice we took only a sleeping bag, some toiletries, and a water bottle. He explained, with a wicked smile, that it was going to be a stiff climb. He did that, too, and very understandable broken English that I am not going to copy here for two reasons; firstly it's been a long time and memory fails, secondly I would not wish to be accused of mocking and that is because I had the greatest admiration for the way that that young man had achieved in four weeks a standard in speaking a foreign language which would not have been achieved in that era in four years, in and English Grammar School. In stating this I emphasise the word 'speaking'.

It was a cheerful group of five young people who began the climb. We had begun the holiday not really knowing each other. Neither Sam nor I had known about either Jurij or Sofia. I felt at one point that Sam and Sofia were becoming sweet on each other but that fizzled out and they established a friendship that remained as a pen friendship for a while after the holiday. As for Marian and I; I had gone away on that holiday with the idea that we might become boyfriend and girlfriend after a long pen-friendship but that never blossomed in that way. As for Jurij, he seemed quite antagonistic towards our arrival in his domain at first. Our open willingness to help him to gain direct access to yet another language melted his cold front big time and he learned with such enthusiasm that I envied him his obvious ability.

I use the analogy here that some people are good at music while a few show obvious signs of being geniuses. I was good at languages and could have been better if my parents had been supportive. Jurij though, in just a few weeks had shown me something else. Languages were his music and he played them like a master.

As for the other members of the family, Lando, Lia and delightful little Vita we had made friendships with all three of them; each of us' Sam and I, in different ways but we were both heading towards the end of the holiday with sincere regrets that it was heading that way.

Having diverted from our climb for those last few moments I shall now return to the severe pain that was beginning to hit the limbs of four of the five of us; the exception to this phenomenon being, of course, Jurij himself. His aggressive stance during the first evening of the Road preparation programme now showed itself in all that he did or set out to achieve. He strode up that hill just like he attacked the young man who angered him that evening. Jurij was a very impressive young man.

Just to add here that certain natural characteristics were present in the region with vast beech forests with preserved remnants of primeval forest on Ravna gora and Trdinov vrh. They are variegated by floristically significant meadows and various forest habitats, which evolved under the influence of diversified ecological conditions mostly in Kobila valley. The range is set to be protected as a regional park. I go no further than this; you'll have to visit Southern Slovenia if you want to drink in the beauty of the place for yourself. Tours in Gorjanci offer a great recreational value. There are numerous clearly identified mountain paths and two permanently supplied mountaineering houses at Gospodična and on Miklavž. I am not sure if the one we visited was either of those identified here but as we walked, or puffed our way up that small mountain, I was hoping sincerely that the sleeping arrangements had been updated. from the ones we experience in Ljubljana.

Jurij did show some compassion for us, weaker mortals, by stopping twice for short breaks. We each had water and some food. Jurij kept reminding us that both water and food had to last until the evening of the next day because there was no restaurant at the top.

"This is not Germany." He added with a huge grin. "Where food room comes on magic in all places."

That was serious information for the hungry and weary listener; it was also the English he used as far as I can remember after all this time. Not bad in my view.

After the second stop I actually began to get a second wind. I could begin to breathe properly again. Boy it felt good! As we started off for the third time, I was close to being able to keep up with our demon leader; there were still a few moany grumbles coming from the group, but they were becoming fewer minute by minute.

I would like to add here for the benefit of all travellers who are new to the job that it is much more comfortable to be able to breathe when you are walking and particularly when you are walking upwards on a small mountain. The Gorjanci group of hills and mountains are outstandingly beautiful but I was not able to begin to enjoy the scenery let alone spot some of the fauna until I began to get my second wind almost two thirds into our climb.

Jurij, of course, was not in any way beset with the curse of breathlessness; he strolled up and down slopes and inclines like there was no tomorrow! On the way he pointed out aspects of the passing scenery, as well as flora and fauna to a group that was largely only concerned with the immediate need for breath.

In my second breathing period I did begin to listen. I gathered that it was possible to see the mountain Ibex although we never did but it was exciting to live in hope and expectation. He also mentioned the brown bears that were supposed to live in 'them thar' hills' and we never did spy any of those either although he did show us some extensive claw type markings on a number of trees that he assured us were made by bears intent on keeping their claws in trim. I was not sorry at the time that we never did encounter any of those.

Golden eagles were also on the list, and we did see those. They are beautiful birds and capable of killing a wide variety of creatures from field mice and other vermin to rabbits as well as a range of birds whether on the wing or nesting, through to lambs, and so they can do both good and bad. For most people moreover the simple wonder of seeing these great and beautiful birds strutting their stuff majestically in the air above us gives us to feel that it is a privilege to have them in our lives whatever the cost-benefit balance may be.

We finally walked out of the trees which was the moment that we caught first sight of both the mountain cabin which was our night refuge and our first pair of swooping, soaring Golden Eagles.

The mountain hut looked to be a mere half mile or so away as we first spied it; well, it was about that in fact and in a straight line but what we could not see at that moment was the series of small rifts and valleys that lay between us and the cabin. We struggled for another hour to cover that short half mile. It was quite a relief to reach the door of the cabin. Inside were, first, a reasonable looking kitchen and then the schlaftzimmer with Oh Dear! Those twelve person beds again! I made an immediate decision to sleep under the stars once more. There seemed to be a good number of the bed spaces taken up already by virtue of the number of rucksacks already 'bagging' places. I could not bear the thought of another night lying awake to the beautiful cacophony of the music of another mountain hut night; with its farting, coughing sniffing talking and getting up for the loud pee moments in the tin-can arrangement in the mediocre loo. Sleeping under the stars was much the better decision. I just loved it and that night was as good as the one in Croatia those years prior. Altitude and lack of light contamination improve the 'star' experience a hundred-fold.

The two girls slept inside as usual; their fear of open grass barely allowed them to walk on it let alone sleep on it. We had barely got ourselves settled down when there was a squeal and a cry from one of the two sisters, it turned out to be Sofia who had been the source of attraction for one of the young men in the hut. Sam and I had barely registered what was going on when that same young man came flying out through the window, glass, frame and all! Jurij had acted before we realised that there was something to react to.

Jurij, it turned out was ready for action because he had picked up some vibes of conversation between three of the young Croat lads. He was spring loaded for action even before his sister had reacted to the wandering hand that had tried to creep into her part of the bed. Jurij was there on the scene before you could say "shove it." The young man had committed his crime and it had been discovered; his trial was a short one in the all-powerful Jurij tribunal and so he came out via the window plus most of its frame above me, to the right. His rucksack followed him- HARD! Jurij returned to his sleeping bag and continued chatting to us in his modest way as if nothing untoward had happened that evening. Jurij was just the sort of brother a girl needed way out there in the frontiers of the East!

The stars though were out in force that night. The 'Road to Rome' shone its path in my imagination all the way to that Great City. One thing though that I must admit as I sit here writing about that night, the one that was to be almost out final night in beautiful Slovenia that one thing that I still have in my mind is the vision of that young man flying out of the window and bringing much of it in his wake, yet I have not one inkling of what happened to him after that. We three simply lay there, as I now remember it, chatting and enjoying the beauty of the night. I am now in my eighties, and I can still in my mind's eye enjoy the feeling of freedom I achieved simply from drinking-in the night sky in a way that few of my contempories ever chose to do.

Chapter seventeen

The return Home

The morning came on which we had to leave or fear expulsion from school. I smile now that my one thought at the time was that the homecoming might even have involved expulsion from home! As we left, amidst tears all round. For my part there was the realisation that I would almost certainly never return to that beautiful place again. I did though make the personal pledge, to myself fortunately as things turned out, that I would send to Lando a decent rod and fishing equipment so that he could strut his stuff among the more affluent of the fishing 'fraternity' in Novo Mesto. I did indeed do this. I purchased a beautiful fibre glass rod, state of the art for me, as well as a good reel. I took them home where my Mum helped me to pack them neatly. Immediately I forayed out to the Post Office where it all hit the fan, Big Time!

Remember this was 1958 and we were in a 'cold war' situation with communist countries. It was possible to send the items ,but the red tape and extra cost rendered the whole enterprise an impossibility for me. Thus, even that connection with Novo Mesto was closed by forces beyond my control.

I was ,thereby forced to use the rod etc. myself!

And so we caught the bus to take our way back to Ljubljana and the train from there to Graz. I had travelled to Slovenia to meet a pen friend who I felt might become a permanent but distant for a while girlfriend. What had happened however was that I had fallen in love with the story of a family. It was a family forged through war. I had thought that I had been forged in war which I had but mine was a much different war. There were some dangers some deprivations, but they were distant. I had felt the strength in depth of this tiny family during the four weeks or so that Sam and I had been with them.

I thought first of Lia such a strong person; she had been abused and ill-treated by the most accomplished ill-treating-ist bastards in history. Through thick and very thin she had clung to her two girls through that long and dark nightmare, and she had emerged fighting and determined not to let it ruin her life. I have no idea what was going through her mind that afternoon that I discovered her weeping on the bench by the back door. We had no common language to help us to communicate but she did understand the friendship I offered when I put my arm round her shoulder and gave her a hug. The kiss on the cheek she gave me meant much to me and I hope that my arm around her shoulder meant something to her.

I realise that I have written little about either Marian or Sofia her sister and I am somewhat ashamed of that but, you see, I fell, not in love with a girl but with the story of her family the main actors in which were Lia, Lando and Jurij. Theirs is a general story, many varieties of which have been written about in the annals of the Second World War but for me their story was one that I lived with for four weeks of my young life. I cherish those weeks, not just for my entry into their story but for that episode in my own. I cherish the whole six weeks in addition to the other remarkable times of pure freedom I had spent in my life. Travel doesn't simply broaden the mind; much more importantly it lightens the soul. I don't care who disagrees; I've done it and I'm still doing it and I know!

I think of Lando and Jurij often and the accident of fate that brought them together as well as the strong bond that developed between them and then with Lia and the girls. I am glad that I met them and have mentally wished them well and good health over the years. As for little Vita she was the one that I missed the most but felt that she probably stood the best chance of making a good long life because she had none of the hang-ups that the others had due to their awful experiences. She had a beautiful life with lovely people all of whom loved her dearly. One hopes that that lovely and loving little girl has had a good life to where her current age of early sixties would have been and to many years thereafter. Jugoslavia however has had a very violent history since the death of Marshal Tito in 1980. I provide a synopsis in the following three paragraphs. The full history has delivered many volumes of script violence, so called 'ethnic cleansing' but this is not the place in which to try to encapsulate all that.

Jugoslavia was a state concept among the South Slavic intelligentsia and later popular masses from as far back as the 19th to early 20th centuries and even before that. Its realization finally came to pass after the 1918 collapse of Austria-Hungary at the end of World War I and in the form of the Kingdom of Serbs, Croats and Slovenes. However, the kingdom was better known colloquially as Jugoslavia (or similar variants); in 1929 it was formally renamed the "Kingdom of Yugoslavia".

The former Yugoslavia was a Socialist state that was delicately created after the cruel and arrogant German occupation in World War II. In a federation of six republics, it brought together Serbs, Croats, Bosnian Muslims, Albanians, Slovenes and others under a comparatively relaxed communist regime. Tensions between these groups were successfully suppressed under the strength of leadership of President Tito.

After Tito's death in 1980, tensions re-emerged. Calls for more autonomy within Yugoslavia by nationalist groups led in 1991 to declarations of independence in Croatia and Slovenia. The Serb-dominated Yugoslav army lashed out, first in Slovenia and then in Croatia. Thousands were killed in the latter conflict which was paused in 1992 under a UN-monitored ceasefire. That is as far as I intend to precis the 19th to 20th century tragic history of the former Jugoslavia.

Sam and I left Novo Mesto with heavy hearts. That was mainly of course because we had had such an interesting, terrific, time there. In honesty though I have to admit that there was also a tinge of apprehension regarding the reception that was about to descend upon us back home. There was no avoiding that and so we made jokes about how it might develop; ancient terms like 'hissy fit' and 'carroty fit' breathed life from somewhere. As I write I can understand 'hissy fit' to an extent but 'carroty fit' leaves me baffled. It was one of my Nan's sayings and I know the message that it conveys but what is it about carrots that connect in any way to fits? Language can be such a beautiful mystery at times.

We arrived back in Graz by train with no problems and proceeded to hitch lifts back towards home. I was particularly keen not to enter German territory and so we missed out on several lifts much to Sam's clear annoyance. I understood his feelings but at that stage in my life I was not prepared to cross Germany by hitching lifts. Graz is situated so close to Germany that much of the motorised traffic was heading in that direction. We actually lost a whole day through my total refusal to change my mind. We slept on a grass verge by the side of the road that night

The next morning, we managed to get a quick wash and brush up in a rather dirty and very unpalatable public loo sited in a lay-by by the side of the road. We decided to use the one remaining change of clothes; washed for use by Lia the day before we left, on the morning of a day that looked as if it might be our last one on the road. It had occurred to each of us that our appearance and standard of hygiene had both suffered considerably during our extended periods on the road.

We had decided to try to get to the French border town of Mulhouse from where we had discovered where might well be a direct train to Calais. From Graz we made it in two lucky hitches.

We walked and hitched for nearly two hours. Irritation and desperation began to bite deep into our senses of humour after the first hour. The overhanging shadow of our forthcoming homecoming didn't help much either. We were avoiding talking about it, but it was there well enough and something that we would be facing the next day or the day after at the very least.

A car came along at last and actually stopped as if to give us a lift. When he heard that we were aiming for Mulhouse in France the driver roared out laughing and choked as he muttered something about Verdammt dumme Engländer and drove off still choking enough to swerve severely to the left across the road before quickly regaining control. Another half hour passed, and another car stopped, and we ran forward much more in hope than expectation, but our luck had returned.

The driver was a young Austrian music student about mid-to-late- twenties and driving a lovely French Citroen Traction Avant 6 cylinder in black of course, that looked to be only about two years old. It was just like the one you see in the old Maigret films nowadays. He laughed out loud when we mentioned Mulhouse and my heart sank; thinking that we might be in for a disappointment as before, but no, his name was Mark, and he gave us the good news that we were going back to Zurich again but not this time through Liechtenstein apparently. Whatever! Zurich would do us fine. We would be much closer to Mulhouse that's for sure! In spite of stopping for an hour and a half for lunch we were in Zurich by about 8pm. We ate more sparsely on that occasion than sometimes we had.

Mark was a musician, and the Citroen was his father's car. He made no offer to pay for food for two scruffy Englishmen and no more he should!

We realised that we were only about two hours from Mulhouse when Mark dropped us off by a main road to the north of Zurich. We decided we would try to push on and go the last leg that night. Resting in Mulhouse seemed a more certain plan if we were to get home before the forthcoming weekend. Another hour or so of hitching during which we had to turn down two offers of lifts and finally we caught a ride direct to France and the target town of Mulhouse. We were left, after the lift, with only about a half hour walk to the station where we managed to get some kip in the main waiting room as well as awash and brush up both there and then as well as in the morning.

That time spent restfully and quietly in the station waiting room proved useful because we were able to get ourselves into a more wholesome state prior to boarding the train. We each of us had spare shirt and underpants. There were washing facilities plus we had both had enough experience by that time of 'squat-upon' loos to be able to accomplish even that part of the toiletry arrangements with aplomb. No probs there, not even wet feet!

I cannot remember the train-time, but it must have been fairly early because we had very little time, after purchasing our train tickets to Calais we needed to scrape together enough cash to purchase a bite to eat for on the train. We rushed in and out of a little corner shop and emerged with our twin trophies, all that we could afford; a large fresh French bread [un pain] and a small tin of fish. We boarded the train with these two items clutched closely to our bosoms. There was a major disappointment on the train where, upon opening the tin of fish we discovered that they were anchovies and tasted horribly salty. We had been so much in a rush in the shop and the tin was remarkably similar to the tins of sardines that Mum often bought that I hadn't bothered to actually read the tin.

The journey from Mulhouse to Calais we knew was going to take about ten hours and so we realised that the bit of food we had was going to have to last us until we arrived home the next morning. It is true that the journey time can be much shorter these days but in those days travel across Europe could be much slower. We had our boat cum train tickets already purchased on a period return basis from Calais through to Lower Edmonton Train Station. My Dad had stipulated that, as a condition of our ever leaving the country.

As it turned out though, that ten hour or so journey proved to be a one final hurrah for me on the holiday front. Minutes after we took our places in the compartment a young woman with two children, one a baby tried to struggle in together with a suitcase. It was one of those compartment types that you don't see these days; two rows of four seats facing each other with a corridor running along the train on one side of a set of four or five such compartments. Each compartment had an entry door to and from the platform at the opposite end of the compartment to the corridor. The young woman was trying to climb up from the platform with her load some of which was apparently struggling to impede all of her efforts. I intervened as soon as my mind caught up with the situation;"

« Puis-je vous aider Madame ? »

"May I help you Madam?"

With that I grabbed the struggling five-year-old and whisked him upwards. He struggled even harder, but I was bigger than him, so he came upwards anyway. Sam by that time was tackling the suitcase and I offered my hand to help the woman by taking the baby. She clearly wanted to reject that one but ever willing to lie just a bit in the pursuit of gallantry; I lied.

« Tout va bien Madame, je suis douée avec les bébés. »

"It's alright ma'am, I'm good with babies."

That was a complete expansion of the truth. I had, once or twice in my life been allowed to hold a baby other than my little sister and then only under the strictest supervision. The very idea if me being allowed to swing one up from a station platform under the eyes of its terrified mother would have horrified my erstwhile baby hoist controllers. Nonetheless the baby arrived safely and, unlike big brother, with something akin to a giggle. Mum arrived under her own steam but flustered just a few moments later.

« Un grand merci messieurs. Je vois que mes bébés sont en sécurité. »

"Many thanks, messieurs. I see that my babies are safe."

« Les remerciements ne sont pas nécessaires madame. L'aîné s'est un peu battu mais je crois qu'il m'a pardonné maintenant. »

"Thanks, are not needed Madame. The older one put up a bit of a fight, but I think he's forgiven me now."

We all settled down with the older child still glaring at me very suspiciously. I couldn't really blame him either.

« Bonjour mon jeune homme. Comment tu t'appelles-toi ? »

« Je m'appelle Jean-Luc monsieur. »

The Journey from Mulhouse to Calais took close to ten hours. The whole journey was undertaken in French except for short conversations between Sam and me. For that reason, I am hereby asking any reader to assume that all such conversations were conducted as I have just outlined.

I must admit that the prospect filled me with real contentment. It meant for me a total distraction for the period of the doom and gloom that I just knew was about to descend on me as soon as I arrived home. That train journey and using French was a welcome extension to the holiday.

« D'accord Jean-Luc ; Quel est le livre que tu tiens en main là-bas ? »

"What is the book you are holding in your hand there?"

He held the book towards me so that I could read the title. 'Les aventures d'Alice au pays de merveilles.'

"Oh yes", I said; "I know that book very well. Every English child knows that story."

"Do you know the story yet?"

"Well, yes, he replied, [in French] my dad has read it to me before, but I like it so much and this book has lots of pictures. It's a good story…I really like it."

I began to tell the story reading in French to my newfound friend and with the permission of his mother as he sat beside me on the bench seat of the carriage. He looked up at me with that 'well get on with it look of impatience to hear the story that they already know and love.' I begin here with a brief beginning in both French and English.

« Il avait une fois il y a très longtemps une fille qui s'appelait Alice, un après-midi ensoleillé, la petite Alice s'ennuyait, assise dans l'herbe... Quand un Lapin Blanc passe en marmonnant devant elle, Alice le poursuit jusque dans son terrier. Elle suivait le lapin vers le trou…mais le lapin est disparu…Un instant plus tard elle y pénétrée à son tour, sans se demander une seule fois comment diable elle pourait bien y sortir. Sa chute l'entraîne au centre de la Terre, où elle fait d'étranges rencontres : un Chat qui sourit, un Loir qui boit du thé, et une horrible Reine bien décidée à couper la tête de tout le monde ».

"Once upon a time a long, long time ago there was a little girl called Alice. One sunny afternoon little Alice was bored, sitting in the grass ... When a White Rabbit passes by muttering in front of her, Alice follows him to the burrow, Alice pursues him to his burrow. An instant later she entered it in her turn, without once asking herself how the devil she could get out. Her fall takes her to the centre of the Earth, where she makes strange encounters: a Cat who smiles, a Dormouse who drinks tea, and a horrible Queen determined to cut off everyone's heads."

After this beginning to remind Jean-Luc of the beginning of the story I began to ask him questions about the wildly interesting story written by Lewis Carroll aka Charles Dodgson.

"Well Jean-L who is your favourite character from the story of Alice? " And that's how we passed a lot of the time between Mulhouse and Calais. I read the chapters one at a time whilst discussing the characters with him so that he could put the whole thing into context by the time we had finished. There was a lot of headshaking and laughter on the way.

In the meantime, Sam had fallen asleep in the corner of the carriage with the baby also asleep in his arms. The Mother was quite amused that her charges seemed to have been 'abducted' in this way. After a while she even asked me if we would mind the children for a few minutes while she 'took a break'. She gave Sam and the baby a worried look.

"Don't worry!" I said. "I've got my eye on him. The baby won't fall."

Nonetheless she could not help giving one last nervous look back over her shoulder as she passed into the corridor on her mission. I, in my turn, felt 'made up' that she trusted us in that way but, on the other hand she would have needed to make at least one trip of that type on that journey. How would that have been accomplished without someone's help?

She returned after a longer period away than I had thought, then I saw why; in her hand she held two packages of food. Two baguettes in each, a croissant together with a small bottle of a fruit syrup drink. She handed one packet to me and put the other one down near Sam and the baby. She had clearly understood some English because earlier in the trip we had spoken in somewhat humorous terms about our lack of both food and money and the diet that we would be on until we got home tomorrow. Maybe even long after that if my Mum's mood could be judged accurately ahead of time.

I thanked her profusely and commented on her obvious understanding of English. She replied, for the first time in English that was quite good but simply lacked a touch of confidence. She made it clear that she had brothers and that when young men were talking about being hungry the language was universal!

I managed to restrain from attacking my food until Sam came back from his slumbers with his newfound friend. He was quite surprised that he had gone to sleep with the little one; even more so that his Mum allowed it and moreover that she had actually left her kids with us to make her 'corridor' trip. Nonetheless he was 'up for' having a bite there and then. We did agree to leave some for later though. The morning, we decided, would have to look after itself.

Sadly, that train journey came to an end. I say sadly because it definitely completed the holiday for me. All I had to look forward to was an eon of naggings and a return to a set of study subjects that I just couldn't look forward to with any kind of enthusiasm; especially after having spent a summer where I had frequently experienced the tremendous joy of conversing in another language.

....

Mum's reaction to my late, my very late, homecoming was pretty much as expected. As a parent and grandparent now, I can understand her feelings very well. I was neither of those things then though and I did feel indignant and trapped by her emotional reaction. Callow Youth at its zenith I suppose!

"What about the cards Mum? I explained it all in the cards."

"What bloody cards? You idiot boy how long did you think it might take cards to get from there to here?"

Well, she was right there; the several cards I had sent started to arrive home about three weeks after me. She had lost some of her anger with me by that time and the cards were placed on the mantle shelf in the kitchen but mostly as a trophy reminder as to the brainlessness of youth.

I didn't see Mum at first as I approached the house. She was on her knees, red leading the front step; a weekly routine as many tasks were for women in those days. In that kneeling position she was hidden because between the front gate and the front step there was but a very short few steps to the front door.

Mum stood up and simply glared at me as I ease past her to make my way into the house.

"Mind the step!"…"I've just polished it!" I stepped over the step and walked into the house towards my room on the ground floor, halfway down the passageway and at the bottom of the stairs. I dumped my rucksack at the foot of the bed sat heavily onto the bed and braced myself for the emotional onslaught that was to come.

"You wait 'till your father gets home!" She always used the term 'father' rather than 'dad' when she wanted to use him as a weapon. Every time I came near to her over the next hour it was the same clammer.

"You wait 'till your father gets home."

After a while I decided to make a break for a while and get myself down to the Town Hall for a very welcome and much needed bath. There were of course no facilities for that in our house at the time. I realise as I write at this moment that Dad had, in fact, recently had a bath with hot and cold running, installed in the scullery but there was still no automatic privacy unless the bath-time was clearly understood. Mum was in no mood to make it easy for me at that moment. I decided to clear off for a couple of hours and make myself clean at least for Dad's return home from work. The day was Friday. My next school day was not until the following Tuesday, not a pretty thought!

"You wait 'till your father gets home."

It rang in my ears as I closed the front gate behind me.

I really enjoyed that relaxing bath after which I took the opportunity to take a walk around the Green and enjoy simply being back in familiar territory. Leaving the Green, I took a turn up Balham Road past the wastepaper collection depot and so into Croyland Road, not back over the Iron-Bridge but round to Bury Street Hill, past the Rising Sun Pub and round to No.222 Winchester Road, Nan's house where my reception was quite different.

I enjoyed Nan's welcome home and took time to describe as much of the holiday as I thought Nan would take in. I then took my leave and returned home; well in time to be there when Dad got home from work. I owed him that at least; to be there as he came through the front door and not to be simply a myth that had returned from 'walkabout'.

I sat in my room listening to 'Prince Igor' on my multi-stack record player. My new set of these records was sequenced in such a way that as they dropped one at a time to tha deck they played a complete half of the entire work. Once the set had played in this way, one only needed to turn the whole stack over in order to finish listening to the whole work. Borodin's Prince Igor was the first long work that I had acquired that had been recorded in such a sequencing style. I was very proud of it.

On that day though, I played it because it was long and often quite loud. It had a capacity to drown other noises out!

The chant "You wait 'till your father gets home." Had become something of a mantra when I heard Dad's key in the door. As I left my room to go into the passageway to greet him, I felt my Mum's presence to my left at the kitchen door. I turned right into the passage towards him. As soon as he saw me, he grinned hugely and gave me such a hug of welcome that I nearly burst' both from lack of breath as well as enormous relief.

MUM DIDN'T SPEAK CIVILLY TO EITHER OF US FOR ABOUT THREE WEEKS!!

In The Meanwhile, an Interlude.

Well, school began again on the Tuesday after we returned from Europe. I really was not looking forward to the next three terms. I knew for an absolute certainty that my parents' hopes and dreams for me were going to be dashed big-time. I returned to school with a very heavy heart both for what had been lost and for what was to come.

Sam and I remained friends but did not keep close contact. This was for no other reason than that we had different interests and were in different study groups at school. This was a similar circumstance to me and Bill at Burgess Hill although we did at least manage to team up on several occasions.

Robin Wilks was a friend I made when he and I were in the Science 6th form together at Latymer. We became good friends in a friendship that continues to this day. He though was very interested in and able to dedicate his studies to the maths and science subjects studied in that form. I, on the other hand, was not. I think that he sometimes despaired at my clear ineptitude at the subjects that he loved and worked so hard to understand. We were good friends and I respected him. I visited him from time to time at his home in Enfield somewhere near the top of Forty Hill if my memory does not fail me. One day he showed me a book Called "Mathematics and the Imagination." It may have been in an attempt to cultivate some interest in me for the subject. Well, I did read the book and enjoy it but did not help me much with the Pure Mathematics that was proving such a stumbling block against my parents' ambitions for me. I do have to thank that book for an understanding of the name of the modern search engine launched by Larry Page and

Sergey Brin in 1998 and named I believe after the mathematical term Googol. If you look it up, you'll begin to understand why!

The fact is that I forgot to give Rob's book back to him; even when he visited us in Sittingbourne in the early 1960s.It is also true however that the book survived several 'book collection thinning out sessions' I undertook over the years. On each occasion that Rob's book came to the surface as a possible thinning out candidate I managed to reject the idea and so 'Mathematics and the Imagination' survived to fight another day. Many years later, somewhere around 2016, Rob endeavoured to make-contact with me once again. Under the impression that over the decades we might have moved he had the foresight to contact the school secretary. She contacted me for permission to reveal my contact details and the rest is history as they say. And so, after a period of about fifty years I was able to ease my sagging conscience by returning Rob's book to him. I had long realised that it might be even more precious to him by virtue of the fact that it had been presented to him as a school prize at the school he attended before coming to Latymer.

There were other friends in the sixth form, and I write of two of them in the next chapter. It was only the thought that I had those regular friends that that kept me sane at the thought of what that year was likely to bring. One other bonus that brought me some relief once a week was that one of my legal free periods coincided with one of the A 'level French conversation periods; this was with a French speaker hired by the school to help the A 'level students with in-house conversation. Having spoken to a few of those students and having voiced an interest they suggested that I should simply join the group and blend in. They maintained that the French lady would not know the difference and it would not be putting her to any inconvenience. Without boasting I am able to say that I was more than able to keep up with the group in terms of my ability to converse. That group was my one highlight of the week and totally illicit' with the help of my friends in 'A' level French. Many thanks to all of you!

Despite my strong feelings of doom and gloom regarding the forthcoming year the first few weeks of that year began quite positively for me. Two events served to bring some light into the early days of my dark-looking future in the Upper sixth Science!

Firstly, there was the announcement of school Prefects. This was a tradition at the beginning of each school year. It was a long-standing tradition in a school that was proud of its history.

The Latymer School was founded in 1624 when a City merchant Edward Latymer bequeathed certain property to trustees on condition that they were to clothe and educate "eight poore boies of Edmonton". The trustees are under a duty to carry out the provisions of his will "unto the end of the world" .see; https://www.latymer.co.uk/school/history. I have committed the earlier spellings of some word to the unwilling memory of the Microsoft Word dictionary.

It was at the beginning of the first school assembly in the Great Hall. That the school year officially began.

[The Great Hall, science laboratories and South Block were opened in a ceremony in 1928 by the Duke and Duchess of York. Fully equipped with stage and seating for over 1,000 people, the hall is used for school assemblies, concerts, drama productions and other major events. ibid]

The Great Hall truly merited its name. It was a truly imposing space; a large ground floor overlooked by a gallery on three sides. It also boasted a stage that was capable of presenting events to a professional standard. On the ground floor just below the stage and to the left of it as you looked at it was a concert grand piano. From time-to-time gifted students at the school were asked to play a chosen piece at the end of a school assembly. I remember one in particular a fellow student, Allen Sheller, a friend but not a close friend, who played piano very well and was asked to play on several occasions. The Great Hall also housed the wonderful Davis Organ.

Assemblies began with a short introduction by the Headmaster or another senior member of staff followed by a short selection from the Bible. N.B. the Head would almost certainly have been a man in those days. It is a welcome aspect of the slowly changing times that the current holder of the post is a woman.

The first meeting of the year however had other matters of business to deal with; there was the traditional Bible reading by the Head followed by the announcement of school prefects for the year. To my astonishment and welcome surprise, I was one of those. It was very welcome because it came with certain privileges one of which was legal access to the boys' prefects' room. This was situated at the end of a former short corridor leading to a now-closed side entrance to the school. In the fullness of time that unlikely entrance had been sealed off and so there was very little traffic along that short corridor; very convenient when you wanted some peace and quiet! The tradition was that even teachers would knock on the door before entering.

Pertaining to the girls' prefects' room though it was a horse of a very different colour! It was simply a former teaching room, requisitioned for the purpose but in quite a busy corridor of the school. The room even had a door with a four panelled set of glass windows. We young men all agreed that ours was a far superior arrangement.

Following the usual selection of welcoming speeches, the Head concluded the meeting with the instruction that we should all repair to our respective Houses for the election of House Officers.

The Houses at Latymer, there were six; each had almost two hundred members. This was as large a population as had some schools. They were Wyatt, Dolby, Ashworth, Keats, Latymer and Lamb. Each House had its colour and badge Wyatt was yellow Dolbé: royal blue. Ashworth; Sky Blue; Keats Red; Latymer Green; and Lamb was bedecked in Purple.

Two Houses take their names from local historical figures Charles Lamb and John Keats, while Richard Ashworth and Charles Dolbé were former head-teachers. Edward Latymer was the founder of the school and Anne Wyatt was a generous patron of the school

The elections for Head Girl and Boy were held and by some mysterious process that is lost in the years that have passed; I was elected as Head Boy of Wyatt House. Being a prefect and Head boy of Wyatt House actually and very surprisingly held some kudos at home. Dad was a keen reader of books such as Tom Brown's Schooldays and others of that ilk. I did read the book but was not so keen. It represented very strongly for me the class differences that continue to damage the social fabric of Britain both then and now. I always preferred 'Just William'.by Richmal Crompton. She wrote about a boy to whom I could relate my own life.

The Head Girl elected was Joyce Baldwin. We knew each other by sight from various activities within the school but had not taken much notice of each other up to that point nor really until the Christmas that followed a few months later.

I am currently having a disagreement with that former Head Girl of Wyatt House as to the site of the Wyatt House Meetings She is not sure, but I am certain that it was the Gym. As she is not certain and I'm the author of this piece it now goes into posterity as the GYM.

A major downside to being a prefect was that one had occasional monitoring duties of school lunches to perform. My early wars with 14-year-old boys were based directly on the use to which food should be put. My view – Food is fuel- should never be air-born – from the plate direct to the mouth Yes! - Flying food No! - Food as weapon. No!- Food anywhere but plate or mouth. - No! My rules and we stick to them – absolutely - Yes!

I discovered then.by that early acquaintance with the difference of opinion that I generally have with fourteen-year-old boys is that there are certain techniques that can come into play. First and foremost, actual violence is totally out of the question. Even in those days mere prefects did not have that method in their legal armoury. There were though certain stances, certain facial expressions, and certain tones of voice that were both legal and effective because they could threaten much more that they could deliver. The fourteen-year-old on the other hand was packed full of cheek and mischief but not yet fully conversant with the legalities of the situation. After a mere few hours of practice, I was able to do my duty in a comparatively peaceful dining room where food behaved itself i.e. it travelled from plate to mouth without finding itself splattered on my back!

After we got ourselves to that civilised understanding about the behaviour of food, I actually began to enjoy those lunch duties. I got to know quite a few of the younger boys and girls of the school and what they did what sports they liked etc. Conversations were held without the need to duck minute upon minute! Lovely jubbly!

At the end of that first term of that my final year at Latymer I did something that I had never done before due to my evolving Jewish identity. I elected to go Carol Singing with a group of senior students at the school. I did this after a plea in assembly for funds for a favourite charity supported by our comparatively new Headmaster Dr Trefor Jones. For the life of me I just cannot remember the name of that charity, but I am eternally grateful that I made the effort. It was during that door-to-door Carol Singing collection that I came into closer contact with Joyce, the then Wyatt House Head Girl, my opposite number. I fell for her sweet singing, and we are due to celebrate sixty years of marriage on the 7th July 2022. I am still ashamed to say that I allowed her to walk me home that night as my house was on her way home from the finish of our Carol Singing. Joyce Baldwin did me the honour of becoming Joyce Kreit on 7th July 1962, just three days after I was discharged from my two years National Service.

<u>Chapter Eighteen</u>

<u>Walking the Downs to Tring</u>

It was the spring of 1959. My friend Rod, Rodney, by some unknown route, had come upon the book and had read it the previous weekend. Now he wanted to visit the town 'Tring' that featured in the title. *The Tragedy near Tring, a novel by John Knox Ryland, 1934.* We argued: he insisted; "Where else are you proposing?" It was true; we had been discussing just that point for at least half an hour. We would need to arrive at a conclusion soon. We were in the boy prefects' common room on a Wednesday lunchtime which was rapidly coming to an end, and we would have to return to our respective lesson periods. I was, for my sins and by my parents' insistence, in the science sixth. The other two Rod and John were in arts groups. Generally speaking, we only ever met in the prefects' room but had nonetheless become quite good friends.

That specific prefects' room was rather grandly named because it was not in fact a room at all. It was, as previously stated, the rump end of a short corridor within the school that had been closed off at one end and into the stud wall of which an entrance door had been introduced. From this a corridor led back into the main school. This corridor was little used other than to get to the prefects' room. It was a small room at best but had the one advantage that it there were few passers by other than those whose intentions were to visit our common room. The girl prefects, on the other hand had been allowed to settle themselves into an actual school room which was a more comfortable, square, room situated right in the centre of the school. The disadvantage of this room, however, from a noise point of view, was that there was a lot of passing traffic. There was therefore a passing bedlam of noise whenever classes were not in session. The room was also too accessible to the teaching staff, those who might 'pop in' far too casually and often did so.

My friends were Rodney Fox and John Thornbury. John lived in Enfield near the bus route that we would need to catch in order to get to Dunstable which was due to be our 'jump' off point for the Chilterns and our walk down to Tring. The walk across the Dunstable Downs to Tring was going to be a shortish walk of 10-12 miles, maybe a bit more, depending on the twists and turns we might decide to build into it. The Chilterns and the Downs hold beautiful memories for me.

Over the years since Dad purchased his little black Ford Anglia NXY 705 we had visited and pick-nicked in the area between St Albans and Dunstable. These visits often included a few hours in Whipsnade Zoo, the off- London Arm of the Zoological Society of London. Dad always carried the makings of a cup of tea in the boot of the car. He had a methylated spirits stove; a kettle a teapot cups saucers etc. and a fold-up wind shield to protect his stove from the wind by the side of the road. He loved his pauses for a cuppa. As I write this, I realise just how much I miss my Mum and Dad while at the same time regretting the terrible life, they made for each other as well as the effects of that on my young sister and me. What a tragic mess!

The whole area presents you with some delightful views of rolling countryside and villages all redolent of past history as well as current beauty and interest. We had decided that we would be in no hurry to get to Tring. We simply wanted to enjoy the walk.

While still in the prefects' room we came to the early decision that, in order to beef up the interest during the walk we would each tell a story ["Chaucer" style you see] but without any of his political cum religious overtones. By a weird election process that I did not fully grasp it was decided that I would go first as soon as we began to walk. Rod would come next, and John would conclude the walking seminar. In view of John's Mum's reaction to one of the opinions I expressed later, in her home shortly after we met up there, my choice of tale to tell was particularly pertinent in that it broke, quite unintentionally, the recently established moratorium on political overtones; more of that later.

Rod and I met up just a few yards from John's home. We walked across the front garden together. John's Mum answered the door and glared at Rod who had given the door a fierce whack with the knocker and still had his arm raised towards the door, as if intending to repeat the event, when she opened the door. "Are you trying to bash the door open?" She continued to scowl at Rod as he squeezed nervously past her into the house. I noticed a slight but distinct accent as she spoke those few words. I walked into the room with the smug cockiness of he who has caused no offense. A smugness that was to be short lived, however.

John came into the room from the kitchen where he had just finished making his sandwiches for the walk to Tring. Like Rod and I he had packed a change of clothes together with some food and drink into a small rucksack. We were ready to go when suddenly I made my faux pas, totally unintentionally but dramatically, nonetheless it was all John's fault!

"I see you've met my Mum." He said then continued. "She's from Belgrade…" "Oh!" I said, interrupting knowingly from the wide experience of my two trips to Yugoslavia. "That's the capitol of Yugoslavia". Mrs. Thornbury reacted furiously "There is no Yugoslavia! Serbia is my country. Belgrade is my town, my capitol! I don't care what that thief Tito says." She put her angry face right close to mine. "You understand boy? I from Serbia – no from Yugoslavia. No place, is it? -Yugoslavia phfeh!" And there it was, in quiet suburban Enfield, a tiny representative kernel of the emotions that later brought about the breakup of Yugoslavia together with the bitter wars and ethnic cleansing that dragged and scarred the final decade of the 20the century in Slavic/Balkan Europe. I tried a stumbling apology without coming to terms as to why I should do so; what had I done or said to cause such an angry reaction?

When Marshal Tito, president of Yugoslavia, died on May 4, 1980, the representatives of over a hundred world states, including an impressive array of world leaders, attended the funeral of the man who was almost universally hailed as the last great World War II leader for, as well as being the first communist leader to successfully challenge Stalin, he was the founder of "national communism." Above all else, Tito was universally praised as the creator of modern Yugoslavia, the leader whose wisdom and statesmanship had united Yugoslavia's historically antagonistic national groups into a seemingly stable federation.

We left John's house and his still peeved but gradually calming-down mother and proceeded into Enfield Town in order to catch the bus to Dunstable and the beautiful Dunstable Downs. Dunstable is a market town and civil parish located in Bedfordshire, England. It lies on the eastward tail spurs of the Chiltern Hills, just about 30 miles north of London. These Downs are part of the Chiltern Hills, in southern Bedfordshire, England. They are established as part of a chalk escarpment forming the north-eastern reaches of the Chilterns. At 797 ft., Dunstable Downs are the highest part of the county of Bedfordshire. Trig point, marked by a small stone obelisk, is the highest part of the Downs themselves.

As we walked away from the house, I could not keep myself from thinking of the woman and the man who met up along the way, she with her two young daughters and he with his newly adopted boy and they made their long hard way back to Yugoslavia and to Slovenia. They were offered a cottage under provisions made by the Tito Government. The cottage lay just on the outskirts of a town in southeast Slovenia called Novo Mesto. That is where they were still living at the time that my friend Sam and I visited them in the summer of 1957. By that time, they had completed their family by having a child together, a little girl Vicki who was about 18 months old when we knew her; a lovely, lively and happy child. I mentally compared the miracle of the formation of that family with the horrendous war that developed in those Slavic countries following, not long after Tito's death with dark shadow of 'ethnic cleansing' that raised its evil head throughout that period.

The walk that I took that day with my two school friends took place in the spring of 1959. I have to admit here that I have always enjoyed writing as well as painting and drawing. I have never, however, kept any notes as I did so. I have relied very much on my memory which has always served me well because my philosophy has ever been that past events are how we remember them. Bearing that in mind I must admit that there are some details, such as the path we took from Dunstable to Tring are a bit too vague after all these years. I am writing this in August 2018. I have used 'Mr Google' as a very useful aide memoire for the route. I do however remember the weather and other details very well particularly elements of conversation.

On the way to Dunstable on the bus I was still reeling somewhat from Mrs. Thornbury's sudden and very angry reaction to my use of the title 'Yugoslavia' for the country that I had visited twice in the previous couple of years. For that reason and in my youthful arrogance I had therefore considered myself to be an 'expert' on the place. In the mid-fifties people were still not travelling to such places anywhere nearly as frequently or with such ease as nowadays.

We left Dunstable by one of its Western exits roughly southwest across the A5183. We were happily greeted by the sudden panorama of the Chilterns across the valley together with the colour contrast of the White Lion carved onto the hillside to the Northwest. On the way to Dunstable in the bus I had been reminded that I was to have first turn to tell a story. This was at the very beginning of the walk just as we made our pleasant way down the hillside towards the village of Edlesborough.

In order to ease my wounded feelings, I decided to regale my friends, like it or not, with a very short tale relating to Marshall Tito from my visit there during the previous summer. "I want to tell you a short story about Marshall Tito." A low joint groan was my sole reward for this gem of information. I felt no guilt, however. Marshall Tito was a hero of mine, and it was a pleasure to have the opportunity to talk about him to a captive audience.

"Well then, it's like this; last summer Sam and I stood on a curb-side in northern Yugoslavia, in Slovenia and not ten feet away from the one of the greatest wartime leaders of the Second World War, Marshall Tito." "Yeh right." Was Rod's instant response, the smile on his face was a 'go pull the other one' smile. John's reaction was more dramatic. "That's totally impossible! The man is the Dictator of the illegal federation of Yugoslavia. You should listen to my Mum, she knows, Tito is totally unapproachable!" He had turned in his tracks to glare at me, in doing so he tripped on a lumpy turf and fell backwards down a bit of a slope. He didn't hurt himself other than his pride but smacked my hand angrily away when I offered to help him up. I suddenly realised the need for extreme diplomacy in the 'John's Mum' department, but I was not going to be categorised as a liar by a woman who was not even present; neither with the three of us there on the Downs nor the previous summer in Novo Mesto with Sam and me.

"Look John I'm not having a go at your Mum. I never would." Pausing for breath I had stopped walking for a moment whilst the other two walked on a few paces. John turned to look at me. "Last summer when I returned home from Yugoslavia, I had the same argument with my Dad. He's a communist and at the other end of the political scale, I would guess, from your Mum – same argument different people. Let me explain as we walk. This was planned as an enjoyable walk, not as a 'glare off' between you and me."

John's face did relax slightly as I walked up beside him. I put my hand on his near shoulder as we walked which freed my left hand for gesticulation as I tried to emphasise and walk on rough, sloped ground as I did so.

"Last summer Sam and I were hitching down to Novo Mesto in Slovenia." "Yes, we know all about that you've only told us about two hundred times already." I grinned at that. He didn't seem to like me grinning though. "Well, we had to take a train into Slovenia from Austria because they would not allow us to enter Yugoslavia on foot for some reason' or maybe because it's a mountain crossing, anyway we ended up staying in a campsite in Ljubljana for a night before taking a bus to Novo Mesto and our hosts. "So, what's all that got to do with Herr Tito?" "I was just coming to that I needed to fill in some background." To be frank his really determined negative attitude was beginning to piss me off. Rod appeared to be immune to it all; he just kept plodding along the other side of John. In fact, although I really wanted to tell the story of nearly 'meeting' the great man as it truly happened in my previous story re Novo Mesto, I decided to shorten it by telling the essence of the 'Tito' bit without any preamble. Here follows the shortened version:-

"When we finally arrived in Novo Mesto you couldn't move for the crowds lined up along both sides of the road. It didn't take a genius to realise that something out of the ordinary was happening, or was about to happen, it wasn't easy to see or to understand. We could hear and feel the growing excitement of the crowd but not comprehend the nature of the occasion. We both felt that something important was in the wind but had no idea what it was." John spoke sharply at this point, but he seemed both irritated and interested. "Well then, come on get on with it. You've created your mystery now get on and solve it before we both go to sleep on our feet."

"Well, with a bit of pushing and shoving we managed to get to the front of the crowd; it was Sam who noticed it first." "Look!" He said to me. "There's some sort of cavalcade coming down the road; an open tourer type of a car, some sort of a soldier geezer sitting on raised seat arrangement over the back seat. He must be important, they're all cheering him, waiving at him, blowing kisses even!"

"You're really milking this aren't you?" John finally offered up a weak grin here. I began to hope that he had returned to the original idea of three friends having an enjoyable walk in an England mercifully at peace, a peace that had eluded us and our country for much of the 20th century up to that day.

I grinned back. "I'm getting to the nitty gritty now." "'Bout bloody time." This time it was Rod who chipped in. "Who pulled your chain?" John demanded to his right with an even bigger grin. Great! Things looked as if they were back on course. I continued my story.

"The cavalcade came closer and closer as the front car drew ever nearer; I became more excited. I began to interpret some of the excitement and warmth of the crown towards the striking figure of a man who was sitting; smiling with appreciation of the crowd and waving happily back at them." At this point I paused for breath in order to get back to the moment; to retreat from the scene of the previous summer in Novo Mesto. I looked directly at John.

"I have to tell you John that that man was Marshall Josip Broz Tito. The crowd was fervent with its warmth of feeling towards him. There was little obvious security around him, and he was sitting high on a kind of raised rumble seat and in a lovely and very open car. He appeared to be very comfortable and totally at ease with the moment." John looked away but gave no comment or argument.

That memory is one of the major moments of my life; that as long as I live, I shall be able to say that I once stood within ten feet of one of the great heroes of the Second World War as he drove past on an ordinary street in a fairly ordinary town in Slovenia. He is also the one man who, during an extremely important period in European History, had stood up against both the power of Hitler's Wehrmacht and Stalin's Kremlin.

"By the way – you can have one guess each – what car was he in, this famous Communist Leader?" And, as we stumbled down a fairly steep section of the path I concluded. "That will be the end of the Tito intermission." "Oh, right on! What do you want to know?" "It'd easy, I just want to know what make of car do you think he was in? My Dad wouldn't believe me for a while and he's a communist." "Oh, that's got to be an easy one. He was being driven in some 'perk' car made for communist bigwigs in Russia. One thing is absolutely certain, it wasn't a Trabant!"

Rod's guess was way of the mark, so I turned back to John. "What about you John. What car was this man in?" "Well." He began. "This is unfair; I've seen a couple of his state car collections and they have both been purpose-built Mercedes limos so that's my guess and I'm certain that I'm correct because I've also seen them on a documentary film." I scrambled over a few awkward lumpy bits at the bottom of that section of the path. "So, I'm very happy to say that you're both wrong. Marshall Tito on that day was the proud owner of a light tan Rolls Royce Silver Wraith purpose-built tourer. I've done a bit of research on him since that holiday. Our Marshall Tito is one big 'High Life' player who loves beautiful cars and, as the Wicked Queen would say to herself and to the mirror on the wall, 'Rollers' are the most beautiful of them all!" With that we decided to have a break and some food. We sat down in the sunshine to have our picnic.

Back at school during the planning stage we had developed a fairly clear outline. After veering southwest towards the village of Edlesborough but not walking into it the path turned leftish to skirt around Whipsnade Zoo, the 'country' development of the London Zoological Society. It was just past the Zoo that we had paused for a break and a bite. The next part of the walk would be to continue in a clockwise curve passing both Holywell and Dagnall. After Dagnall one walks a long zig zag route down towards Tring Train Station. After that it is a short walk into Tring. I understand that this comprises the Icknield Way and the Ridgeway. We did not know that at the time. We just walked a route that looked right on the map. It is a walk of just over 14 miles. We reckoned, back at school, that it would take us between 4-5 hours. Our reckoning was off!

The Whipsnade White Lion can be seen just over a mile southwest of Whipsnade village and 1 mile North of Dagnall on the Dunstable downs in south Bedfordshire. It is situated facing West on a gentle slope below Whipsnade wildlife park. These downs are a continuation of the range of chalk upland that also includes the Chiltern Hills and the Berkshire downs. The end of the Ridgeway long distance footpath is 2 miles away to the West at Ivinghoe beacon which offers a good view of the Lion as do other hills to the west. The gentle slope makes the Great Cat difficult to view from close quarters. It is close to the B4506 but is obscured by hedges.

The B4540 offers some good side-on views of the Lion from just below a conveniently placed car park. It can also be well-viewed from the B489, but the best view is from several vantage points on the A4146 leaving Dagnall. The Whipsnade White Lion is a modern monument of the 20th Century as it was created in 1933. At the time of our walk the Lion could have been regarded as a home for escapees from the Zoo at Whipsnade. Not dangerous ones though, but interesting, nonetheless. There had been escapes of both Cavies and, more famously, Wallabies that had made their escape and had become established as significant breeding colonies on the downs. In that way the 'Home' counties may well have had the largest colony of breeding wallabies outside of Oz.

We rose reluctantly from our short rest. The day was beautiful. We had had sun all the way thus far and not baking hot either; just nice heat in which to walk with a slight westerly breeze. We pushed Rod to tell his story. We all felt that I had used the time available to me with my Tito story although I had been intending to tell the tale of 'The Chiltern Hundreds'. I felt that I could still easily manage to fit it in, but the others would not hear of it. I tried to argue but the chorus against was too fierce to combat. I yielded, very reluctantly, as you will soon find out.

Rod began just as we must have been passing the village of Holywell. "Well." He began almost apologetically. "My story is not as long as Tony's." "Thanks-be to Heaven!" John interjected with ungraciously deep feeling I felt. "My story is about a tin of pineapple." "Yes" he continued after catching the suddenly amused expressions on both of our faces!" "Yup, I guess you both remember rationing?" "Why, has it ended already?" I joked. Rod ignored me.

We all remembered, only too well, the complicated nature of the different types of rationing, food, clothing fuel; all of which had certain sub-divisions elements of which ended at different times. Food rationing finally ended in 1954. That was only four years ago at the time of our trip to Tring. Yes, indeed we all remembered Wartimes indeed we all remembered War-Time rationing. Even after years of official enforced rationing had ended, many, many consumer items were rationed for many years by virtue of scarcity and cost. Wartime rationing had been in place for most of our lives.

"Is your story about rationing then?" I asked our eager storyteller. "Well, yes, it is in a way. I was going to call it 'The last tin of Pineapple. I've changed my mind though. I'm now calling it 'The first and last tin of pineapple."

"It all started with my Uncle Bob." He began. "Bob had been a soldier during the war. He served in North Africa and was one of the famous 'Desert Rats', The British 7th Armoured Division. He was away from home and England for nearly six years all-told. You talk about Tito well Bob is my hero, a family hero at that. He signed up for the British army right at the outset of war. Having chosen the 7th he served in the front line throughout the War; Sidi-Barrani, Rommel, El-Alemein, Italy then Normandy, Ghent Hamburg Berlin Bob served every day of that war." Rod paused at this point, both for breath and to collect his thoughts. We all paused with him. Bedfordshire, like most British counties is beautiful. During the pause we were able to take in the outstanding beauty of the Downs. There was a soft summer breeze blowing; one of those elements that make you feel that England is 'home'. Rod continued:-

"Finally, the poor sod was badly wounded by a sniper just three days before the end of the war. He was shipped back to England for treatment only to find that the girl he was going with before the War, with whom he had been exchanging letters all through the bloody thing, had married some Yank serving in the RAF in 1943. She hadn't told him about the news by letter because she didn't want to hurt him whilst he was away serving his country!"

"The silly cow went to the hospital with her new husband, arm in arm just like they were on a regular visit there to a friend. They gave the news still arm in arm and hoped that they could all be friends once he got better. Bob had never been short of a few swear words, but the standard of invective had broadened over six years in the 7th. He began loudly with old favourites such as 'You can just Fxxx Off you Bastards and it all went rapidly up-and-downhill from there!' The stream of invective followed them from the ward; it drifted down the corridor and could still be heard by them and anyone else in earshot. As far as we know old Bob never saw either of them again. They rapidly retreated through the front entrance of the hospital. They were lucky that times were hard, and they had not been able to take him some fruit because that would have given our Bob some solid ammunition to hurl at them. Jean, which was her name and her American wisely gave up any further attempts at reconciliation."

"It was well into 1946 before Bob came out of convalescence. He made the journey home to stay with his Mum and Dad. He informed them, when they dared to ask, that he had forsworn at further ideas of any dealings with women. Life treated him badly, well, in truth it was he who treated life badly. Like many men Bob had begun to smoke in the Army but now he also began to drink heavily and often."

"Uncle Bob treated women badly; he showed no respect for any woman. Bob got into drunken fights and almost always came off the worst for it because he was usually too drunk to stand up. His parents became really 'pissed off' with him; several times his Dad chucked him out and finally made him sleep in the old 'Andersen' 'till he mended his ways. For nearly three years he went downhill big time!"

"I thought that this was going to be a short story and was to be a bout a tin of Pineapple chunks, the first or last of that ilk I don't care." John glared a challenge at Rod.

"Well, it's about my favourite Uncle. Once I got started, I began to get carried away."

"Well don't!" came the unhelpful response. By this time our walk had proceeded, and we had just passed by Dagnall having skirted round Whipsnade and passed Holywell as we did so. The weather was great and I for one was enjoying our decision to engage in story each. I had had my turn which allowed me to relax and enjoy the efforts of others.

Rod just grinned and continued unabashed. "Well then, as I was saying before I was so rudely interrupted." He aimed his sarky grin at John.

Bob continued to go downhill, and the slide continued until the SSAFA Christmas Dance in December 1950 when he met Margaret. I should say, in truth that she met him because he was slouched in a chair at the edge of the dance floor and showing a total disinterest in anything especially the dance and particularly not one iota in any of the girls there."

Margaret just happened to be walking across the dance floor and skirted past this loudmouth yob called Bob who she vaguely remembered from school those many years ago. As she passed him, she accidently knocked into his chair which caused him to spill some of his precious brew.

"Watch it you clumsy bitch"! Was the darling, sweet man's response.

Margaret did no more; she turned back towards him and gave him such a belt across the kisser that he spilled more of his beer. She then removed the glass, with the remainder of the beer still in it, from his astonished grasp and poured it over his head to a very heart-felt cheer from several people in the crowd.

"You ever swear at me again you f-ing foul mouthed lout and I'll hit you with anything I can lay my hands on".

 Margaret then turned and walked away but not before she gave him a piercing stare that, for all the world, seemed to say 'you're mine you ape. You just don't know it yet but you're mine'.

Within days Bob had come out of the doldrums. He seemed to begin to enjoy life and to entertain some thoughts of living once more. I can tell you one thing. His Mum and Dad felt the difference in so many ways. They came back to life alongside their son, so long a distant son but now, bit by bit, little by little their old son began to return to them from the depths.

 "I suppose this story does have an end? "Queried John once again. "And just when do we get to the bloody pineapple?"

"I'm getting there, I'm getting there. Don't be so damned impatient!"

I thought that this would bring John to the boil, but he did manage to control himself. He, after all, had already listened to one story, mine!

Two days later Margaret turned up at his front door. "Hello Mrs Baker. You probably don't remember me from when we were at school, but I did meet up with your son Bob a couple of nights ago."

Bob's Mum folded her arms across her chest, leaning her right shoulder against the door frame she asked.

"Are you the one who belted my son across the chops?"

Margaret was totally unabashed at this appearance of sternness on the older woman's part. "Yes, I damned well am and if he ever tries talking to me again the way he did that night he'll get more of the same and worse. He was behaving like a lazy, idle, foul-mouthed lout and I have no time for him if that's the way he wants to live his life."

Mrs Baker smiled a wide smile. "You'd better come in girl." With that she turned on her heels and disappeared into the house, leaving Margaret to shut the front door behind her as she entered and followed.

Mrs Baker led the way through the house to the kitchen at the rear. Bob was sitting at the table finishing off a late breakfast. He looked up as the two women entered the room. "Well young lady." Mrs Baker looked towards her son as she spoke to Margaret. "This, I believe, is the… what was it...the lazy, idle, foul-mouthed lout you were looking for." Margaret blushed somewhat at the introduction but managed a restrained "Hello Bob – how are you?" And that's how they made peace; with a simple greeting, exchanged blushes and reconciling smiles. Mrs Baker, after the few seconds that assured her that there was no question of the two young people continuing their physical combat in her home, retreated from the kitchen.

Margaret made good her resolve to 'get her man'. They began to 'go out' together from that day and Bob soon realised that he was head over heels in love with the girl who, by clouting him hard, had brought him back from the 'never, never' land of his deep depression. Within weeks they had planned to get married and, as was the usual practice they planned an engagement party. Bob did what was still expected in those days; he asked Mr Watts' permission to marry his daughter Margaret and the party date was set. It was on the day of the party that Bob disgraced himself once more.

No! It wasn't through drink it was all because of a missing tin of pineapple and the telling of a fib, some would call it a downright lie but I'm trying to be as kind as possible. On the day of the party Bob offered to help Mrs Watts to prepare the food in the kitchen. She fell in willingly with his offer as she wanted to get herself dressed and ready. So, as it turned out and much to Bob's eventual disgrace, he was left to his own devices for quite a while.

Mrs Watts' last instructions to her future son-in-law before she left the kitchen were "You'll see some tins of fruit in the larder Bob. Could you open three of them for me please, to make a fruit cocktail, only I find that tin-opener a bit of a bugger to use."

That was the opening gambit towards the loss of grace for Bob. It needs to be explained here that in about 1942 tinned fruit was placed on the Government's schedule of rationed foods. Bread was also 'on ration' like many other foods until 1954. Mrs Watts, in order to make her daughter's engagement party in 1950 had had to use her family entitlement of coupons plus using up some begging and borrowing favours to scrape together the food for the party. That, of course, included the tins of fruit.

Bob's eyes widened considerably when he saw the tins. There were two tins of mixed fruit, a tin of peach slices and, wonder of wonders, a tin of pineapple! Bob chose one of each type leaving a tin of mixed fruit in the pantry, he opened the pineapple first of the three; he stood back as if to behold the wondrous sight of all those pineapple chunks swimming in their own juice.

'Just one!' he thought I'll just try one to see if I can remember the taste. Just one won't hurt they won't know. So Bob tried just one chunk of pineapple. He remembered at once exactly why it had always been his favourite fruit especially pineapple chunks swimming in their own juice. 'One more won't hurt'; thus continued the devil seemingly sitting on his left shoulder and so on and so on until dear Uncle was staring uncomprehendingly into half a bowl of juice and no chunks.

"What the hell have I done?" He muttered, suddenly realising the enormity of his actions over the last few minutes. Bob quickly drank the juice; not really noticing how beautiful it was. He was suddenly overcome with the guilt of his actions. He knew only too well how hard Mrs Watts had scrimped and scraped under the hardship of rationing to put together the food for his and Margaret's party. He just wanted to get rid of the evidence.

Then he had a brainwave. The mixed fruit contained some small pineapple sections. He grabbed the second tin of mixed fruit from the parlour and mixed the remaining three tins of fruit in together hoping that no-one would notice a missing tin of pineapple until he could scrounge one from somewhere. 'I'll get one on the black-market if I have to' he thought. At that moment however his few seconds of solace took a dramatic dive. A small crowd of three people entered the kitchen. Margaret and both of her parents bustled into the room with the simple intention of checking on his progress.

"How's it going?" Mrs Watts smiled hugely as she asked the question. After all, what could go wrong?" She very quickly noticed something amiss, however. "Where's the pineapple?" She made a sudden dive for the larder where there should have resided an intact tin of that precious fruit.

Her face paled suddenly as she realised that the difficult to get, hard-won and long-awaited tin that had been destined to remain safely intact for that party on that day was not where it should be! She rounded on Bob; her face transformed into red accusing fury.

"Where's my bloody tin of pineapple?" The words spat out of her mouth with the ferocity of a sub machine gun. There was no offer of a negotiated peace in her tone if she did not receive an immediate and satisfactory response. It was this ferocity and immediacy that drove Bob to make his second and, as it rapidly became clear, his more serious mistake of the morning. In his panic he lied which once you begin down it, is a difficult row to hoe.

"Don't know Mrs Watts ain't seen one of those." Then he added the one word that finally condemned him into the liars' corner. "Honest."

Both Mr and Mrs Watts looked at him with a withering disgust that shrank him visibly. They left the room swiftly clearly showing their dislike of being in the same room as him. Margaret strode across the room clearly having no intention of letting him off so lightly. "You ate those dammed pineapple chunks you low down two-faced lying bx! You just have no idea about how much you've hurt my Mum today you bloody toad. Now piss off and don't show your face around here again."

"Well, of course it didn't end like that. Bob had ended up as something of a pariah in the Watts household. Margaret was totally ashamed of him; much more for the lie than for eating the pineapple chunks. For Mrs Watts the balance between was about equal and, strangely, Mr Watts could see the funny side of the whole business right from the start. He even left the kitchen chuckling which annoyed the hell out of his misses. They had a row which put Mr Watts in the doghouse for a while. He and Bob met by chance in the 'The George and Anchor' a local pub one evening. They got chatting and hatched a plan which gradually made the way for Bob's re-entry into the good graces, first of Mrs Watts and then, with more difficulty, with Margaret who still had strong feelings for her 'Bob'. They were married a few months later but never tried to hold another engagement party. No pineapple was served at the Wedding Breakfast'!"

Rod finished his talk as we strode down a hill away from Dagnall and in the general direction of the village of Ivinghoe Aston. We stood and rested for a few moments both for Rod to take breath after regaling us with the tale of his Uncle Bob and for all three of us to enjoy the still distant view of Ivinghoe nestling in small woodland and the spire of St Mary's Church just peeping out above the trees.

Ivinghoe is a small and very pretty village situated on the edge of the Chiltern Hills Area of Outstanding Natural Beauty. It is an important point on the Icknield Way. The Icknield Way is claimed to be the oldest road in Britain, dating back to the Celtic period, though this, as is often the case where British Historical claims are concerned, has often been disputed.

Today the village is known as a starting point on The Ridgeway, which is a popular route for hikers and cyclists and which uses part of the Icknield Way, running for 87 miles to Overton Hill. You can always check, as I did, and often do, with 'Mister Google' for more information.

Further to this, Ivinghoe Aston is a hamlet which lies within the parish of Ivinghoe. Its name refers to a farm which can be found to the east of the main village. This hamlet has four farms, several houses and at the time of my research a pub, The Village Swan, which was bought by local residents in 1997. If you do your research, you will see that it is a case of a 'Mermaid that has metamorphosed into a Swan.

"Well then…" I broke the silence generated by our brief sojourn into sight-seeing. "It's your turn John now, for your story." "What's it called?" This came from Rod who had suddenly woken up from a reverie about pubs and how many we might find in Tring. Remember there were no quick reference tools like MR G in those days!

"It's like this." John hesitated. "I've decided to call it; The Worst Bloody Christmas Ever!" He turned back down the slope and began…

"It was the Christmas before last. I was in the final throes of working towards my batch of O'levels [exams before GCSEs]. I had been hoping for a quiet Christmas holiday so that I could do some revising in peace. What does my Mum do? She invites the whole bloody family to stay with us over the Christmas and New Year!" He paused. "Eleven of the buggers from both sides descended on us the day before Christmas Eve."

John sighed a sigh of profound resignation and continued. "My Mum knows full bloody well that her family and Dad's family just do not mix well."

"To top it all" he added with one extra deep sigh. "My Mum and her Mum are often at daggers drawn"… one extra sigh as if the world were on his shoulder.

"It began from the moment that they arrived. We have four bedrooms which normally gives my brother and me a room each. With the mob coming we were told that we had to share. He was moved into my room on a 'put-u-up' bed – no room to move and buggered up my revision plans for the whole ten days of the occupation by the hoards. This then; over the very last decent period for revision before the exams". John looked at me as if he thought that there was something I could have done to rectify a situation that had taken place two years previously. After a few moments he continued:-

"Yes, it really did start from the moment my Mum's Mum entered the house. She sees the room that she and my Grandad have been allocated and it's not good enough. It's really my brother's room and it's the best room available. It's a bit bigger than my room but the view isn't good enough for her".

"I didn't ever know how Mum put up with her or why she ever dreamed that she would become easier to live with. There are eleven people coming to stay with us for ten days. She's been offered the best room and she's moaning about the view! Mum comes downstairs in tears. Dad wants to know what's going on. He's usually a quiet man but the expression on his face changes as he listens to the tale". "Don't worry love I'll deal…"

"With that he bounds up the stairs like a goat. We hear some muffled raising of Dad's voice, a short silence and he's downstairs again." "What happened? What did you say to her?" "He smiled softly…"I simply told her how hard you had worked to try to please her and informed her that if she didn't like the arrangements that you had made in your own house that she could clear off home back to where she came from so that we could all enjoy this holiday together".

"Did you really tell her to clear off?" "I certainly did, and I meant it. I'm beginning this holiday the way I mean to go on. She's bloody well not going to spoil it for you."

That was quite a good and entertaining start to the Christmas but, unfortunately, my Mum's Mum was not to be the only joker in the pack!"

At that point our walk was continuing very well. The sun was still shining. I remember that it was about 3pm as we turned away from the direction of Ivinghoe; we were walking now roughly south towards Tring Railway Station. John looked at his watch; the time was gone 3pm. Not late but we had hoped to be a bit closer to Tring by this time. We had not booked ahead for a room for the night so we had to hope that there would be a pub, possibly in the High Street, that could put us all up in one room. That would cost less than having to pay for two rooms.

John continued his, rapidly developing, lurid, family story. "Now my Mum has a sister Clara who is quite a bit younger that she is. Clara has two boys who are now in their teens. I say Clara has them because she and her husband Paul are separated, pending divorce due to admitted adultery by Paul. My Mum threw a spanner into the works by inviting Paul to Christmas dinner to give him a nice family occasion with his boys. That was a kind thought for both Paul and the boys, but my Aunt Clara took offence in a big way. She then went totally 'apeshit' when Mum threw her the added piece of information that Paul, a few days after he received his invite, 'phoned Mum to thank her for the kind invite and announce that he was proposing to bring his new 'amour' Wendy. After all, he reasoned, he couldn't leave her at home alone on Christmas Day, could he?"

John Paused for breath before continuing. "I have to say that after that the Christmas holiday went downhill bigtime and that I for one could understand Clara's point of view. It wasn't Mum's finest hour. The boys were ok about seeing their Dad but were really upset that he was intending to bring with him the woman who they blamed for breaking up their family and for making their Mum so unhappy".

"Clara was totally incensed and refused to be mollified. It was only my Dad's intervention that persuaded her not to return home there and then. By now we had got to Christmas Eve and Clara was still threatening to go home for the day, the next day. She made it very clear that she was not going to be in the house at the same time as Wendy. Dad was furious with Mum; his Mum gave him a right rollicking for not supporting his wife's good intentions and Clara would not speak civilly to anyone, not even her boys who had both commented that they wouldn't mind seeing their Dad for Christmas. A cloud of deep gloom and anger had descended over the whole family"

"Christ John, that's a bit of a story. How the hell did it all end up?" "Well, that's the thing, the day was finally saved by Clara's older boy; another 'John' I'm afraid. He took it upon himself to 'phone his Dad and tell him how much he and his brother would like to see him over Christmas but that they both thought it would be a bad idea for him to come at that time. John junior pointed out that no-one would enjoy the experience. He took it upon himself to arrange for the two of them to visit his Dad for New Year. And so the whole situation was saved but Clara remained cold towards her older sister for much of the rest of the holiday". Deep breath: - "They've just about mended their bridges by now though".

And thus, we completed the telling of our three stories at just about the right moment…Just as John was finishing the last few words of his story Tring Train Station hove into view. We very quickly realised however that the Station is slightly miss-named. By rights it should have the Name Aldbury rather than Tring because it is much closer to that village than to Tring. We still had a one and a half mile walk along the road before getting into the market Town of Tring. In order to pass the time productively and to take our minds off the extra walking that we were now forced to undertake I decided to regale my friends with some interesting information regarding the History of the Chiltern Hundreds. This decision was not greeted with universal enthusiasm, but I disregarded that on the basis that they were tired and needed cheering up.

 "So", I began somewhat pompously as the three of us strode down the country road towards Tring. I was rather pleased about my new raft of knowledge. "It used to be that the Chiltern Hundreds was simply an ancient administrative area in this county". I spread my arms wide as if to indicate thereby the whole of the county of Buckinghamshire whilst suddenly realising that we were probably in Hertfordshire by that time... "That is Buckinghamshire which is composed of three hundreds"….. "What's a hundred?" Rob spurted out, grinning, and apparently determined to spoil the flow of my masterpiece. "I'm just about to tell you if you let me!" I responded tetchily. "Sorry, I'm sure." He grinned and I glared at him as I continued. "The three hundreds lie partially within the Chiltern Hills. A 'hundred' I explained was traditionally a section of an English County that had the capacity to raise a hundred fighting men for the King". I paused for breath to allow them to absorb this gem of information. John began to whistle the 'Teddy Bears' Picnic' and grinned in joking; "You've spent more time swatting up all this rubbish than for your 'A' levels you daft bugger".

Despite a distinct lack of any obvious enthusiasm for me to continue my story about the Chilterns I was determined to press on, nonetheless. In fact, their seeming lack of interest fired my stubborn enthusiasm for delivery more than they will ever know. I had boned up on all this stuff and they were damned well going to get it, like it or not! I continued: "Do you realise that the phrase, 'Taking the Chiltern Hundreds' has crept into the English language in a parliamentary sense?" I felt that this might at least have aroused some glimmer of interest. I explained; "Under normal conditions an elected M.P. is not allowed to resign from his seat in Parliament. Taking the Chiltern Hundreds' refers to the legal procedure that gives effect to the resignation of an M.P. from the British House of Commons."

"You see?" As I continued to try their patience. "A sitting M.P. may not at the same time hold a Crown Office. To take a Crown Office position effectively relieves the M.P. from his/her duties as an M.P. The ancient office of Crown Steward for the area (in full Crown Steward and Bailiff of the three Chiltern Hundreds of Stoke, Desborough and Burnham), was reduced to a mere sinecure by the 17th century, and thus became the first to be used in this resignation procedure a century later. Other titles have also been used for the same purpose, but nowadays only the Chiltern Hundreds office and the Crown Steward and

Bailiff of the Manor of Northstead are used…Now then wasn't that interesting?" It was at that moment that I noticed the sudden exchange of surreptitious grins between my two friends. They had feigned a total lack of interest in order to wind me up. "Right, you buggers, I muttered. I've not yet finished after all." We were rapidly approaching the country town of Tring, but I now felt strongly that I should make time to finish the full delivery of my new knowledge. I had one more card to play.

"Who do you think was the first to use the device to relinquish his position as a sitting M.P.?" Blank stares all around!

The procedure was, in fact, invented by John Pitt, as a means to vacate his seat for Wareham in order to stand for Dorchester but could not be a candidate for the one while he was still an MP. Pitt wrote to Prime Minister. Henry Pelham in May 1750 reporting that he had been invited to stand in Dorchester and asking for "a new mark of his Majesty's favour to enable him to do for him these further services". Pelham wrote to William Pitt (it was the elder) indicating that he would intervene with King George II to help. On 17 January 1751 Pitt was appointed to the office of Steward of the Chiltern Hundreds, and was then elected unopposed for Dorchester.

The Manor of Northstead was first used as a pretext for resignation on 6 April 1842, by Patrick Chalmers, Member for the Montrose District of Burghs.

These two examples just show the importance of the ancient adage… "Where there's a will there's a way." One also needs to have a willing King or Queen in one's armoury.

By the time that I had finished we found ourselves striding hopefully into Tring High Street.

Tring is a small market town and civil parish in the Borough of Dacorum, Hertfordshire. The town is situated in a gap passing through the beautiful Chiltern Hills, which are classed as an Area of Outstanding Natural Beauty. Tring is linked to London by the old Roman road of Akeman Street; now the modern A41, as well as by the Grand Union Canal and by rail lines to Euston Station.

Tring is not a large town and has a population of only about 11,000 these days. I have no idea what it was in 1958 nor did I give the matter a second thought at that time when our sole intention was to have a pleasant walk through the Dunstable Downs and the lower edge of the beautiful Chilterns in order to find out more about the author and the book mentioned at the very beginning of this story.

In fact, our first and immediate task was to find somewhere to stay for the night. As we were looking for a reasonably priced pub we pushed on into the High Street as the most likely place.

We were much luckier than we deserved because we had done no hard-core planning such as consulting phone directories and making 'phone calls in order to book ahead for a room for three in a pub in the High Street which is exactly what we did get at the very first pub that we tried. The few memory cells that I still have working have convinced me that it was the Bell Inn and they had just one room left with accommodation for three, a double and a single. The room overlooked the High Street. I do remember that because I did only partially enjoy going to sleep and waking up to the music of the various noises, some loud, some animal and some distinctly inebriated human, in the High-Street Tring!

By the same bizarre election process that had decided that I would go first as a storyteller at the beginning of the walk it was determined, later that evening that I would share the double with John and that Rod would get the single. By the time that all that had been settled we had booked ourselves in for dinner at the pub. We made our way back downstairs very well aware that, as guests residing at the pub, we would not be subject to the same licensing restrictions as walk-in customers.

For young men of our ages that seemed like a big deal. In fact, I was the only one of the three of us who was actually over 18 and could prove it because, by chance, I had my provisional driving license on me. The landlord used that to take our collective word that we were all 'of age'. We had no intention of 'putting him straight' on the matter.

We found ourselves quite popular towards the end of closing time, 10.30pm in those days because, as residents, we were allowed to have guests to stay awhile to enjoy a few drinks with us. That was the landlord's interpretation of the rules provided that it was we who paid for the drinks; a rule that was very easily overcome on the face of it, a simple pre-drink collection served the trick. To this day I am not certain of the Landlord's interpretation of the law but who were we to argue? It gave us more drinking time in company that was becoming more convivial by the minute. It also gave us the opportunity to quiz some friendly natives about the 'Ryland' novel.

The compulsory carrying of identity cards, apart from during wartime, has always been treated as a potential infringement of civil liberties in Britain. In this day and age, the balance has changed somewhat in that most of us carry I.D. around on a daily basis; the huge difference being that it is not compulsory to do so. The pros and cons of that argument I will not enter into here.

As for the original quest re the book we drew a blank all round. To tell the truth by the time we had had a few drinks we were not really in a mood to delve too deeply into the issue anyway. We did quiz some of our newfound friends in the pub; on the basis that they were locals and might just have heard about John Knox Ryland and his book but there was no joy in that direction.

The next morning, we had breakfast after which we paid our bill and left the pub to have a walk around the town. We made the gesture of trying our luck in a couple of antique shops that we discovered had opened for a few hours but no luck there either.

As I began this story, I tried to get myself a copy of the book from Amazon, but they have it listed as out of stock. Since that I have tried the British Library. They do have it listed but I am now at the end of the story and have lost interest in the book itself. It was not my concern in the first place anyway, it was Rod's. For anyone who finds themselves interested you will find the British Library reference below…

- **Title:** The Tragedy near Tring. A novel. - **Author:** John Knox RYLAND

- **Publication Details:** London : Stanley Paul & Co., [1934] - **Language:** English

- **Identifier:** System number 003210213 - **Physical Description:** 288 p.; 8°.

- **Shelfmark(s):** General Reference Collection NN.22120.

- **UIN:** BLL01003210213

<u>Chapter Nineteen.</u>

<u>I Don't Do Plumbing</u>.

Joyce would be very relieved that I am about to disclose these forthcoming events and to finally get them off my chest, and into the public arena. In that way to finally eradicate my potential to tell and retell this story any time that the subject of DIY hoves into view. My Mum's reaction, on the other hand, to the title itself, would have been more on the lines of, "thank the good Lord for that!!"

The day was a Sunday, a very long Sunday whose date I remember well. It was Sunday May 31st, 1959.

I have good reason to remember the date. I have always disliked Sundays as a reaction to what they were for me as a child growing up. It was a time and a climate when Sundays had to be revered, venerated, and respected to a degree well beyond any possibility of enjoying them. Nothing was open. None of your friends was allowed to play out. As a young child one had to be up early, polished until your face shone. You were then placed in your best clothes, so that you could not move for fear of damaging them, or anything else within reach of your, by now, very limited range of movement. Nor was there any refuge to be had at the cinema. I am absolutely convinced that film producers and directors in those times guided their worst failures towards the Sunday market. They sold these failures cheaply, as 'B' films for the one Sunday showing allowed in those days. It was usually a relief to stand up for the National Anthem which signalled going home time at the end of the film.

My very worst nightmare though, again as a young child, was the one Sunday a month when my best clothes were put into 'proper' use when I was dragged out of the house, mentally battered, and frogmarched over to Cheshunt to see my great grandmother; my Mum's grandmother and my great grandmother who used to dress in the mode of Whistler's Mother. There were two ladies and a dog residing in that small cottage in Cheshunt. The main source of my nightmares, though, was the dog, or should I say bitch? Her name was Becky Sharp and oh how she deserved that name! That house was a "Children should be seen and not heard" abode, not uncommon in those days but Becky Sharp acted as if the sentiment of the saying was her own province to preserve.

That little dog made my life more of a misery than even the visits themselves. My allocated seat during those sessions was on a stool near the fireplace. If I ever tried to move away from the stool the dog would get me. Her favourite form of torture was to give the ankles of sharp nip with her needle like teeth. In this way she kept me in my place for years. I was about four when I was first press-ganged into those 'family' visits. By the time I was six I had not only had enough of Becky Sharp long since, but I became better capable of inflicting surreptitious 'dog control'. The day then came when Becky Sharp met her match in the form of a determined six-year-old boy.

The ladies were having tea and in deep discussion while, as usual, leaving me to fend for myself under the control of the dog. I moved my right leg as if to stretch for comfort. Becky reacted as I knew she would. Just as she lunged forward to grab my ankle, I folded my leg again so that my heel struck her a sharp blow on the snout. She yelped in some pain but mostly in surprise. The ladies turned to see what had occurred, but I simply sat as if bent on reading eagerly from a lovely old book called Wee Gillis. I say reading; I was six at the time and could make out some individual letters, but pictures were much more at my level, and that book had some wonderful illustrations. I recommend it thoroughly for young children if you can get a copy these days. The book also helped my cover in my one and only contest ever with the erstwhile redoubtable Becky Sharp. She was a game dog and returned to the fray a couple of times more. I think that her nose became quite sore before she gave up the ghost and yielded victory to that small boy; he who had had enough of going home with both ankles smarting from the attentions of a dog called Becky.

Back now, however, to the morning of Sunday May 11th 1958.I was nineteen and still, just, a teenager. I was, therefore, still keen to keep up the usual Sunday morning tradition for teenagers everywhere, the lie in. Mum, lived by a quite different code, however. Her code was "once I'm up you're all up!" She emphasised her application to this code with the aid of her vacuum cleaner which she produced every Sunday morning and proceeded to hoover the carpets on the landing and stairs just outside my bedroom door. It was much more than a hint, moreover, because she kept it up until everyone she wanted to rouse was up. It was a crude tool, but it was hers and she used it to good effect, from her point of view.

Reluctantly and solely under the duress caused by the racket made by that infernal 'hoover' I roused myself and got up. I would not have been a pretty sight. We had no water plumbing upstairs in that house. Neither was there any internal sanitary plumbing. Each family member had his or her own piece of plumbing replacement equipment tucked under the bed for which he or she was personally responsible. Mum wanted no part of that for others and I for one do not blame her. Shortly after that particular Sunday morning I moved to a spare room downstairs and made that my bedroom firstly, away from other bedrooms and secondly possessing a downstairs window. At two in the morning in the cold of winter I no longer needed to go out into the freezing depths of the cold night air to do a pee. I just opened the window and did it on the coal that was handily stacked right outside. There was seldom any smell associated with this operation but on the odd occasion my Mum simply blamed next door's cat. I never did like that cat anyway.

As I got out of bed I noticed, and not for the first time the there was a loose floorboard just underfoot a few steps away from the bed. It was right next to the one where years before I had secreted the stolen piece of lead in a large jar. It had not been moved. The squeaky board needed to be fixed in place, I reasoned. I then set in motion a series of events that were to change the whole nature of the day. I made my way downstairs still haunted by the persistent sound of Mum hoovering on the landing, this time just outside my sister's room. I went straight to the cupboard under the stairs where Dad's few DIY tools were kept. I returned to my room, lifted the small scatter rug and the section of lino that covered the loose floorboard. With thoughts that I was doing my good deed for the day I proceeded to hammer a couple of nails, one in each end of the short board that my investigations had shown to be loose.

I had just made my first big error. Just as I was about to get myself up from the floor, with my one single thought that the good deed was now done I heard the terrible sound of water hissing from below the board. Sudden panic took over and I made my second mistake. I found a screwdriver and lifted the board to see what damage I had done. In lifting the board, I also removed the nails from their newly made holes in the water pipe below. All sorts of possible consequences now began to flood into my head. Firstly, my bedroom was right above the kitchen where my Mum had only the day before had a plasterer in to make her a brand-new ceiling. The old one had become very tatty over the years. Dad had recently purchased the house after years of renting it. Now that he owned it, he had decided that he could spend money on it in order to begin to make it more pleasant to live in. Oh God! I thought what do I do now? I did not know where the water stop cock might be, my brain had decided to neglect me, big time!

Dad caught wind of the noise I was making; he came upstairs to see what was occurring. His sudden anger did nothing to improve either my feelings or my performance. As we made our way I managed to let him understand that I was trying to locate the water stop cock. He dived into the same cupboard under the stairs. He emerged after several very long seconds with a four-foot-long metal rod that had an eyehole at one end and an inverted metal half tubed fitment at the other end. "It's in the front garden." He yelled at me.

My brain clicked back into gear for a moment. I suddenly remembered the small metal plate in our tiny front garden. It was about a foot to the right of the very short path as you left the house and about the same distance from the front wall of the house. I hurried to lift the small plate and quickly located the tap neatly sited about eighteen inches to two feet down; hence the long rod as a stop key. By this time Dad had located the rod that fitted into the eyehole to enable the key to be turned from above once the end fitment had been placed over the tap. I gave the rod a hefty twist clockwise. At that precise moment two things happened. I heard a huge crash and a scream from my Mum as her new ceiling came very noisily to the kitchen floor. I also heard the terrible noise of rushing water from down in the hole because I had sheered the tap from its base.

At that point Dad showed tremendous restraint, he didn't kill me! He was not calm, but he did not kill me. We had a phone, there were not so many about in those days. He phoned the Water Board. This was a public concern in those days, well before Mrs Thatcher began to sell the public utilities back to selected members of the public, the ones who self-selected by being able to afford to buy stock market shares. I have to say that the men from the Water Board came very quickly but made it clear at once that they could do nothing until the water flowing into our garden had been turned off. This they informed us could only be done from the main cock in the middle of the road. That meant that the water for half the street would be turned off until they were able to dig themselves down to the level of our erstwhile stop cock to give them elbow room to fix it. Once they heard about my part in the ongoing calamity they kindly gave me the job of going round to the neighbours to let them know about the forthcoming drought.

By this time, it was mid-morning on a Sunday; the one day of the week when, from time immemorial the Englishman expected to have his Sunday roast. I was about to advise all of our friends and neighbours that, today and for one day only, lunch would be delayed! It did not go down well. I do not have to go into details but that is one half-hour of my life that I would not like to have repeated. Years of friendship were as nothing apparently. Neighbours who had known me all my life were not happy to see me. We had gone all through the War together. Even that was forgotten in those unhappy hours that meant that lunch would be late that day! And that my friends, is why I do not ever Do Plumbing!

<u>Chapter Twenty</u>

<u>Working at Chase Farm Hospital</u>

The summer of 1959 saw my educational star fall out of the sky big time as far as my parents were concerned. Very unfortunately they had both passed away by the time that I did begin to resurrect that star much more strongly in the 1980s but in subjects chosen by me. They died within two years of each other in the early 1970s. 1959 though was very much the year of the falling star! Of my 4 A' Level Exams, taken in June of that summer, I passed only one and that was in Applied Mathematics. Apart from that I received O'level passes in Pure Maths Chemistry and Physics. That was not at all what my parents had hoped for or expected. The only surprise to me, however, was that I actually got a half-decent pass in the Applied Maths.

The fact is that it was my parents' dream for me that I should go off to college and become a doctor. I had never wanted to enter the 6th Form to do the science subjects. My parents knew that well enough but insisted on coming up with parental arguments that prevailed in those days; about security and work balance against earning potential etc. etc. My nearly six weeks in Europe the previous summer had sharpened my taste for language study and that added to my natural disinclination for hard work at that time in my life, added to the firm probability that my final year of A Level sciences would end in tears.

Three changes took place in the year 1959/60; firstly, at some pressure from my parents I did enrol at Ponders End Adult Education College with the vague and unenthusiastic promise that I would attempt a re-sit my failed exams. Secondly, in order to mitigate against some of my squashed pride at having proved myself to be such an exam booby I started to apply for jobs. I was very successful very quickly. I got a job as a trainee theatre technician at Chase Farm Hospital. Additionally, I made the decision to cease my struggle against being conscripted into Her Majesty's Military Service and finally, under Dad's tuition, I learned to drive a car and successfully passed my driving test.

I can deal with the exams very quickly because I went to the college with the attitude that I did not really ever expect to do well in either Pure Maths or in Physics. There was little point in working hard for either of those subjects. I attended the college part-time for a few months but spent most of my part-time hours there playing cards, bridge in fact, with some other nere-do-wells. I actually worked up quite a good game of bridge in the time that I was there. My other claim to fame was that I managed to crash a friend's beloved motor bike in probably the shortest bike ride ever recorded!

I do not accept the full responsibility for that crash, however. I had never ever expressed any desire to ride a motor bike. I had always been much more interested in cars. My friend kept insisting that I would be hooked once I convinced myself to try it under his guidance. My strong claim is that it was he who in this fashion put his own beloved bike into harm's way. That's my story and I have, or had in the early autumn of 1959, witness evidence to prove my case. In any case I'm sticking to it!

So, what actually did occur? Well, I had recently begun to; learn to drive a car with my Dad as my instructor. That fact received the first guffaw from my low-interest group of friends. We were waiting for the Maths lecturer who was almost always late for class. He never seemed to be that interested, in fact. We, a group of about seven would-be re-sits, were discussing the pros and cons of motor cycling vs car driving and ownership. For my part I had never been at all interested in motor cycling. I have been on various motor bikes over the years but always, always since the day in question in fact, always as a passenger. I can readily understand the joy, the pleasure and interest that others may have but I just don't have it for myself. I never did have it but my erstwhile friend just could not bring himself to believe it.

My friend pestered me and cajoled me until finally I agreed to descend to the yard of the college and into the large quadrangle where he parked his motor bike. That was his first mistake. He decided that that quad would be a good place for me to begin my entrée into the wonders of the motor cycling world. I could see at one glance that it was no-where large enough for my needs but he would not be said! The details of gear changing, and braking were carefully explained until he was convinced that I had enough knowledge to be trusted with his beautiful, olive green, 1954 Royal Enfield Clipper 250. I knew in both my heart and the bottom of my stomach that he was going to be proved wrong and just how was I correct! I started the bike OK and put it into gear just as I was shown but I immediately revved the engine far too much for the space that I had available. After that the bike took over entirely. It and I travelled about 15 yards before we both hit the side wall of the quadrangle.

The damage to my feelings was minor compared to the damage to the poor lovely old bike. My friend could not believe what he maintained I had done to his bike, but I rested my defence firmly and defiantly on the "I told you so!" explanation and reasoning. I'm sorry to confirm that the event put to death, at that embryo stage a budding friendship. It was, as I say, both a very sad as well as a short motorcycle experience for me and one that I have had no desire to improve upon at any time since. I have long appreciated the joys that many people experience from their motorcycles, but it is not for me. I would add that even as the event described did have the additional effect of ending my embryo friendship with that young motorcycle owner. I would still claim that the major responsibility was his.

The year between July 1959 and July 1960 was a big year of many changes. These changes moved my life into a totally different direction from that had been planned for me by my parents. I had received my first set of call-up papers from the War Office just before my 18th birthday. I had been able to defer my military service on the acceptable grounds that I was in higher education. At the beginning of the year in question I was still firmly inclined to continue with the deferment route. By the end of the year, I had decided that military service would allow me a break from home-life over which my parents would have no control. This was not an easy decision for me but was one that I felt was necessary for me at that time for the reason given above. It was certainly not a welcome decision for me to arrive at; however to go into military service was definitely a way to make a no-fault break with my parents and their influence on my life. I decided that The UK Government could help me to do that. When I had first received my call up papers in 1957 it had been both a blow as well as a relief to realise that there was something 'out there' that could be even more powerful in my life than my parents. By 1960 it had now become a tool that I could use.

I began to do part time work as a trainee theatre technician at Chase Farm Hospital in Enfield in order to earn some money, ostensibly as a precursor to going off to college to study medicine. This however had become more and more a dream of my parents than of mine. I had wanted to study languages, but my parents could see no financial future in that. That was the game of the day; the job had to be able to ensure a worthwhile and financial future. I think that Dad might have accepted 'solicitor' or 'accountant' as alternatives, but those possibilities had not even been thought of. After many unpleasant family arguments and discussions on the subject I simply took the route of least opposition and spent my time perfecting a quite decent game of bridge. I finally took a set of three 'A' levels in the February at which point I upped my hours at the hospital to full-time. Those were the days when there was a great deal of flexibility in the jobs market. I learned of the inevitable failure of those exams in the June of that year by which time my route into the RAF had already been settled…

 I enjoyed the months that I worked at the hospital very much. I was able to pay my Mum some housekeeping money. It was not much because the pay was not so good, but it did make me feel better. I believe very strongly that she envied me my emerging range of liberty. Dad had always refused to permit her to go out to work. There was never any real discussion on the subject he just said no and that was that in those days. I am not prepared to explore this further in this story, but I do try to put some 'meat on that bone' in later stories when I discuss separately the deaths of my parents.

Chase Farm hospital has its origins in what was a Poor Law orphanage established in 1886. The oldest part of the hospital, the "Clock Tower" building, was formerly the main part of the orphanage. Middlesex County Council started to admit elderly people to the facility in 1930 and it had developed into a care home for elderly people by 1938. The facility became a part of the National Health Service in 1948. Moving forward; after my short association with the Hospital a new surgical block; known as the Highlands Wing was opened in 1995 in memory of the local Highlands Hospital which had recently closed. In 1999 the hospital became part of the Barnet and Chase Farm NHS Hospitals Trust.

By the time that I came to be a worker at the hospital my parents had moved home from Winchester Road Edmonton to Peartree Road Enfield. The new house had decent gardens, front and back, a shared driveway to the garage and, wonder of wonders, an indoor loo. I must add here that my Dad was very proud of his garage. He was the only man I have known in my life who always kept his car in the garage overnight. That was in spite of the fact that manoeuvring the car into the garage was not without its difficulties. The shared driveway was quite narrow. At the garage-end of the drive it became divided 'V' shaped into two short sections, one aimed at each of the two garages; there was thereby one for each of the two houses sharing the drive.

The entry into each garage did thereby involve a zig zag of manoeuvres. The garages were only just big enough to allow for this as well as to permit room to exit and to access the car once inside that only-just adequate building. There was definitely no room to allow for the car to be turned around for the return journey and so one had to reverse either into or out of the garage. Whether you reversed into or out of that structure did not matter it was 'well tricky' either way! [See my next story re Clutch plates for another, fuller, tale regarding that driveway!]

Working at the hospital became my first real employment and I was able to enjoy it for a number of reasons. It began my road of separation from under the wing of my parents. When I first received my call-up papers some years before, I had resented the idea of an entity that had more 'power' over my life than my parents. By the time of which I am now writing I was looking for ways of separating from parental power as gently as possible. Don't get me wrong, I loved them both but there does come a time…

To come back to the subject in hand; Chase Farm Hospital was an ideal place for me to begin working. It was close to home, by which I should explain that it was within walking distance from home. It was a tidy walk but, nonetheless, walking was definitely an option for me in those days. It was also very achievable by bike, and I still possessed the old Claude Butler of my teenage years. There was also a very handy bus available from Enfield Town centre, just round the corner from our house. I was able to pick and choose from those options according to my mood and the weather, the first of these often being determined by the second.

My duties were simple in reality although I knew in my heart that my parents were hoping that the association with the hospital would lead me back towards medicine. There was not a remote chance of that as far as I was concerned. It was just a job, pure and simple, to give me space to think about a better path. It was, though, interesting enough in its own way.

First and foremost, the job entailed being part of a team dedicated to keeping the operating theatre and environs clean. The theatre itself needed to be kept super-clean; as close to surgically sterile as possible. The actual equipment used for operations was, of course, required to be sterile. Contamination of sensitive 'high impact' surfaces can be from body fluids, human tissue and other more mundane debris such as dirt, dust, paper products etc. through direct means or from cross contamination via touching potentially contaminated surfaces. Microbial contamination during a surgical procedure is a continuing and contributing factor to a surgical site infection. As I remember it there was a between-operation procedure and an end-of-day more thorough routine. Each of these had to be followed scrupulously. Medical science has been on a steady learning curve on these matters ever since and continuing….

An example of a major difference, a then and now example, is that much of the direct surgical equipment such as knives are now 'single use' pieces of kit prepared and produced in sterile packages by the manufacturer. In the operating theatre at Chase Farm Hospital in 1959/60 such equipment was sterilised 'on site' by a nurse trained for the purpose using a sterilising autoclave.

There was a team of theatre technicians of which I was the youngest and least experienced. I came to understand, much to my surprise that as one aspect of the job was to make sure that the equipment was always 'to hand' for the medical staff, I needed to be 'gowned up' and available myself during operations. Thus, during my months working there I was able to observe many operations as they were being conducted. I was still 20 when I started working there and my eyes were opened to the realities of life in surgery very quickly.

My first shock came with my introduction to the sluice room. This was a small room positioned between the two theatres. Its main function was a place in which the initial cleaning of articles was completed, such as the initial washing of surgery tools was undertaken before they had to be taken away for sterilisation; linen was gathered together and bundled up for sending to the laundry. My first impression of the sluice room was that it was a place of blood and gore. Second and third impressions did nothing to dispel my first impression. Having said that it is truly surprising just how much one's sensitivities can be crushed by experience. It was not long before I was able to eat my lunch sandwiches in that erstwhile abominable place.

Morning theatre sessions lasted as long as was necessary. The senior theatre medical staff did try to judge the list so that they were able to run to a timetable. Those timings were very much like trying to tie a piece of string round a football. There was always the likelihood that the subsequent loop would slip to either side of the ball. It usually slipped to the side whereby the list ran on longer than planned. That would mean that the time between morning and afternoon lists could evaporate rapidly. The theatre had to be cleaned of course which meant that lunch had to be taken 'on the move'. I learned rapidly that work in the real world does not obey the rules about timekeeping that you learn at school. Yes indeed, I quickly learned to eat my lunch in the sluice room simply by being hardened, even to the point of brushing aside some of the 'blood and gore' to make a space!

It was, I think, as early as my second week that, on the Monday morning, I was informed that I had been assigned to the plaster [fracture] clinic for the next day. I took the news quite non-committedly assuming quietly that I would be required simply to keep supplies going for the medical operative on duty in the clinic. I was quickly disabused of this naïve notion. I attended the clinic room the next morning with one of my theatre technician colleagues only to discover that 'we were it'. The process was that the injured person would attend the fracture clinic staffed by medical doctors. X rays and other tests were done. The person would then be sent along the corridor to us with instructions as to what type of plaster to apply. "It's all quite simple really" was the advice from my colleague.

My colleague explained that there were certain fractures that were more common than others forearm fractures of either the radius or the ulna bones in the forearm, sometimes of both. These needed to be constrained by the same style of caste; from the wrist to the upper arm about 4" above the elbow with a bend in the elbow. These restrictions were necessary to prevent movement of the radius and ulna which would of course harm the healing process. It all seemed quite straight forward as I assisted my colleague Ron with a couple of these fractures during the very first morning.

It all went off very well until My colleague, Ron, left me alone to deal with a fracture of the type with which I had assisted him a couple of times. I was thus left to my own devices for a while. I assumed an air of total confidence as I approached my unsuspecting victim. I asked him to sit down by the plaster table as I cut an appropriate length of stockinet. This was used both to protect the arm from irritations and to help to prevent a very painful removal of the plaster were it to have trapped most of the hairs of the arm during its residence there, without such 'depilation' protection.

It then came to selecting lengths of plaster strip. Now if I have one inherent weakness it has always been that of 'adding a little bit extra'. I have done this all my life with 'a few more potatoes to the stew, another spoonful of oats to the porridge another helping of formula to the baby's bottle…I guess you get the idea by now. Well, this 'additional bit' attitude was with me, sitting there on my left shoulder, as I applied just a bit more plaster to the man's arm. It didn't seem that much more to me while I was applying the strips. I just wanted to make the cast just that bit stronger. I was only trying to help to secure my unintended 'victim' from further injury! It wasn't until I had finally finished, and the plaster had set that I began to become aware of the look of puzzlement on the man's face…

"I can hardly bloody-well lift my fxxxxxg arm"; he growled at me through gritted teeth. "You some kind of sodxxg moron or what?" Just at that point my own 'witch-finder general' entered the room; ostensibly wanting to see how I was doing.

The theatre sister who also had responsibility for the plaster theatre was the second person in a matter of minutes to glare at me that morning. She gave me that 'I knew you were going to be trouble the first time I saw you', look. A lot of strongly felt meaning can be contained in certain facial expressions. Sister had them in abundance. She was concentrating them fully on me! I stepped towards her, mumbling some inane offer to help 'fix' my mistake. The glare became more intense, sister simply lifted her arm, without a murmur or a word she pointed at the door and her meaning was very clear – OUT!

My interview with Sister later that morning was not pleasant, but it was educational. I am not going to elaborate on that side of things, but she did make her feelings very clear on the subject of following instructions to "The Letter" in future. She added in true 'witch-finder' fashion that she would be watching me, very carefully adding, rather unpleasantly I felt, that my future "in her hospital" was far from secure…

My second 'run-in' with Sister was to be my last. As a member of the 'theatre' crew, albeit a very minor member, I became privy to witnessing a wide range of medical operations, both major and minor.

Before I come to my final confrontation, however I would like to dip-over to the more minor side of the medical operation regime. It was scheduled as a 'faecal disempaction' and everyone I asked about the meaning of this simply grinned and walked away.

It was the final 'op' booked into theatre one Wednesday afternoon. As soon as the poor guy was wheeled in under anaesthetic, I became aware of a certain light-hearted and ribald atmosphere that had become established. I also noticed that the Consultant surgeon had left the theatre. His senior registrar was now in-charge. I also noticed the singular lack of surgical equipment that had been sterilised and laid out for the 'op'; one dessert spoon to be precise. Then it slowly dawned on me the meaning of the actual words; faecal disempaction. The poor chap had been unable to 'go' for I do not remember how long. The result being that he had become impacted and that it was felt that a dessert spoon was the ideal 'weapon of choice' as the means whereby to relieve him of the major part of his blockage.

I believe that the intervention was successful, and that the poor fellow was relieved of his encumbrance. I do realise that I have referred to a certain ribaldry that developed as this patient was wheeled into theatre on the trolley. There was no disrespect however that I ever witnessed among the varied emotions that were extant from time to time in theatre because emotions there were, and any voiced expressions were simply ways of reducing the tensions experienced by human beings doing a difficult job. My parting comment on this specific intervention however is short and sweet. In all the months that I worked at the hospital I used the staff canteen but rarely. I never did though, ever, choose a meal that required the use of a dessert spoon!!

My final confrontation with Sister came shortly after the 'disempaction' event. I caught the full blast of 'Sister's careful watching eye' on me during a D&C afternoon list in theatre. I came to the conclusion that she was disapproving possibly that such a young man should be allowed into such intimate surgery.

Perhaps I should explain the term D&C before I continue in order that you will understand more completely the discussion that took place later between 'the dragon' and me.

Dilation and curettage (D&C) is a brief surgical procedure in which the cervix is dilated and a special instrument is used to scrape the uterine lining. Entry of course is via the vagina.

A woman may need a D&C for one of a number of reasons. It may be needed in order to: remove tissue in the uterus during or after a miscarriage or after abortion or to remove small pieces of placenta after childbirth. This procedure helps prevent infection or heavy bleeding.

Alternatively, it may be recommended to the patient as a way to diagnose or treat abnormal uterine bleeding. A D&C may help diagnose or treat growths such as fibroids, polyps, hormonal imbalances, or uterine cancer. A sample of uterine tissue is viewed under a microscope to check for abnormal cells. As I remember it the procedure usually took a short while only, perhaps 15-20 minutes after which the woman had to be returned to the ward by me and one of my colleagues for a short period of recovery.

I have to confess that my period spent in the hospital was a long time ago. According to my memory of those times the women undergoing D&C did so under anaesthetic and so needed time in the hospital to recover from that. On the afternoon of a D&C clinic therefore there were a number of those patients in the recovery ward, which was where I had to regularly run the gauntlet of their perverse humour.

Most of the patients had seen me in the operating theatre just prior to their anaesthetic taking effect. It quickly became established on the ward that there was this young 'kid' working in the theatre who was 'fair game' for some teasing. Every time that I ventured up there, I had to brace myself for some very ribald but always good-natured joshing from 'the collective' there. The theatre sister became aware of this and sought to challenge me over it but not from the angle of my comfort or self-esteem; not that that aspect of the situation worried me much anyway.

Sister's office was not a cheerful place; there were no items of personalisation apparent there, either on the bookshelf or on her desk. She was all business it seemed.

"I'm taking you off of working in the theatre during the D&C clinic". This was her opening comment to me as I entered her domain following the peremptory summons there.

"You are too young to be seeing some of the things that you experience there."

"There are other people who are younger than me working in theatre sister."

"Those are all females."

"And there we have it. It's not my age you're having trouble with. It's the fact that I am male."

Her lips tightened she said nothing but remained firm. She was clearly resolved to have me out of theatre.

"Have any of the female patients complained?" I asked. I was beginning to firm up myself now. Her meaning was becoming clearer by the second and I didn't like what I was feeling and thinking although she was clearly determined not to actually voice them.

"Have any of the theatre staff complained?"

Sister's face reddened with anger, her lips tightened further, now lost their colour, nearly white.

"Are you daring to suggest that I am using these poor, uncomfortable women unconscious and with their legs in stirrups, in the most ungainly and unbecoming positions as free porn sister?"

I felt that she might burst now such was the sense of anger and frustration she was clearly experiencing. She was clearly not used to being cross-questioned by such a lowly person as me. Something had to give, and it wasn't going to be me; not over this anyway. I was feeling angry and also just a bit frightened. I was 20 and almost totally without either experience or qualifications worth bragging about. I tried clenching my jaw at a time when I really felt like biting my tongue but neither would have cut the mustard to use one idiomatic expression after the other.

"Well Sister, I'll tell you what I'm thinking. I'm thinking that you're way off track. You've totally misread a situation and you've jumped in without even speaking to me before you've made up your mind. I'm only 20 years old, seeing as you are objecting to my age. The women who come to this clinic are all much older than me. They are in their 30s. Many are in their 40s or even 50s. How attractive or appealing do you think they are to me, trussed up as they are like chickens in a coconut shy?" I paused to catch my breath. She reeled visibly at my somewhat gross and dramatic description of the scene.

"No sister I was thinking of the indignity of the situation and of some of the unpleasantness, the loss of dignity as well as the pain and suffering that woman go through in order to bring their families into the world."

"What would you know about all that?" Her voice had softened.

"Personally nothing of course, but don't forget sister when I was a child there was no NHS. Babies were born at home. I heard my Mum have two miscarriages and one live child all by the time I was 8 and all in the room next to mine. I was too young to know exactly what was going on. I was only eight when my sister was born but I could understand pain when I heard it and then I also saw the blood on the sheets. As we all know a little blood goes a long way." I felt I had said enough. It was the thought of my Mum's hard life that had made me so bold in fact. I made to move towards the door. She had one more arrow to fire.

"What about all the unseemly banter in the recovery ward. It only happens when you're up there. The ward sister has told me that much."

"Oh dear, sister!" I sighed. Was this never going to end I wondered?

"Did that sister ever deign to also tell you that it's all good natured and that it is the patients who start out on me? It began the first time that I entered the ward after a clinic and, like a race batten; the 'goading-Tony' batten has been passed on somehow from clinic to clinic." She stared at me her expression now changed, now to sympathy and that was not what I had intended.

"Look sister, don't you think that some of those women just want and need a release from the tension and the indignity of it all? They've had their children and now just want to get on with their lives, but they still have to undergo the humiliation of being treated as inanimate objects by the NHS and having their private parts pushed and poked about by its workers, mostly men. They need to joke a bit and perhaps pull someone's leg like they do me." I was just about to go through the door when I pulled out another arrow of my own.

"You know sister; the same thing happens inside the theatre itself even among the great, the good and the mighty."

"What on earth do you mean?" The voice rising again!

"Well, to break the tension of difficult situations the doctors will often begin to crack jokes. Those joking sessions would often seem to be totally inappropriate and disrespectful to any casual observer, but they are nothing of the kind. They are simply a way of easing the tensions of difficult situations."

I thought that I might get the push from working in the operating theatre altogether after my outburst in sister's office but nothing of the kind. She seemed to mellow into a period of resigned acceptance that a young man might be ok to work in her hospital for the time being at least.

I enjoyed my work there or, rather, I enjoyed the experience of it all. It was from that experience though that I began the path of understanding the harder life and road that women have to travel than we men. I also began to put a context around it. For example, my Dad's absolute and resolute refusal to allow my Mum ever to go out to work whilst he was alive.

"No wife of mine is ever going to need to go out to work for her living. I am the provider for this family."

I can still hear him in my mind, saying it, as I write this. There was no question that his decision had to be obeyed. Mum never did go out to work, while he was alive, although she often tried to get him to change his mind. It was no use and their relationship worsened over time so that any conversation between them ended in a spiteful argument. She did not go out of the house to work until after Dad died. That is a story that I explore more fully when I write about their deaths; the last two stories in a later series. My Dad's attitude would have been seen as quite normal by many in those days. In the modern era however, his behaviour would be seen to be very controlling and even grounds for divorce. Times change and attitudes fall into line. Maybe?

It was at the hospital though that I began to put it all in a social context for myself. Dad was not a bully nor was he an unkind man. I felt then and now that he was himself trapped in the pervading social context that it was his job to provide for his family. I am writing about events from 1959. I am writing them down in 2018 just two months before the beginning of 2019 by which time it will be sixty years on from those times. Society has moved and developed a very long way from the 50s and even now it still has a long way to go. Sexism lives! Along with a whole range of discriminations we still have a road to travel but that, for now, is another story.

Virtually all doctors were men and nurses were almost exclusively women in the era of which I am writing. Legislation has done much to change social attitudes and behaviour over time, but most would agree that we are nowhere nearly there yet.

During my months working in the theatre, I saw a wide range of operations and procedures. I saw very complicated orthopaedic procedures as well as several caesarean births. I also saw several appendectomies which are operations to remove an appendix. These are usually fairly quick operations as I remember it because the appendix is usually not so difficult to find and the warning signs that it needs to be removed are well known and understood. Things become much more complicated for the surgical staff if the appendix ruptures.

I witnessed several caesarean sections during which surgical procedures were turned on their head. Under normal procedures a surgeon will enter a body tying off blood vessels as he or she goes. The operation will be completed to his or her satisfaction and the exit is completed again making sure that all blood vessels are tied off where appropriate and that all surgical material such as swabs is removed.

A caesarean operation takes on a different priority from the very beginning. The emphasis is to save the baby so that the entry is done as swiftly as possible and the tying up of the blood vessels is done as the wound is closed. The baby is usually delivered in about 5 or 6 minutes. That is my memory of the operations that I witness and of the conversations of the medical staff at the time. If my memory is incorrect in any way, then it is probably all to the good that I never did take the parental path to medicine.

As far as orthopaedic surgery was concerned it was, as with all surgery, very skilled and sometimes physically hard work. I remember one surgeon who referred to himself rather dismissively as a 'bone carpenter' which in some respects he was. He was also much more of course than that. I remember one young man who had been in a traffic accident in which he had been a motor cyclist colliding with a car coming along a country road in the opposite direction. It is clear that a motorcycle is never going to win that contest! The lad was in a bad way. The surgeon and his senior registrar spent several very painstaking hours re-constructing his legs. When they had finished the senior man thanked his registrar at which point, he stopped to pause a moment to whisper what seemed like a short prayer. He then wished the unconscious lad the best of luck before he left the theatre. It was a memorable moment.

I would like finally to emphasise that I was a medically unqualified observer of all the procedures mentioned in this short story and that I am relying on my memory over a 60-year time span. All my poor jottings must be read with a full recognition and understanding of these facts. Similar limitations apply when one considers that the techniques themselves will have changed, sometimes radically, over the same time span.

In the March of 1960, I reached the grand old age of 21. Later in the Month, I cannot remember the exact date; I received what was clearly a final letter from the War Office regarding my National Service call-up. They had apparently had enough of my continued deferment without clear evidence of higher academic achievement. In the letter I was given a date for a medical with a doctor in High Holborn and the news that I was to be 'recruited' into the RAF. That at least was good news as that, after the Navy, was my second choice of the three choices on offer. By that time in the game though it suited me to cease to struggle against the inevitable. I decided that I would attend the medical and submit to the findings thereof. All of that is described in the first chapter of my first book 'A Road ran Through It'. A good and easy read although I say it myself.

In the meantime, I continued to work at the hospital. I am becoming quite used to the routine there; so much so that, under pain of near death if I should let her down again, 'sister' had allowed me back into the plaster theatre. The interview in her office when she announced her change of heart to me was far from easy. She did admit that my work had improved but that was as far as the positives were to go. "Rules are there to be obeyed!"… "Instructions are given for the protection of patients as well as for the education of operatives!"… "And I am the final arbitrator on both of those issues. Do you understand what I am saying?" That was the short version of the pre-change of circumstances interview. What could I say? "Yes sister," was all I could come up with. I would like to think that I noticed the wisp of a smile as I left her office…

I would like to terminate this story of my first real-life work experience on a lighter, if somewhat embarrassing note. It all began just towards the end of my lunch break one Thursday afternoon. As usual I had taken my break in the sluice room because we had been working hard during the time between AM and PM theatre sessions to make the theatres ready for the PM list, general surgery.

The nurse approached me with a huge grin on her face and presented me with the contents of her hands, a mug of warm water, a bar of ordinary soap, a small towel and a safety razor. She also obliged me with the ward name as well as that of the patient, a man in his thirties and due for an appendectomy early in the afternoon list. I groaned inwardly. The task that I was about to perform was usually done by the ward nurses and but for some unusual conspiracy of circumstances that would have been the course of events that afternoon.

As I climbed the stairs and made my way to the ward for my next engagement, I tried to recall all the euphemisms that I could conjure up for 'Penis'; Captain Winky, Cock,

Corporal of the Guard, Cyclops, Energizer Bunny, Godzilla, Dick, Todger, Jimmy, One-eyed Monster and for obvious reasons 'Joystick'. These are just a few. Believe me there are many, many more. Just consult any one of any number of sources on the 'net' if you need confirmation! Men have been most enthusiastically inventive regarding the choosing of names for their 'best friend' over the years. I engaged in this mental activity to try to take my mind off of the next job in hand. Oh God! I realised – 'in my bloody hand'!

I tried to forget the enormity of my near future as I approached the ward but to absolutely no avail. I prayed that my approaching activity would not be so dreadful. My optimistic prayers that my 'adversary' would be unconscious from pre-op medication were doomed from the moment that I saw him. He was a man in his mid-thirties Strong, fit, bushy eyed and glaring fiercely at me from the moment that he saw me walking towards him, razor and shaving mug in hand. He sat bolt upright in his bed and glared at me all that long walk down the ward to his bed. It did not help that each of the several ward nurses smiled sweetly at me and said "Hi" in turn. What, I wondered fiercely, had been the bloody emergency that had kept each of them from performing the duty to which I had been so suddenly and unexpectedly assigned?

One of the nurses made a drama out of swishing the curtains round the bed as I came close. Despite myself I could not refrain from chuckling as I caught sight of his indignant posture when I came to the bedside.

"What the fxxx r'you giggling at?" I could not reply to this for fear of making it worse by laughing even louder.

"Right" I tried to sound business-like, professional. "We both know why I'm here; best get on with it." With that I pulled back the light bedclothes. I got a full view of my task. I was horrified. He had the bushiest dick you could imagine! It was not circumcised fortunately, I thought, which mercifully meant that I had something to hold it up with without having to make a full-handed grab when I needed to get to the underside. I whipped up a bit of foam with the now only warm-ish water and the soap and began to shave downwards from just below his belly button. My intention being to work in that direction as fast as possible in order to get the job over and done with ASAP. As I made my first downwards stroke however the full horror struck me that the razor, they had given me was as blunt as a bullock's backside.

In an act of self-preservation, I asked one of the nurses for a pair of scissors so that "I could cut some of the forest down" before trying to finish the job. It was not going to be a speedy activity. In fact, I swear that it seemed to me that I seemed to take longer doing the shaving than the surgeon finally took to do the appendectomy! I also spilled just about as much blood; what with the inevitable nicks that are result of shaving with a blunt razor. There came the moment when I had to shave the lower part of his belly, that part in the shadow of his Todger. I moved slowly around to the other side of the bed so that I could do the 'holding' with my left hand, that is strictly the thumb and fore-finger and by pinching the end of the poor sod's foreskin.

Mercifully there did come to an end, for us both, of this medical house of horrors event. He though was the one who's lower belly looked as if it had been given more than a once-over by a bunch of angry rooks. I apologised to the poor chap without any response from him. I returned to my duties in the theatre and waited for the afternoon list to begin. To my horror my erstwhile victim was the first to appear. This time however he was unconscious. The surgeon took one look at the carnage around the general 'One-eyed Monster' area and burst out laughing. "Well then, I bloody well hope that he had a general anaesthetic for this piece of work!" I edged slowly backwards, towards the sluice room.

I finally received the results of the last set of science/maths exams that I would ever attempt. As expected, they were no better than not quite enough…I had become resigned by now but not content by any manner of means that I was moving towards my enforced enrolment into the RAF. It was and always had been the case that I saw it as a form of theft, a theft by the government of two years of my life during which, without consultation with me, I could be put in harm's way. I did see it though as a means to an end. The end being a move away from my parents and towards the young woman, Joyce, with whom I had fallen in love. See my book 'A Road Ran Through IT' [Amazon]. During the months immediately before my RAF training began at RAF Bridgenorth my Dad taught me to drive. That was a good period for us both. It took the focus away from exams and studying subjects that did not interest me, as well as from the tensions surrounding all that onto something much more mundane. It was also something that Dad could do for me and that we could achieve together. He did try to teach me 'double declutching' in a fully synchromesh car, to no avail however with that one. Nonetheless I'm not certain which of us was the more pleased when I passed first time…

Chapter Twenty ONE

Clutch Plates for an old Austin 14!

I have never longed to own a motor bike; cars have always been my love and preference after I gave up riding my beloved Claude Butler bicycle at the age of 16 or 17. I was already familiar with the controls of a car despite not having yet passed my test. That is an admission that I did not have to make to my pater because he caught me out just three days before my driving test. The ensuing interview with him was not short nor was it sweet!

The first car I ever owned was a very second-hand Austin 14. I bought it for £10 cash in 1960, just a few days after I passed my driving test and shortly before I was due to enter, very unwillingly, into the Royal Air Force as a National Serviceman. I felt that I deserved that small luxury because I was almost at the end of a year's work as an operating theatre technician at the Chase Farm Hospital.

I called the car 'Goosie' for reasons that shall remain lost in the mists of time. I have never given a car a name since. My memories of events surrounding this vehicle do not include the purchase of either Road Tax or Insurance, for which I now apologise sincerely to the authorities. My only excuse for these omissions is that this was my first car and my excitement of owning it did not leave space in my poor brain for such mundane essentials. I had after all already made the considerable outlay of £10!

I bought the car simply on the basis that it had no rust, that it was cheap and that it had a nice leathery smell inside. It was also a reasonably big car, not huge but big enough to satisfy my preference for large rather than small in the world of cars. I just liked the way it stood on the car lot. It was my first car purchase and I consulted no-one before buying it.

I first noticed problems with the car on my drive home from the lot. Once the engine housing had had time to truly warm up, the clutch began to slip. I was nearly home by this time and managed to make it with little problem although I fully realised that my first venture into car ownership had suffered a serious setback. I parked my new £10 acquisition on the road in front of my parents' new house. Our new semi-detached home in Peartree Road Enfield.

I have referred to the house as new, it was, in fact, some 20 years old but new to Mum and Dad and my Mum's pride and joy since we had moved in about 18 months before that, the day of my entry into car ownership. The property was a definite cut above their previous house, a terrace house in Edmonton, with outside toilet and a tin bath in the scullery. That place did have hot and cold running water though, which was a definite upgrade by Dad from the old tin bath we had had for many years. A bath in front of the kitchen range on a Friday night, one at a time in the same water. The new property moreover actually had its own garage where my Dad religiously kept his car, a black Ford Anglia that he had owned from new in the early 1950s. This garage was accessed via a joint drive with the house next door. The drive divided, once past the houses, into a space for the two garages of our house and that of Mr Bell, our neighbour.

My next move, optimistic as it seems now, was to walk into town and buy a workshop manual to help me to repair my recent purchase. I also managed to get to a garage that could supply me with the correct clutch pads for the car. I wanted desperately to impress my Dad that, even if I had bought a 'pig in a poke', I was intending to make it good by repairing the clutch. I had the offer from two friends who said that they would give me a hand. That was good to know but, as they both lacked any substantial knowledge or experience in the work, their offer only contributed some very welcome muscle to the equation.

The actual repair was fraught with difficulties two of which were well to the fore; firstly, I had no experience at car maintenance, secondly, we had no appropriate place in which to undertake the repair. The first of these, namely my total lack of experience, I decided to ignore based on my acquisition of a car repair manual for the Austin 14. To deal with the second I decided that the only sensible place to do the work would be at the beginning of the joint car drive between the two houses. That, I reasoned, would be a lot safer than attempting the operation in the public road.

A further problem was that we had little in the way of tools to undertake the work. We did have a car jack together with some spanners and things that I found in Dad's garage. The total provision of equipment, however, would have fallen far short of what a real mechanic would have considered necessary or even safe!

We took one look at the workshop manual, then another at the underside of the car, once we had raised its front end on bricks. We decided that the only way we were going to get to the failing clutch pads was to unbolt the clutch and gear assembly from the engine block and try to lower it, attached to the drive shaft, onto a safety net of ropes that we had strung between arms of the car's chassis. In this way we hoped to gain access to the clutch sufficient to change the worn pads. It seemed feasible but we had reckoned without 'neighbour delay'.

The fact is that the story of the changing of the clutch pads fades dramatically against the developing story of neighbour delay and neighbour anger that began almost at the moment that we had successfully unhinged the clutch from its safe haven attached to the engine block. It was at that moment that Mr. Bell appeared on the scene and demanded that we move the car so that he could get his car out of his garage and take his dear wife to town so that she could do some shopping.

I tried to explain, as politely and in as conciliatory manner as I could, that the car could not be moved at that precise moment. I tried to explain the fix we were in and apologised profusely, many times, for my lack of foresight in beginning the work on the car without consulting him first. From the beginning of these exchanges, I could see quite clearly that the man had right on his side. I was, after all, blocking his rightful exit, by car, from his property. My conciliatory attitude began to wane drastically, however, as the exchanges continued.

Neighbour delay set in quite quickly, because Mr Bell began to return every ten or fifteen minutes to badger us into speeding up the process. I was indeed under the car on about his third or fourth re-entry from the outer space of his anger. He began to bang on the car to attract my attention. He certainly did that because he had alarmed me enough to make my exit from that position very speedily. We had the car raised onto a quite Heath Robinson collection of blocks and bricks. I was not totally confident that the combination was up to a physical attack such as my neighbour appeared to be prepared to mount.

Once that I had extricated myself from the underside of the car I faced my neighbour, still wishing to be polite but with a new determination to be firm. I pointed out that, although he had right on his side, he was now delaying our attempts at making progress to rectify the situation. I added that he had put me in danger by banging on the car. At that point the man's language deteriorated profoundly. He strode around me and up our garden path towards the front door. He began banging loudly on the door. "I'm going to discuss this with your father". He added heavily whilst managing to glare fiercely at me over his shoulder.

Well, I knew that he would have no luck at speaking to Dad because he was at work. Mum came to the door after some delay and additional banging. I could see, even from twenty feet away and past Mr Bell's shoulder, that she was irritated by the interruption to her 'quiet' time. The neighbour began with a tirade of invective against me once he had ascertained that Dad was not home. If he had thought that, in this way, he could bully a 'mere woman' in the absence of the man of the house he had sadly misjudged the situation. Mum was a Londoner who had survived many trials and tribulations and, in any case, in neighbourhood squabbles, her initial instinct was always to protect and defend her own, in the absence of any concrete evidence to the contrary. Mr Bell had put himself on very shaky ground by opening up with an angry barrage. That was no way for him to get Mum's listening ear, no, not at all.

Mr Bell moved from angry to incandescent. During this transfer he crossed another boundary into difficult country for maintenance of his case. He began to swear. Now, my parents could argue, in fact that was what they did, and had done, for much of their married life together. They did not, however, use profanity. Whilst Mr Bell did not actually swear directly at my Mum the mere fact that he began to lower the tone in that direction brought my own protective instincts into play. The truth was also that I was very happy to see the man begin to put himself in the wrong and, by so doing, divert the spotlight somewhat from yours -truly. I strode along our garden path towards that angry man, I was suddenly full of righteous indignation. I told him firmly to move away from our front door and my Mum. By this time, I had stood myself between him and the house. For just a moment I thought that he was going to hit me. Fortunately for both of us this did not happen.

There had to come a point when angry sentiments began to cool but it took the separate arrival of three new players to begin the process. Mr Bell did not actually strike me. At the precise moment when this might have happened, a very distraught Mrs Bell opened her from door in tears and demanding that we should all cool down. Mrs Oxley, our next-door neighbour on the other side opened her front door to see what all the 'racket' was about. A couple of minutes later, at which point Mrs Oxley had begun to take charge of the consoling of Mrs Bell, my Dad came wandering into the situation having just arrived home from work. This being Saturday he had hoped to enjoy some peace and quiet in what remained of the afternoon. That hope was rapidly dashed to the ground as he turned to walk up our front garden path.

The group of, now, five people coalesced into a minor parliament at our front door and discussing the rights and wrongs of my behaviour. Mr. Bell's behaviour was, apparently, no longer on the agenda. I made my way quickly back to the car for want of anything better to do. Just before I managed to seek refuge under my old Austin I glanced back towards the house. I immediately wished that I hadn't done this. I took one look at my Dad's face and realised that the rights and wrongs of the argument had moved strongly back towards Mr Bell, as far as he was concerned.

It was, in fact, my Dad's judgement that concerned me the most. He was a hardworking man. The thought that I had involved him in a pile of grief at the end of a long, hard week of work and mind-bending rush hour travel really upset me. Mum was still intent on battling Mr Bell's attitude but this, I could hear, was cutting no ice with Dad. Mrs Bell's tears were abating but she was still too upset to join in the general verbal assassination of yours- truly. Mrs Oxley was the only one of the five who seemed prepared to verbally defend me. Her evidence, however, came solely in the form of a character reference. This bore no weight as far as the two men were concerned!

There was no actual punishment, though, that could realistically be imposed on me. By the time that they got to the point of discussing retribution I had installed the pads and, thankfully, moved the car back out of the drive and onto the road. Dad's verdict, as I walked slowly towards them was that I had to get rid of that offending vehicle at the earliest opportunity. I had already decided that I wanted no more to do with my Austin 14 so that did not come as too harsh a sentence for me to bear. I pretended to protest, mainly for Mr. Bell's benefit, but I had, in fact, just sold Goosie to one of my helpers, Rodney, for £30, a profit of £10 once expenses were taken into account. Thus, was ended my very first venture into car ownership.

It was upon returning home later on, after one very successful morning selling and disposing of the car that I found the brown envelope waiting for me on the hall table. I opened it with some trepidation because I knew what it would contain. It was a missive from a power greater than that of my parents. For the first time in my life something was about to happen to me over which they had no control, absolutely none. It finally signalled both the end of childhood and the beginning of adult responsibility.

<u>A Final Chapter</u>

…The brown envelope that I held in my hand was the latest of a series of such envelopes that I had held in my hand over the years since my eighteenth birthday. I had usually greeted the contents with a mixture of disdain and concern. I realised at once that this slim brown container held yet another attempt by Her Majesty to obtain my services for two years in defence of her realm. The disdain came not from a conscience that objected to that activity as a matter of principle it was the notion that there was a legal force somewhere out there and far beyond my experience that could require me to do what I did not want to do; and for two years at next to no salary. The concern was based on the renewal of the realisation that that force was even more powerful than that of my parents. On this occasion however I remember tapping the envelope on the fingers of my left hand to the thought that maybe just maybe I could use the previously unknown force to my advantage on this occasion. Then I opened the envelope and read the contents whereupon my previous concern rose to the level of actual anger.

Basically, and not too loosely translated the missive was advanced notification of a hostage taking, without the possibility of ransom. I was advised somewhat brusquely that I was to attend for a medical at the surgery in Holborn of an RAF doctor at a date in June. I would be advised further depending on the outcome of that medical examination. If I failed to attend for the medical, they were going to come and get me!

I have intended to use this, the final chapter of this my second book, to connect as smoothly as possible with the beginning chapters of my first book 'A Road Ran Through It'. Published in Amazon. I am arrogant enough to believe that I have had an interesting life, less so than some but more so than others. My parents, and I must begin with my parents, were both kindly, caring people and I loved them both; separately. As a joint enterprise though I am obliged to say that there were times when I did not even like them. They argued incessantly; usually when my sister and I had gone to bed. I have indicated my feelings about possible reasons for this apparent lack of fondness between them on several occasions. Whatever that case maybe it can never be decided absolutely now, simply because they are not available to answer to Denise and me. I am absolutely certain on one point; however, that if they even suspected that I felt this way about their relationship they would have been mortified. That is where I intend to leave the matter. The reasons are as dead as they are, and I do have some very good memories of each of them. I hope sincerely that that is also true for my sister.

Now however I had in my hand the implement which finally ended my legal Childhood This fact was confirmed in other ways. Firstly, during the period about which I am writing a person did not reach the age of majority until he or she was twenty-one. That document I realised, not for the first time, was the one that could and would, with some relief on my part, release me from the emotional control that my parents had held over me, more so as I grew older. I was able to use the nature and tone of the letter as a means to leave home without the 'personal blame and recrimination' that would have ensued from any other route that I might have chosen at the time.

I was not overjoyed to receive the missive from H M War Office, but I did see it as a reality that I had to face. I had never been a conscientious objector. I did in fact apply for selection as a trainee pilot in the RAF. I had attended a three-day selection course at RAF Hornchurch towards the end of 1958. I had been told during the three days that I had done well. I had believed that, because quite a high percentage of the initial candidates were sent home at different stages of the selection process. I was one of the few who remained to finish the three days of selection.

Post-War. In the 1950s, entrants hoping to become pilots first had to pass through the Aircrew Selection Centre at RAF Hornchurch. Pilots were selected on the basis of aptitude and physical condition so only the most promising applicants were selected. After enlistment, aircrew cadets would have undertaken a 12-week ground course at the Initial Training School at RAF Kirton-in-Lindsey. I did eventually attend a training course at RAF Kirton-in Lindsey later, towards the end of 1960 but as a trainee pay accounts clerk, not a trainee pilot.

The three days came to an end and those of us who remained were told that we would hear in due course the result of the selection. I waited for several months as my hopes gradually faded away. It all eventually came to a dreadfully disappointing conclusion several months later when I received the rejection letter from the War Office. I had not been selected. My Dad then let me know that he had feared that result all along and had based his fears on the fact that he was a registered member of the Communist Party. I did not believe that at that time. That the British Government could be so mean spirited. Later events though, which are outlined in my first book came back to hit me in the face with the very probable truth in my Dad's opinion on the matter of my rejection for training as an RAF pilot.

And this was the way on which my childhood finally ended except, some would say, for the second one through which I am now passing…

<u>Closing dedications</u>

Peter Vansittart who taught me to love my own Language.

Ruth Richards who taught me to love French.

Don Brown: People who knew us both will know why.

Cyprian Lunga who gave me sound advice and always solid support for both of which I am ever grateful.

Last but by no means least I enclose a final grateful dedication to my friend Robin Wilks and his partner Jan. In November of 2021 I needed a sub-tibial amputation of my right leg. Travel has been all but impossible throughout the Covid pandemic, but Rob and Jan have been consistent in contacting me throughout what has been a difficult period. Many thanks to you both. T.

Now, - Your Clue for the short fictional piece.

"It was about two, on one of three and yet it was a tale of four."

And finally, a dedication the reason for which has only occurred during the very recent few weeks. I have made reference several times throughout this manuscript to my Aunt Joann and her love and friendship towards me during the whole of my life. On those previous occasions I have made the point that she was still with us. Sadly, very sadly Aunt Joan passed away on 14-04-22 Joan will be missed not just by me. She had family and friends who will all miss her. Joan was a Christian Lady and so my final words to her are by way of a huge Thank You and God Bless! From your loving nephew Tony. HUGS! xx